Nineteenth-Century Women Philosophers in Britain and America

This book advances the rediscovery of forgotten women philosophers in the nineteenth century, who have been unjustly left out of the philosophical canon and omitted from narratives about the history of philosophy.

Women often did philosophy in a public setting in this period, engaging with practical issues of social concern and using philosophy to make the world a better place. This book highlights some of women's interventions against slavery; for women's rights; and on morality, moral agency, and the conditions of a flourishing life. The chapters are on the following: Mary Shepherd's idea of life; the collaborative authorships and feminist perspectives of Anna Doyle Wheeler and Harriet Taylor Mill; the roles of Elizabeth Cady Stanton and Lucretia Mott in the American women's rights movement; the influence of classical German philosophy on Lydia Maria Child's abolitionism; George Eliot's understanding of agency; the views of agency and resistance developed by Harriet Tubman and Elizabeth from within the abolitionist tradition; Annie Besant's search for a metaphysical basis for ethics, which she ultimately found in Hinduism; E. E. Constance Jones on the dualism of practical reason; Marietta Kies on altruism and positive rights; and Anna Julia Cooper's black feminist conception of the right to growth. This book unearths an important and neglected chapter in the history of women philosophers, showing the variety and vitality of nineteenth-century women's intellectual lives.

Nineteenth-Century Women Philosophers in Britain and America will be of great use to students and researchers interested in Philosophy, Women's Studies, and the politics of gender at the heart of British and American societies. This book was originally published as a special issue of *British Journal for the History of Philosophy*.

Alison Stone is Professor of Philosophy at Lancaster University, UK. Her interests span the history of philosophy, post-Kantian European philosophy, feminist philosophy, and aesthetics. Her books include *Being Born: Birth and Philosophy* (2019), *Frances Power Cobbe* (2022), and *Women Philosophers in Nineteenth-Century Britain* (2023).

Charlotte Alderwick is Senior Lecturer in Philosophy at UWE Bristol, UK. Her monograph *Schelling's Ontology of Powers* (2021) connects the history of philosophy with contemporary metaphysics; this is indicative of her philosophical approach. Charlotte is now working on eco-philosophy and the contribution that historical philosophies of nature can make to this area.

Nineteenth-Century Women Philosophers in Britain and America

Edited by
Alison Stone and Charlotte Alderwick

LONDON AND NEW YORK

First published 2024
by Routledge
4 Park Square, Milton Park, Abingdon, Oxon, OX14 4RN

and by Routledge
605 Third Avenue, New York, NY 10158

Routledge is an imprint of the Taylor & Francis Group, an informa business

© 2024 British Society for the History of Philosophy

All rights reserved. No part of this book may be reprinted or reproduced or utilised in any form or by any electronic, mechanical, or other means, now known or hereafter invented, including photocopying and recording, or in any information storage or retrieval system, without permission in writing from the publishers.

Trademark notice: Product or corporate names may be trademarks or registered trademarks, and are used only for identification and explanation without intent to infringe.

British Library Cataloguing-in-Publication Data
A catalogue record for this book is available from the British Library

ISBN13: 978-1-032-52172-5 (hbk)
ISBN13: 978-1-032-52173-2 (pbk)
ISBN13: 978-1-003-40551-1 (ebk)

DOI: 10.4324/9781003405511

Typeset in Myriad Pro
by codeMantra

Publisher's Note
The publisher accepts responsibility for any inconsistencies that may have arisen during the conversion of this book from journal articles to book chapters, namely the inclusion of journal terminology.

Disclaimer
Every effort has been made to contact copyright holders for their permission to reprint material in this book. The publishers would be grateful to hear from any copyright holder who is not here acknowledged and will undertake to rectify any errors or omissions in future editions of this book.

Contents

Citation Information   vii
Notes on Contributors   ix

Introduction

Introduction to nineteenth-century British and American women philosophers   1
Alison Stone and Charlotte Alderwick

1 Mary Shepherd and the meaning of 'life'   16
 Deborah Boyle

2 "Political…civil and domestic slavery": Harriet Taylor Mill and Anna Doyle Wheeler on marriage, servitude, and socialism   34
 Helen McCabe

3 Elizabeth Cady Stanton and Lucretia Mott: radical 'co-adjutors' in the American women's rights movement   52
 Lisa Pace Vetter

4 Lydia Maria Child on German philosophy and American slavery   67
 Lydia Moland

5 The fragility of rationality: George Eliot on akrasia and the law of consequences   83
 Patrick Fessenbecker

6 "Count it all joy": black women's interventions in the abolitionist tradition   100
 Lindsey Stewart

7 "Friendly to all beings": Annie Besant as ethicist   116
 Kurt Leland

8 E. E. Constance Jones on the dualism of practical reason   135
   Gary Ostertag and Amanda Favia

9 Marietta Kies on idealism and good governance   151
   Dorothy Rogers

10 Race and the 'right to growth': embodiment and education in
   the work of Anna Julia Cooper   166
   Kevin Cedeño-Pacheco

   Index   181

Citation Information

The chapters in this book were originally published in the *British Journal for the History of Philosophy*, volume 29, issue 2 (2021). When citing this material, please use the original page numbering for each article, as follows:

Introduction
Introduction to nineteenth-century British and American women philosophers
Alison Stone and Charlotte Alderwick
British Journal for the History of Philosophy, volume 29, issue 2 (2021)
pp. 193–207

Chapter 1
Mary Shepherd and the meaning of 'life'
Deborah Boyle
British Journal for the History of Philosophy, volume 29, issue 2 (2021)
pp. 208–225

Chapter 2
"Political…civil and domestic slavery": Harriet Taylor Mill and Anna Doyle Wheeler on marriage, servitude, and socialism
Helen McCabe
British Journal for the History of Philosophy, volume 29, issue 2 (2021)
pp. 226–243

Chapter 3
Elizabeth Cady Stanton and Lucretia Mott: radical 'co-adjutors' in the American women's rights movement
Lisa Pace Vetter
British Journal for the History of Philosophy, volume 29, issue 2 (2021)
pp. 244–258

Chapter 4
Lydia Maria Child on German philosophy and American slavery
Lydia Moland
British Journal for the History of Philosophy, volume 29, issue 2 (2021)
pp. 259–274

Chapter 5
The fragility of rationality: George Eliot on akrasia and the law of consequences
Patrick Fessenbecker
British Journal for the History of Philosophy, volume 29, issue 2 (2021)
pp. 275–291

Chapter 6
"Count it all joy": black women's interventions in the abolitionist tradition
Lindsey Stewart
British Journal for the History of Philosophy, volume 29, issue 2 (2021)
pp. 292–307

Chapter 7
"Friendly to all beings": Annie Besant as ethicist
Kurt Leland
British Journal for the History of Philosophy, volume 29, issue 2 (2021)
pp. 308–326

Chapter 8
E. E. Constance Jones on the dualism of practical reason
Gary Ostertag and Amanda Favia
British Journal for the History of Philosophy, volume 29, issue 2 (2021)
pp. 327–342

Chapter 9
Marietta Kies on idealism and good governance
Dorothy Rogers
British Journal for the History of Philosophy, volume 29, issue 2 (2021)
pp. 343–357

Chapter 10
Race and the 'right to growth': embodiment and education in the work of Anna Julia Cooper
Kevin Cedeño-Pacheco
British Journal for the History of Philosophy, volume 29, issue 2 (2021)
pp. 358–371

For any permission-related enquiries please visit:
http://www.tandfonline.com/page/help/permissions

Notes on Contributors

Charlotte Alderwick is Senior Lecturer in Philosophy at UWE Bristol, UK. Her monograph *Schelling's Ontology of Powers* (2021) connects the history of philosophy with contemporary metaphysics; this is indicative of her philosophical approach. Charlotte is now working on eco-philosophy and the contribution that historical philosophies of nature can make to this area.

Deborah Boyle is Professor of Philosophy at the College of Charleston, USA. The author of *Mary Shepherd: A Guide* (2023), and *The Well-Ordered Universe: The Philosophy of Margaret Cavendish* (2018), plus articles on Shepherd, Cavendish, Shepherd, Conway, Astell, Descartes, and Hume, she also edits the *Journal of the History of Philosophy*.

Kevin Cedeño-Pacheco is a dual-title PhD candidate in Philosophy and African American studies at The Pennsylvania State University, USA. His research focuses on the overlap between aesthetics and politics in the critical philosophies of race and gender advanced by African American, Latina, and Chicana women philosophers.

Amanda Favia is a bioethicist and philosopher. She is currently Associate Professor of Philosophy at Nassau Community College, USA. She has held fellowships at the Icahn School of Medicine at Mount Sinai. Her research ranges from metaethics and epistemic injustice in health care to the history of women in philosophy.

Patrick Fessenbecker is a teaching faculty member at the University of Wisconsin-Madison, USA. His book *Reading Ideas in Victorian Literature: Literary Content as Artistic Experience* was published in 2020.

Kurt Leland is an Independent Scholar based in Boston, USA. He is the author of *Invisible Worlds: Annie Besant on Psychic and Spiritual Development* (2013) and *Rainbow Body: A History of the Western Chakra System from Blavatsky to Brennan* (2016).

Helen McCabe is Associate Professor of Political Theory at the University of Nottingham, UK. Her first book was *John Stuart Mill, Socialist* (2021); and the second book was *Harriet Taylor Mill* (2023). She is currently working on a book about Mill and Taylor Mill's collaborative writing relationship.

NOTES ON CONTRIBUTORS

Lydia Moland is Professor of Philosophy at Colby College, Waterville, USA. She is the author of *Lydia Maria Child: A Radical American Life* (2022); *Hegel's Aesthetics: The Art of Idealism* (2019); and *Hegel on Political Identity* (2011), as well as numerous articles on German Idealism. She is co-editing the forthcoming *Oxford Handbook of American and British Women Philosophers in the Nineteenth Century*.

Gary Ostertag is a faculty member at both the Philosophy Program in The Graduate Center, CUNY, USA, and the Department of Philosophy in Nassau Community College, Garden City, USA. He works primarily on questions in the philosophy of language and in certain overlapping topics in metaphysics.

Dorothy Rogers is Professor at Montclair State University, USA, where she teaches courses on philosophy, education, and feminism. She has published several articles and books about feminist social/political thought, across race/culture, and women in the history of American philosophy in the nineteenth and early twentieth centuries.

Lindsey Stewart is Assistant Professor at the University of Memphis, USA. Her research focuses on developing black feminist conceptions of agency. She is currently working on a manuscript, tentatively titled *Fever*, which tells the story of how conjure women emerged in the US South, how they were thrust into the heart of national conflicts, and how they have shaped our American culture in response.

Alison Stone is Professor of Philosophy at Lancaster University, UK. Her interests span the history of philosophy, post-Kantian European philosophy, feminist philosophy, and aesthetics. Her books include *Being Born: Birth and Philosophy* (2019); *Frances Power Cobbe* (2022); and *Women Philosophers in Nineteenth-Century Britain* (2023).

Lisa Pace Vetter is Associate Professor of Political Science and an affiliate faculty member of the Gender, Women's, and Sexuality Studies Department at the University of Maryland, Baltimore County, USA. She is the author of *Political Thought of America's Founding Feminists* (2017) and *"Women's Work" as Political Art: Weaving and Dialectical Politics in Homer, Aristophanes, and Plato* (2005).

INTRODUCTION

Introduction to nineteenth-century British and American women philosophers

Alison Stone and Charlotte Alderwick

Since the 1980s, an immense wave of scholarship has recovered the voices of the many women who contributed to early modern philosophy, transforming our picture of the period. It is now typical for accounts of early modern philosophy to cover Elisabeth of Bohemia, Margaret Cavendish, Mary Astell and Catharine Trotter Cockburn, to mention just a few. Similarly, it is now generally recognised that women made massive contributions to twentieth-century philosophy – on both the 'continental' side, as with Arendt and Beauvoir, and the 'analytic', as with Anscombe, Murdoch and Foot.

Women's contributions to nineteenth-century philosophy, however, largely remain to be rediscovered. It remains standard for histories of nineteenth-century philosophy to include no coverage of women at all, or very little (see, e.g. Mander, *Oxford Handbook of British Philosophy in the Nineteenth Century*; Wood and Hahn, *Cambridge History of Philosophy in the Nineteenth Century*; Stone, *Edinburgh Critical History*; Moyar, *Routledge Companion*; Stedman Jones and Claeys, *Cambridge History of Nineteenth-Century Political Thought*; Goodman, *American Philosophy Before Pragmatism*).[1] Admittedly, nineteenth-century philosophy as a whole tends to be somewhat forgotten within the history of philosophy, sandwiched uncomfortably between the early modern and twentieth-century periods that draw the lion's share of attention. But within this already somewhat overlooked period, women are overlooked even more.

Now, however, feminist-informed historians of philosophy are increasingly turning attention to women in the nineteenth century. A pioneering study here was Dorothy Rogers's *America's First Women Philosophers* in 2005. Rogers looked at women connected to the idealist tradition: Susan Blow, Anna Brackett, Grace Bibb, Marietta Kies, Ellen Mitchell, Eliza Sunderland,

---

[1] Although Claeys and Stedman Jones include Lucy Delap's chapter "The Woman Question and the Origins of Feminism"; Wood and Hahn include Christine Blaettler's "Social Dissatisfaction and Social Change"; and Mander includes Barbara Caine's "British Feminist Thought".

and Lucia Ames Mead. Within its longer timespan of 1600–1900, Mary Ellen Waithe's *History of Women Philosophers*, vol. III, includes chapters on the nineteenth-century authors Clarisse Coignet, Antoinette Brown Blackwell and Julie Velten Favre, with shorter sections on nine further nineteenth-century figures, amongst them Catharine Beecher, Harriet Martineau, Harriet Taylor Mill, George Eliot, and Christine Ladd-Franklin. In addition, the fourth, twentieth-century volume of Waithe's *History* features several authors who began publishing at the end of the nineteenth century, such as E. E. C. Jones, Victoria Welby, and Mary Whiton Calkins. A 2004 special issue of *Hypatia* on nineteenth-century American women philosophers (see Rogers and Dykeman, "Women in the American Philosophical Tradition") dealt with Beecher, Julia Ward Howe, Ednah Dow Cheney, Lydia Maria Child, Anna Julia Cooper, Kies and Ames Mead, and – extending into the early twentieth century – the pragmatist Jane Addams. Also notable are *Contributions by Women to Nineteenth-Century American Philosophy: Frances Wright, Antoinette Brown-Blackwell, Marietta Kies*, edited by Dorothy Rogers and Therese Boos Dykeman, and Catherine Villanueva Gardner's *Empowerment and Interconnectivity: Towards a Feminist History of Utilitarian Philosophy*, on the nineteenth-century authors Anna Doyle Wheeler, Catharine Beecher, Frances Wright and Harriet Taylor Mill. The most comprehensive studies so far, in terms of mapping the overall nature and trajectory of women's contributions in the nineteenth century, are both anticipated: the *Oxford Handbook of Women Philosophers in the Nineteenth Century (The German Tradition)*, edited by Kristin Gjesdal and Dalia Nassar; and the *Oxford Handbook of British and American Women Philosophers in the Nineteenth Century*, edited by Lydia Moland and Alison Stone.

We mention these studies, though, as exceptions to a wider pattern of neglect. Moreover, general histories of nineteenth-century philosophy have as yet accommodated little of the above scholarship. This prompts the question: What have been the obstacles impeding women's inclusion in histories of nineteenth-century philosophy? After all, women *were* philosophically active in that century. It is not the case that no women engaged in philosophical discussion at that time. That much is evident from the works on nineteenth-century women which we have just mentioned. Yet the contributions made by women have tended to get forgotten, be eclipsed, and go unacknowledged. Nineteenth-century women's fate is the same that Eileen O'Neill diagnosed for women in the history of philosophy generally (O'Neill, "Disappearing Ink"): the problem lies at least as much with how we *narrate* the history of philosophy than with the actual intellectual contexts about which we are narrating. Whereas both women and men were philosophically active in the nineteenth century, it is only (some) men's contributions that are remembered by historians.

Unfortunately, once canons that omit women have been established, changing them is difficult (Rée, "Women Philosophers"). These canons shape our sense of the trajectory of philosophy within a given period: what positions and landmarks existed in the then philosophical landscape, what its key issues and debates were. Thus, our sense of trajectory further cements existing canons, creating a double-bind. We will come back to this problem below.

First, we note another obstacle to including women in the history of nineteenth-century philosophy: the obstacle presented by what we count as philosophy in the first place. Consider the immense amount of abolitionist and women's rights activism in the nineteenth-century United States. The two movements intertwined: some female abolitionists came to chafe against the sex-based restrictions that they encountered – as when the Grimké sisters (Sarah Moore Grimké (1792–1873) and Angelina Emily Grimké (1805–1879)) found themselves castigated for publicly speaking against slavery. Thus discovering that they were not regarded as equal partners in the anti-slavery movement, the sisters came to advocate women's rights in the later 1830s (see Birney, *Grimké Sisters*). From another angle, some – such as Elizabeth Cady Stanton (1815–1902) – argued that women's prominent role in abolitionism was evidence of women's more developed conscience, or moral sensibility, or powers of empathy, on account of which women deserved rights, including voting rights. These kinds of beliefs about women's moral superiority were widely held in the nineteenth century (see Stoper and Johnson, "Weaker Sex"). The same beliefs were also regularly used to support opposing, anti-feminist conclusions: that women should not have the vote, or rights to higher education or professional jobs, because their superior moral faculties could only be properly exercised in the home, especially in care of family and maintenance of personal relationships. Otherwise, the self-interest that organizes the public domain would contaminate and degrade women's higher, special moral sensibilities.

What all this brings to light is a rich world of public argument and debate in which women were heavily involved on all sides. This included opposition to women's rights. Catharine Beecher (1800–1878) was one who objected to the Grimkés' public oratory.[2] Women were chief architects of the 'angel in the house' ideology of women's special moral capabilities – see, especially, Sarah Lewis's classic statement in *Woman's Mission* of 1839.[3] And, later in the century, Mary Augusta Ward (1851–1920), or Mrs Humphry Ward as she

---

[2] See Grimké Weld, *Letters*, in which she replies to Beecher.
[3] Before Lewis, the Evangelical author Hannah More (1745–1833) is another source of these views. In her 1799 *Strictures on the Modern System of Female Education*, More advanced her view of women's moral role and the proper purpose of women's education in opposition to Wollstonecraft's radical egalitarianism. On the Wollstonecraft/More disagreement, see Taylor, *New Jerusalem*, 13–15.

preferred to be known, organized and authored the 1889 "Appeal Against Female Suffrage", objecting to women's suffrage on the basis that women's proper sphere was home and family, and by extension philanthropic work in wider society, but not national government as such.[4]

On the other side of these debates, advocates of women's rights made arguments as to what rights women should have, and why; and women abolitionists similarly advanced reasoned arguments as to why slavery was wrong, and about what actions and political changes ought to follow from that given the nature of equality and justice. Female abolitionists and women's rights advocates aimed to persuade, but to do so in part by deriving their conclusions from reasoned arguments. As such, women's anti-slavery and feminist advocacy was philosophical, even if most of it was not done as professional philosophy. The same goes for arguments for and against the idea of woman as 'the angel in the house', and of women's superior moral capabilities; and for arguments made apropos of other social campaigns, such as Josephine Butler's (1828–1906) campaign for the repeal of the Contagious Diseases Acts of 1864, 1866 and 1869. These Acts, eventually repealed in 1886, authorized certain police forces to arrest any woman suspected of prostitution and subject her to regular physical inspections. Butler saw these Acts as enforcing a sexual double standard – only women could be arrested under their terms – hence as an instrument of patriarchal control (see Caine, *Victorian Feminists*).

Some might baulk at the suggestion that these public-focused arguments constitute philosophy, preferring to say that they merely contain material that is of philosophical interest. Why might someone thus doubt the philosophical credentials of this public-focused work? One reason offered might be that these arguments were not being authored by professional philosophers. Yet it was only over the course of the nineteenth century that philosophy became professionalized – along with many other academic disciplines, including the various natural and social sciences. Consequently many already-canonized nineteenth-century philosophers were not professionals, such as J. S. Mill – whose *Subjection of Women* (for one) is nevertheless generally regarded as a work of philosophy.

Even had professional philosophy been fully developed, this was a century when women were generally excluded from higher education. Indeed, what level and kind of education women should be allowed to have was itself a matter of philosophical debate. Emily Davies (1830–1921) argued for women to study the same university curricula as men, *pace* advocates of different or special education for women such as Henry Sidgwick (see, again, Caine, *Victorian Feminists*; and Davies, *Higher Education of Women*).

---

[4]Interestingly, Ward was influenced in these views by T. H. Green's idealism; see Loader, *Mrs Humphry Ward*.

Women began to enter higher education in growing numbers from the mid-century onwards, partly thanks to activism by figures such as Davies. But women remained largely blocked from holding professional academic posts right across the period. For instance, in the U.S., Eliza Sunderland (1839–1910) obtained a PhD in philosophy in 1892 on "The Relation of the Philosophy of Kant to that of Hegel". But despite students petitioning the University of Michigan to appoint her when openings arose in the philosophy department (one insisted: "I *know* that Dr Sunderland is second only to Dr Dewey"), the university stood by its policy against hiring women (see Rogers, *America's First Women Philosophers*, 119–20). A few women did start to take up professional posts in philosophy from the 1880s and 1890s onwards. One was E. E. C. Jones (1848–1922), who became a lecturer in Moral Sciences at Girton College, Cambridge, in 1884 – the college Davies had co-founded in 1869. But women such as Jones achieved this against a wider background where professional exclusion remained pervasive.

To philosophise in the nineteenth century, then, the majority of women perforce had to do so outside professional academic settings and in other contexts – such as social and political activism, campaigning and philanthropy; or religious and spiritualist thought;[5] or around the banner of 'literature';[6] or in connection with the education of children, a field in which many women were involved (from amongst the American Hegelians, Susan Blow (1843–1916) founded one of the earliest kindergartens in 1873 while Anna Brackett (1836–1911) became the first female secondary school head in 1863; while Mary Everest Boole's (1832–1916) programme of work disseminating and fulfilling the legacy of her late husband, George Boole, included

---

[5]Notably, several religious movements that sprang up in the century, amongst them Christian Science and Theosophy, were female-headed – respectively by Mary Baker Eddy (1821–1910) and Helena Blavatsky (1831–1891) succeeded by Annie Besant (1847–1933). Overlapping with these movements were the emergence of Spiritualism, in which women were also central (see, inter alia, Owen, *The Darkened Room*), and Black spiritual traditions such as hoodoo (discussed here by Stewart). By bypassing established churches, these religious currents allowed new openings for women. Spiritualism, for instance, retained the idea of women's self-sacrificial, submissive nature and yet turned it around subversively, changing it into the idea that women are especially receptive to spirit communications, capable of spirit possession, and attuned to spiritual and religious truths. Such views provided a background that enabled women to say things, when possessed, without having their speaking authority questioned as it would be if they were directly speaking in their own voices. Stewart explores this here apropos of Harriet Tubman. While these alternative spiritual traditions might seem esoteric to many contemporary naturalist-inclined philosophers, at the time they interested many philosophers, William James – who co-founded the Society for Psychical Research in 1884 – being a case in point. Moreover, some of the work by these religious or spiritual women is itself directly philosophical, as with Besant: e.g. her discussion of materialism in philosophy of mind in "Why I Became a Theosophist" of 1890. Arguing against Vogt's materialism, Besant claims "We study the nerve-cells of the brain; we find molecular vibrations; we are still in the object world, amid form, colour, resistance, motion. Suddenly there is a THOUGHT, and all is changed. We have passed into a new world, the subject world" (*Why I Became a Theosophist*, 8).

[6]It is striking just how many philosophical women of the period wrote fiction. Amongst those mentioned in this introduction, this goes inter alia for Ward, Boole, Martineau, Lee, More, and Shelley.

writing the 1909 children's book *Philosophy and Fun of Algebra*).[7] In sum, "we often have to look beyond academic philosophy to find the women who were influential ... philosophers" (Whipps and Lake, "Pragmatist Feminism").

Along with this, we need to be open to forms of writing and communication beyond the conventional philosophical treatise. To be sure, there were women in the period who wrote straightforward articles and books of philosophy, such as Mary Shepherd (1777–1847), with the *Essay upon the Relation of Cause and Effect* of 1824; Caroline Frances Cornwallis (1786–1848), with *Philosophical Theories and Philosophical Experience, by a Pariah* in 1841; Frances Power Cobbe (1822–1904), with the *Essay on Intuitive Morals* of 1855/57 and "Darwinism in Morals" of 1871; Constance Naden (1858–1889), who defended induction in *Induction and Deduction* of 1890; and the aesthetician Vernon Lee (1856–1935) with such works as *Art and Life* of 1896. Others philosophized within popular tracts, essays, pamphlets and speeches, as with, e.g. Frances Wright (1795–1852) and Annie Besant. Others philosophized within the medium of literary work – for example, Mary Shelley's (1797–1851) incredibly successful 1818 novel *Frankenstein* advances a philosophical stance on children's rights (Hunt Botting, *Mary Shelley and the Rights of the Child*), and equally is a thought-experiment about the possibility of artificial life, while George Eliot's (1819–1880) novels embody her distinctive version of evolutionary and socially progressive positivism.

There is also translation and editorial work. Harriet Martineau's (1802–1876) two-volume condensed translation of Comte's *Cours de Philosophie Positive* as *The Positive Philosophy of Auguste Comte* (Martineau, *Positive Philosophy*, 1853) reflected, and tacitly expounded, her own interpretation of positivism – meaning that positivism as received in Britain effectively bore Martineau's stamp.[8] Likewise, Ada Lovelace's (1815–1852) translation of Menabrea's "Sketch of the Analytical Engine" in 1842 includes her extensive notes on the topic, the touchstone for her own views on artificial intelligence (as we now call it).[9] And Eliot, we should remember, before turning to fiction, translated Strauss's *Life of Jesus* (in 1846), Feuerbach's *Essence of Christianity* (1854) and Spinoza's *Ethics* (in 1856, although this remained unpublished

---

[7] And on Mary Everest Boole's broader programme, see Valente, "Wings to Logic".

[8] Martineau's influence on British positivism is rarely acknowledged – but on one occasion when it is, by Mike Gane, he complains that Martineau "dumbed down" Comte (Gane, *Comte*, xiv); apparently, she was "insensitive to theory", as she was "a novelist" (23). Martineau did write the novel *Deerbrook*, as well as a fictionalised biography of Toussaint L'Ouverture, but this was just part of her vast, multi-disciplinary and highly philosophical output; see Sanders and Weiner, *Martineau*.

[9] See Lovelace, "Sketch". Amongst other things, Lovelace here introduces the idea of a "science of operations" – i.e. in effect, computing; and she also claims: "The Analytical Engine has no pretensions whatever to *originate* anything. It can do whatever we *know how to order it* to perform. It can *follow* analysis; but it has no power of *anticipating* any analytical relations or truths". Some have found here a "Lovelace test" for artificial intelligence, different from the Turing test (Bringsfjord, Bello, and Ferrucci, "Creativity").

until very recently, as *Spinoza's Ethics*), also becoming the anonymous co-editor of the *Westminster Review* in the early 1850s (Gray, "George Eliot") – the journal that Mill described as the organ of philosophical radicalism in Britain.

To include women in the canon of nineteenth-century philosophy, then, we need to broaden our conception of what we take the forms, scope, domain, methods and subject-matter of philosophy to be. However, what we have said so far may give the impression that women of the time were very largely occupied with social and political matters, and that the broadening of scope that we are advocating is primarily to recognise social and political campaigning, advocacy, and persuasion as constituting philosophy in an extended sense. This would be an unfortunate position. It would reinforce pre-existing assumptions that women are somehow suited to 'soft', social and political, rather than 'hard' epistemological and metaphysical, theorizing – and perhaps to the even softer 'practice', rather than theory proper. Arguably these assumptions are an indirect legacy of the nineteenth-century idea of women's supposedly greater moral capacity to care for others – indeed to sacrifice their interests for the sake of others – as we mentioned earlier. But as we have also seen that idea of women's moral vocation was double-edged, effectively leading to women's extensive involvement in social campaigning and philanthropy across the nineteenth century.[10] Thus, the study of women in nineteenth-century philosophy helps us to see some of the historical origins of the lingering assumption that women are inherently suited to caring and social matters.

That said, we want to respond to the worry that we are reproducing associations between women and 'soft' social thinking in two ways. On the one hand, women can and do engage in the most abstract as well as more concrete intellectual fields, and so they did in the nineteenth century. Take for example, Lovelace's technical analysis of the principles behind Babbage's analytical and difference engines; Shepherd's metaphysics of causation; Martineau's advancement of naturalism, hard determinism, and an empiricist philosophy of science; E. E. C. Jones's work in logic; and Victoria Welby's programme of 'signifies' within philosophy of language.

On the other hand, given the constraints under which women operated in the nineteenth century, it is not surprising that no small part of the philosophical writing done by women in this period concerns social and political matters or was value-facing. This goes for some of those just mentioned. Welby, for instance, was concerned with meaning both in relation to scriptural interpretation and as the source of value, stating in 1893 that "*meaning* – in the widest sense of the word – is the only value of whatever

---

[10]That activity was manifest, inter alia, in Florence Nightingale's establishment of nursing as a profession, and her work reforming and modernizing hospitals; and in Octavia Hill's establishment of social work and the beginnings of social housing. Hill also co-founded the National Trust. See Boyd, *Butler, Hill, Nightingale*.

"fact" presents itself to us" (Welby, "Meaning and Metaphor", 524). That women of the period often wrote, in whole or part, about value-related topics was a consequence of the fact that, of necessity, women did much of their intellectual work within practical, political, literary, educational, and spiritual contexts – and against a background where their very right and ability to engage in intellectual work was contested.[11] In short, we need to say both that women were perfectly capable of doing abstract, highly technical philosophizing, and that for contextual reasons in the nineteenth century, women often philosophized in value-facing ways.

Let us now return to the pattern noted earlier whereby canons and inherited narratives tend to reinforce one another in feedback loops, impeding us from including women in the history of nineteenth-century philosophy. Our received narrative about the contours of nineteenth-century philosophy is less clear and well-defined than those for early modern (rationalism versus empiricism up to the Kantian synthesis) and early twentieth-century philosophy (the dual revolutions of logical positivism and phenemenology). Potentially, a less settled narrative can be more easily reshaped to take account of women's contributions. Yet one overarching narrative about the nineteenth century has taken a degree of hold. On this, the nineteenth century was marked by a struggle between two central currents – idealism and naturalism (Skorupski, *English-Language Philosophy*; Stern, "Nineteenth-Century Philosophy"; Stone, *Edinburgh Critical History*). These two outlooks divide on whether value and value-related phenomena can be adequately understood naturalistically, i.e. as features of the natural world amenable in principle to empirical scientific study; and on the adequacy of scientific methods for grasping reality as a whole and accounting for the possibility of knowledge.

Roughly, in Britain, forms of naturalism prevailed through much of the century – especially in the guise of utilitarianism, and to a lesser extent of positivism – but became superseded by British idealism as the century closed. Conversely, in Germany, idealism prevailed earlier in the century to become superseded by naturalism after around 1850. The U.S. picture is closer to the German, with transcendentalism (as a form of idealism) prevailing earlier in the century followed by St Louis idealism, with pragmatism – a more naturalistic approach – taking over in the later century. But this picture has been framed with reference to male philosophers – the German idealists Fichte, Schelling, Hegel; the transcendentalists Thoreau and Emerson; the British idealists Green and Bradley; with more naturalistic positions represented by such figures as Bentham, J. S. Mill, Nietzsche, Dewey and James. What happens when we factor women in?

---

[11] Moreover, nineteenth-century American philosophy overall had a marked practical orientation, across its transcendentalist, idealist and pragmatist phases.

We certainly find a divide between more idealist and naturalist approaches in the philosophical writings of many women of the time. For example, as Deborah Boyle shows in this issue, Shepherd takes an idealist view that life requires a non-material explanation. Cobbe argues in idealist vein, influenced by both Kant and transcendentalism, that the moral law is known intuitively, intrinsically obligates us as rational agents, and transcends the natural world. Martineau and Eliot, in opposition, endorsed versions of positivism. And we find in many nineteenth-century women an overarching concern about whether morality and value can be accommodated naturalistically, especially in light of Darwin's work and other scientific discoveries. Cobbe thought they could not; whereas Besant, having been a follower of Cobbe in the early 1870s, came to think in the mid-1870s that morality *could* be put on a scientific, utilitarian and atheist basis that was more secure than the traditional Christian one. But Besant subsequently changed her mind again and came to think that morality did need spiritual underpinning – from the new religious framework she espoused from 1889 onwards, Theosophy (as Leland discusses in this issue).

To some extent, then, existing narratives about the nineteenth century can illuminate the thought of women of that time. Reciprocally, by factoring women's thought into those narratives we build up a richer picture of the range of idealist-to-naturalist perspectives then debated. Including women fills out our sense of the period beyond a few 'big names' – in recognition that these 'big names' operated within a crowded spectrum of figures and movements.

But, in the end, it will not suffice to simply extend pre-existing narratives to women, as this prevents us from genuinely learning about and expanding our conception of the period on the basis of its female participants. We need to read these women's work with relatively open minds as to what they were discussing and arguing about, and what their preoccupations and approaches were. We have to look and see. We can then construct new generalizations about women's overall philosophical interests and agendas at that time, and revise our overall narratives about the period's philosophical trajectory in that light. At the moment, we barely even know what revisions are needed, because we still have so much to learn about nineteenth-century women philosophers.

The goal of this issue, then, is to help to fill in this blank in historical knowledge with ten articles on figures who span the whole century and cross a variety of areas of philosophy. For manageability's sake the focus is limited to authors who wrote in the English language, largely in Britain and North America. The figures covered are Mary Shepherd, Anna Doyle Wheeler, Harriet Taylor Mill, George Eliot (Marian Evans), Annie Besant and E. E. C. Jones from the UK; and, from the U.S., Harriet Tubman, Lucretia Mott, Lydia Maria Child, Elizabeth Cady Stanton, Marietta Kies and Anna Julia Cooper.

Some of the authors covered are well known outside philosophy, e.g. George Eliot in literature; Harriet Tubman (c.1822–1913) as anti-slavery activist. But the philosophical dimensions of these authors' work have been neglected, and are explored here. Other authors covered here have been overshadowed by their male associates, as with Harriet Taylor Mill compared to her husband and intellectual companion J. S. Mill, and Anna Doyle Wheeler compared to her co-author William Thompson. Others of our authors are largely forgotten today – such as the neo-Hegelian political philosopher Marietta Kies, the abolitionist Lydia Maria Child, and the logician and ethicist E. E. Constance Jones. In all cases we hope to help restore these authors to their places in philosophical history.

We begin the volume with Boyle's account of Mary Shepherd's contribution to the nineteenth-century debate on the nature of life. Boyle outlines Shepherd's critiques of Lawrence, one of the most prominent immanentist theorists of the day (holding that life is a property which can be accounted for from an organism's material or structural properties alone). As Boyle argues, Shepherd demonstrates that Lawrence's view merely constitutes a *description* of life, rather than an account of *how* life arises. Using an analysis of Shepherd's critiques of the Humean account of causation, and an outline of Shepherd's own unique account of causation (which looks strikingly similar to contemporary accounts of causation as power-based), Boyle sketches Shepherd's novel version of the transcendentalist view of the origins of life. Boyle argues that for Shepherd, life itself is a distinct kind of causal power, but one which is only effective when combined with the causal powers of mind and body.

McCabe's piece focusses on two British feminists – Harriet Taylor Mill and Anna Wheeler – both of whom co-wrote with their partners (John Stuart Mill and William Thompson, respectively) as well as producing works in their own right. McCabe makes a strong case for reconsidering the role of these women both in the works that they co-authored with their male counterparts, but also for their role in works traditionally considered to be the sole work of their partners. As well as providing arguments for this claim and investigating the nature of these co-authoring relationships, and what they may have bought to the texts, McCabe also gives an account of the two women's positive views. As McCabe demonstrates, both women were committed to a version of the claim that marriage is a form of slavery; both women were engaged in the endeavour of freeing women from patriarchal structures and relationships; and both argued that co-operative socialism was the best way to ensure the emancipation not just of women, but of society as a whole.

Vetter's article focuses on another philosopher who has been historically overshadowed by someone she worked closely with – Elizabeth Cady Stanton is typically seen as a central figure in the feminist movement in nineteenth-century America, while much less is known about the work of her collaborator, the Quaker abolitionist and women's rights advocate Lucretia Mott. However, Vetter argues that despite leaving fewer published works, and taking a less central role in some of the organized events promoting women's suffrage at the time, there is still a distinctive and important philosophical position that emerges with a more careful look at Mott. As Vetter shows, once we reconsider Mott it becomes clear that her quietism on particular issues, her tendency to prefer informal networks of activism, and her lack of published works, in fact reflect a distinctive position, which is more inclusive and therefore more radical in its emancipatory aims than Stanton's.

Another philosopher whose ideas were disseminated through less traditional means (much of her work comes from the column "Letters from New York" which she wrote in her capacity as editor of the *National Anti-Slavery Standard* in the early 1840s) is Lydia Maria Child. As an outspoken abolitionist, Child's advocacy of practical action is apparent throughout her life. However, as Moland argues in her contribution to this volume, Child also drew heavily on classical German philosophy both to provide a theoretical backbone to her abolitionism, and to guide her actions. Moland identifies three central themes from classical German philosophy and demonstrates how each one had a distinctive impact on elements of Child's thinking. First, a Spinozist/Romantic conception of the unity and interconnectedness of nature, inherited from thinkers such as Novalis and Herder, which underpinned her core belief in human equality: as mere parts united in a larger whole, all human beings share the same rights, and all share the same responsibility for promoting the rights of others. Second, a commitment to something like a Kantian account of duty, underpinning her conviction that continuing to take action for the abolitionist cause was always necessary, even if it led to further violence; if an action is right, then there is an obligation for it to be performed whatever the cost. Her own lifelong commitment to activism is itself a testament to her adherence to this way of thinking about ethics. Finally, Child thinks a lot about progress in history, and Moland highlights a Hegelian influence. However, Child's commitment to practical action is also shown to be in play here; she understands progress in history to be driven by morality and individual action, thus underpinning the importance of the abolitionist movement for social change and progress.

One of the better-known figures covered in this collection is George Eliot (Marian Evans), however the paper we include here forms part of a recent recognition of her work as having significant philosophical as well as literary significance. In this paper, Fessenbecker argues that the trend in the literature to see Eliot as primarily concerned with causal determinism is misguided, and obscures the more nuanced and subtle problems of agency that she deals with across her works. Fessenbecker demonstrates that the central issue for Eliot is a specific type of determinism, whereby the agent's past actions (akratic actions in particular) determine her present actions, entailing that she is bound by her past decisions to act against her better judgement. Thus Eliot's 'law of consequences' does not, Fessenbecker argues, refer to external influences determining human action, but isolates the particular cases where a free agent is nonetheless determined by her own previous choices. As Fessenbecker shows, understanding Eliot's view in this way also enables her accounts of the fragility of virtue, the importance of sympathy for moral action, and her critiques of consequentialism to come into view.

Stewart's paper on the role of black women in the abolitionist tradition, focussing on Harriet Tubman and Elizabeth from *The Memoir of Old Elizabeth, a Coloured Woman*, clearly demonstrates the way that gendered understandings of agency and resistance necessitate the erasure of female agency and resistance, and particularly black female agency and resistance. Stewart shows that the abolitionist tradition has historically understood both resistance and emancipation in problematic gendered ways: resistance is exemplified by the black man committing violent acts in order to protect the black woman made to submit to the slave owner; the paradigm case of emancipation is the freed black man. This is exacerbated by a conflation of agency with active and violent resistance: the black woman is overlooked as a genuine agent because of a narrative that depicts black female submission as at the heart of the black man's motivation for resistance. Stewart demonstrates that by rejecting these masculinized accounts of resistance and agency, forms of resistance, agency, and emancipation that black women were engaging in come in to view. Stewart also shows that submission can be a key element of active agency: the struggle of these women to find internal emancipation takes the form of a submission to God and religious joy. This spiritual emancipation in turn leads to non-violent forms of political and religious resistance which, as Stewart demonstrates, deserve to be taken equally seriously as violent forms of resistance.

Another of the better-known figures in this collection is Annie Besant, however again she is rarely seen as a philosopher but rather as a populariser of the views of others. Besant's varied life and involvement with a range of different social and political causes as well as spiritual and religious groups have also led to a narrative that she lacked a consistent view or focus. Leland's paper challenges both of these claims, arguing that Besant should be understood as a philosopher, and specifically as an ethicist whose work is structured by the central question of whether ethics is possible without metaphysics. Leland shows that, far from being disconnected leaps between disparate views, Besant's changes in focus throughout her life stem from her ongoing project to find a satisfying answer to the question of how to ground ethics. Besant finds this, as Leland shows, in Hinduism, as its emphasis on the unity of self and world is capable of providing a metaphysical basis for the virtues of happiness and 'friendliness to all beings' that she had espoused throughout her life.

Ostertag and Favia's paper focusses on E. E. Constance Jones, one of the few women in this collection who was known in her lifetime for her philosophical work. However, while most of Jones' work is in philosophical logic, Ostertag and Favia focus here on her lesser known work in ethics, specifically her response to Sidgwick's dualism of practical reason. They argue that Jones recognized that this issue (that the demands of self-interest and the demands of duty to others provide competing but equally rational bases for action) could only be satisfactorily solved if the different demands entail one another. The paper outlines Jones' 3 different attempts at a solution to the dualism, demonstrating that the view she outlines is unique and provides a promising line of response to this issue.

The other paper which focusses on a women who was recognized as a philosopher in her lifetime is Rogers' contribution on Marietta Kies, one of the first women to formally study philosophy and political theory in the USA, and to work as a professional academic philosopher there. Rogers' focus here is on Kies' political philosophy, in particular her ideas of positive rights and the importance of altruism as a principle for effective states. Drawing on Hegel's conception of the organic state, Rogers shows that Kies is able to mount a defence of the rights of individuals against large-scale industry and the state itself. Further, Kies extends Hegel's account of the state with her arguments that altruism should be a central feature of an effective state: if, as Hegel's account entails, the whole has a mutual relationship of dependence with its parts, this implies that the state should take an active role in redistributing wealth and opportunity to ensure the flourishing of as many of its parts as possible. This argument is then shown to underpin Kies' defences of measures such as taxation, guaranteeing public access to education, and laws to support those members of society who find themselves facing hardship.

We finish the collection with Cedeño-Pacheco's paper on Anna Julia Cooper, whose 1892 work *A Voice from the South* was and remains an important articulation of the claim that both black men and white women and men have failed to grasp the unique and pressing nature of the issues facing black women. As well as writing extensively on black women's experience and emancipation, Cooper also wrote on black issues more broadly, and on the philosophy of education. Cedeño-Pacheco approaches her work through two themes which recur throughout her writing: vitality and corporeality. He argues that by taking this systematic approach to her works and reading them in the context of these themes, new aspects of her view are able to come to light. Specifically, Cedeño-Pacheco argues that his approach enables us to read Cooper as claiming that one of the central ways that black Americans have been wronged is through the denial of their right to *growth* – to freely self-determine their evolution as individuals and a community.

Bibliography

Besant, Annie. *Why I Became a Theosophist*. New York: "The Path" Office, 1890.

Birney, Catherine H. *The Grimké Sisters. Sarah and Angelina Grimké, The First American Women Advocates of Abolition and Woman's Rights*. Boston, MA: Lee and Shepard, 1885.

Boyd, Nancy. *Josephine Butler, Octavia Hill, Florence Nightingale: Three Victorian Women Who Changed Their World*. London: Palgrave Macmillan, 1984.

Bringsjord, Selmer, Paul Bello, and David Ferrucci. "Creativity, the Turing Test, and the (Better) Lovelace Test". *Minds and Machines* 11 (2001): 3–27.

Caine, Barbara. *Victorian Feminists*. Oxford: Oxford University Press, 1993.

Cobbe, Frances Power. *An Essay on Intuitive Morals, 2 Vols*. London: Trübner, 1864. Originally published in 1855 (vol. 1) and 1857 (vol. 2).

Cobbe, Frances Power. "Darwinism in Morals". *Theological Review* (April 1871): 167–192.

Cornwallis, Caroline Frances. *Philosophical Theories and Philosophical Experience, by a Pariah*. London: Pickering, 1841.

Davies, Emily. *The Higher Education of Women*. London: Strahan, 1866.

Eliot, George, trans. *Spinoza's Ethics*. Ed. Clare Carlisle. Princeton, NJ: Princeton University Press, 2020.

Gane, Mike. *Auguste Comte*. London: Routledge, 2006.

Goodman, Russell B. *American Philosophy Before Pragmatism*. New York: Oxford University Press, 2015.

Gray, Beryl. "George Eliot and the Westminster Review". *Victorian Periodicals Review* 33, no. 3 (2000): 212–224.

Grimké, Angelina. *Letters to Catharine E. Beecher, in reply to "An Essay on Slavery and Abolitionism, addressed to A. E. Grimké"*. Boston, MA: Isaac Knapp, 1838.

Hunt Botting, Eileen. *Mary Shelley and the Rights of the Child*. University Park: Pennsylvania University Press, 2017.

Lee, Vernon. *Art and Life*. Aurora NY: Roycroft, 1896.

Lewis, Sarah. *Woman's Mission*. New York: Wiley & Putnam, 1840.

Loader, Helen. *Mrs Humphry Ward and Greenian Idealism*. London: Palgrave, 2019.

Lovelace, Ada. annotated trans. "Sketch of the analytical engine Invented by Charles Babbage" by L. F. Menabrea. *Bibliothèque Universelle de Genève* 82, Oct 1842. http://www.fourmilab.ch/babbage/sketch.html.

Mander, William, ed., *Oxford Handbook of British Philosophy in the Nineteenth Century*. Oxford: Oxford University Press, 2014.

Martineau, Harriet. *The Positive Philosophy of Auguste Comte, 2 vols*. London: J. Chapman, 1853.

More, Hannah. *Strictures on the Modern System of Female Education with a View to the Principles and Conduct of Women of Rank and Fortune, 2 Vols*. Cambridge: Cambridge University Press, 2011. Original publication 1799.

Moyar, Dean, ed., *Routledge Companion to Nineteenth-Century Philosophy*. New York: Routledge, 2012.

Naden, Constance. *Induction and Deduction*. London: Bickers & Son, 1890.

O'Neill, Eileen. "Disappearing Ink: Early Modern Women Philosophers and Their Fate in History". In *Philosophy in a Feminist Voice*, edited by Janet A. Kourany, 17–62. Princeton, NJ: Princeton University Press, 1997.

Owen, Alex. *The Darkened Room: Women, Power, and Spiritualism in Late Victorian England*. Chicago: University of Chicago Press, 1989.

Rée, Jonathan. "Women Philosophers and the Canon". *British Journal of the History of Philosophy* 10 (2002): 641–652.

Rogers, Dorothy. *America's First Women Philosophers*. New York: Bloomsbury, 2005.

Rogers, Dorothy, and Therese Boos Dykeman. "Women in the American Philosophical Tradition 1800-1930". *Hypatia* 19, no. 2 (2004).

Rogers, Dorothy, and Therese Boos Dykeman. *Contributions by Women to Nineteenth-Century American Philosophy: Frances Wright, Antoinette Brown-Blackwell, Marietta Kies*. Lewiston NY: Edwin Mellen, 2012.

Sanders, Valerie, and Gaby Weiner. *Harriet Martineau and the Birth of Disciplines*. London: Routledge, 2017.

Shepherd, Mary. *Essay upon the Relation of Cause and Effect. In Philosophical Writings vol. 1*, ed. Jennifer McRobert. Bristol: Thoemmes, 2000. Original publication in 1824.

Skorupski, John. *English-Language Philosophy 1750 to 1945*. Oxford: Oxford University Press, 1993.

Stedman Jones, Gareth, and Gregory Claeys, ed. *Cambridge History of Nineteenth-Century Political Thought*. Cambridge: Cambridge University Press, 2013.

Stern, Robert. "Nineteenth Century Philosophy". *Routledge Encyclopedia of Philosophy* (1998. doi:10.4324/9780415249126-DC100-1.

Stone, Alison ed. *Edinburgh Critical History of Nineteenth-Century Philosophy*. Edinburgh: Edinburgh University Press, 2011.

Stoper, Emily, and Roberta Ann Johnson. "The Weaker Sex and the Better Half: The Idea of Women's Moral Superiority in the American Feminist Movement". *Polity* 10, no. 2 (1977): 192–217.

Taylor, Barbara. *Eve and the New Jerusalem: Socialism and Feminism in the Nineteenth Century*. New York: Pantheon, 1983.

Valente, K. G. "Giving Wings to Logic: Mary Everest Boole's Propagation and Fulfilment of a Legacy". *British Journal for the History of Science* 43, no. 1 (2010): 49–74.

Villanueva Gardner, Catherine. *Empowerment and Interconnectivity: Towards a Feminist History of Utilitarian Philosophy*. University Park: Penn State Press, 2012.

Waithe, Mary Ellen, ed. *A History of Women Philosophers, 4 Vols*. Dordrecht: Springer, 1987.

Welby, Victoria. "Meaning and Metaphor". *The Monist* 3 (1893): 510–525.

Whipps, Judy, and Danielle Lake. "Pragmatist Feminism", *The Stanford Encyclopedia of Philosophy* (Winter 2017 Edition), ed. Edward N. Zalta. https://plato.stanford.edu/archives/win2017/entries/femapproach-pragmatism/.

Wood, Allen, and Songsuk Susan Hahn, eds., *Cambridge History of Philosophy in the Nineteenth Century*. Cambridge: Cambridge University Press, 2011.

Mary Shepherd and the meaning of 'life'

Deborah Boyle

ABSTRACT
In the final chapters of her 1824 *Essay upon the Relation of Cause and Effect*, Lady Mary Shepherd considers what it means for an organism to be *alive*. The physician William Lawrence (1783–1867) had recently presented a theory of life that historian Stephen Jacyna has labelled 'immanentist'. Shepherd's critique of Lawrence's arguments reveals a specific application of her own anti-Humean causal theory and shows her own affinities with the 'transcendentalist' camp. This paper explores Shepherd's criticisms of Lawrence, offering some suggestions for understanding Shepherd's own account of life as a principle, power, or cause, that, when 'mixed' with a certain kind of organized body, makes that body living.

1. Introduction

Among the women philosophers whose work is now being rediscovered by historians of philosophy is Lady Mary Shepherd (1777–1847), author of *An Essay upon the Relation of Cause and Effect* (1824), *Essays on the Perception of an External Universe, and Other Subjects Connected with the Doctrine of Causation* (1827), and three philosophical essays published in popular magazines. Shepherd's work shows her to be not just a careful, perceptive critic, but also an original thinker in her own right. In the 1824 *Essay*, she takes on Hume's account of causation in terms of constant conjunctions and habit, arguing that causal principles can be known by reason to be necessary truths, and offering a novel account of causation as synchronous necessary connections. In her 1827 book, she appeals to the causal principles established in her *Essay* to provide ingenious arguments against external-world skepticism, and, along the way, offers compelling arguments against George Berkeley, Thomas Reid and Dugald Stewart, and French 'sensationalists' such as Condillac.

In the final two chapters of the 1824 *Essay Upon the Relation of Cause and Effect*, Shepherd considers what it means for an organism to be said to be *alive*. As Shepherd observed, "the *nature of life* is become a question of great interest" (Shepherd, *Essay*, 175); just six years before, Mary Shelley had published *Frankenstein*, in which Dr. Frankenstein sought and found "the cause of generation and life" and became "capable of bestowing animation upon lifeless matter" (Shelley, *Frankenstein*, 79). The nature of life might seem an odd topic to address in the *Essay*, which otherwise focuses on Hume's causal theory. However, Shepherd was interested not just in Hume's own works, but in how her contemporaries used Hume's account of causation. One such contemporary was William Lawrence (1783–1867), who was among the early nineteenth-century scientists, doctors, and philosophers debating the nature of life. Seeing that Lawrence's theory of life was inextricable from his commitment to a Humean theory of causation, Shepherd devoted two of the six chapters in her *Essay* to refuting Lawrence. Her criticisms may seem, at first glance, to be of little interest to twenty-first century readers, since Lawrence is no longer a significant thinker. Nonetheless, Shepherd's critique is worth examining, for it reveals a specific application of her own anti-Humean causal theory.

Section 2 sketches an overview of the two main types of theories of life being debated in Shepherd's day – immanentism and transcendentalism – with special attention to Lawrence's immanentist views. Section 3 examines Shepherd's critique of what she sees as Lawrence's "most dangerous" error. Since this critique pertains to Lawrence's endorsement of a Humean causal theory, Section 4 contains an overview of Shepherd's alternative theory of causation. The paper ends with some suggestions about how to understand Shepherd's own account of what life is; siding with the transcendentalists, Shepherd understood life to be a principle, power, or cause, that, when 'mixed' with a certain kind of organized body, makes that body living.

2. Theories of life in the early nineteenth century

In an 1822 book, Scottish anatomist John Barclay distinguished two types of theorists about life: the "mere materialists", who "ascribe organism and vital phenomena to the chemical and mechanical properties of matter" (Barclay, *Inquiry*, 36 and 38), versus those who hold that "a principle of life is independent of organization, a something superadded to the organized structure" (Barclay, *Inquiry*, 485).[1] Historian Stephen Jacyna has suggested labelling these two camps *immanentist* and *transcendentalist*, respectively (Jacyna, "Immanence or Transcendence", 311). Roughly, immanentists maintained

---

[1] We could call these theories forms of 'vitalism', but Shepherd herself never uses that term. Her contemporaries referred to "vital powers" (Lawrence, *Lectures*, 78), "vital phenomena" (Barclay, *Inquiry*, 21), and "vital principles" (Abernethy, *Inquiry*, 89), but not 'vitalism'. Moreover, 'vitalism' is used in so many ways that using it here would invite confusion. On the complexity of nineteenth-century theories of life, see Benton, "Vitalism".

that life could be explained in terms of features inherent only in living organisms – for example, some quality of the *matter* or some fact about the *structure* of living organisms. Immanentists typically did not deny that living bodies contain some sort of vital force, but they saw this force as emerging from the physical or structural features of bodies. These are the sorts of theories that Barclay labelled 'materialist'. Transcendentalists, on the other hand, held that living entities differ from non-living ones because the former contain a vital principle that is not inherent in matter but is, theoretically at least, separable from it.[2]

German physician Johann Blumenbach (1752–1840) was an immanentist, positing the existence of a special life-force, the *Bildungstrieb*, which was (in historian Timothy Lenoir's words) a "teleological agent which had its antecedents ultimately in the inorganic realm but which was an emergent vital force" (Lenoir, "Kant", 83). Lenoir stresses that Blumenbach thought this *Bildungstrieb* "was not to be considered a kind of soul superimposed on matter" (Lenoir, "Kant", 84); it was itself material. Similarly, French scientist Xavier Bichat (1771–1802) argued that the "vital properties" of a living organism are "inherent" in its matter (Bichat, *General Anatomy*, 10).

The early nineteenth-century debate over the nature of life is crystallized in a dispute between two London surgeons, William Lawrence and John Abernethy (1764–1831).[3] In his 1814 lectures to the Royal College of Surgeons, subsequently published as a book, Abernethy defended a transcendentalist theory of life, writing that "the matter of animals and vegetables is ... as we express it, common matter, it is inert; so that the necessity of supposing the superaddition of some subtile and mobile substance is apparent" (Abernethy, *Inquiry*, 41). The book received a scathing review in *The Edinburgh Review* (Temkin, "Basic Science", 99) and William Lawrence added to the criticisms. In 1816, in his own lectures to the Royal College of Surgeons, Lawrence rejected Abernethy's defense of a superadded source of life; Abernethy replied with an attack on Lawrence; and Lawrence gave an aggrieved defense of himself in his 1817 lectures, protesting that he had been "trampled on, lecture after lecture" (Lawrence, *Lectures*, 3). He published this series of lectures in 1819 under the title *Lectures on Physiology, Zoology, and the Natural History of Man*, and it is to this book that Shepherd responded.[4]

Lawrence was clearly in the immanentist camp, warning his readers not to commit the "error of viewing the vital manifestations as something independent of the organization in which they occur" (Lawrence, *Lectures*, 53). Instead,

---

[2]Immanentism can also be characterized as a form of 'endogenous vitalism', and transcendentalism as 'exogenous vitalism' (see Jacyna, "Immanence or Transcendence", 313). Shepherd echoes this language when she refers to an "extraneous power" (Shepherd, *Essay*, 180 and 182).

[3]In this account of the dispute between Abernethy and Lawrence, I am indebted to Temkin, "Basic Science".

[4]Shepherd gives page numbers from the 1819 edition of Lawrence's book (the first edition). However, all citations in this paper are from the third edition (1823).

he insisted, "vital properties" must be studied through observation of the bodies that manifest those properties. He wrote, "I profess an entire ignorance of the nature of the vital properties, except in so far as they are disclosed by experience; and I find my knowledge on this subject reduced to the simple result of observation, that certain phenomena occur in certain organic textures" (Lawrence, *Lectures*, 12). Living beings can be *described* in ways that distinguish them from the non-living, insofar as only the former have "vital processes" – that is, the actions of muscles, nerves, and capillaries (Lawrence, *Lectures*, 66, 68). The "vital process" of muscles (or "living muscular fibres") was "irritability", and the "vital process" of nerves ("living nervous fibres") was "sensibility" (Lawrence, *Lectures*, 70–71).[5] These tissues and processes can be studied by anatomy, chemistry, and physiology: the anatomist must "demonstrate the structure and unravel the texture of animal bodies"; the chemist examines their composition; and the physiologist "unfolds the nature of life" by identifying the functions performed by the various parts of the living animal body (Lawrence, *Lectures*, 51–2). Lawrence especially emphasized the need for *both* anatomical research (through dissection) and physiological studies (using observation of functions): "anatomy and physiology should be cultivated together" (Lawrence, *Lectures*, 52). To understand life, for Lawrence, is to know how structures in the animal body are correlated with functions.

Lawrence noted that "the ultimate purpose of our researches in natural history is, to penetrate and lay open the secret springs by which the great organization, called 'nature', is maintained in perpetual activity" (Lawrence, *Lectures*, 59), and that in physiology, in particular, researchers want to know "whether the vital processes can be explained on the same principles as the other phenomena of matter" (Lawrence, *Lectures*, 60) – that is, in mechanical or chemical terms. This might suggest that Lawrence thought chemical analysis would explain why some entities are living and others are not. But while Lawrence conceded that chemistry usefully provides information about bodily processes such as digestion (Lawrence, *Lectures*, 63), he rejected the attempt to explain vital processes in chemical or mechanical terms (Lawrence, *Lectures*, 65–6). Arguing that the variety and complexity of forces and motions in animal bodies are so great that it is not humanly possible to do the calculations needed to explain these forces and motions in mathematical terms (Lawrence, *Lectures*, 63), Lawrence thought complete mechanical or chemical descriptions of vital processes would forever escape our human capabilities.

Moreover, even if we *could* describe all the chemical and mechanical processes involved in physiology, Lawrence denied that those descriptions would

---

[5]'Irritability' and 'sensibility' had been key concepts in physiology since the work of Francis Glisson in the seventeenth century and Albrecht von Haller in the eighteenth; see Young, *Mind, Brain, and Adaption*, 65.

tell us *how* living organisms are able to carry out those processes (Lawrence, *Lectures*, 65); while chemical analyses of physiological processes have "thrown great light on both the healthy and disordered actions of our frame … .[i]t is … in most cases the result, and not the operation itself, that we learn from chemistry" (Lawrence, *Lectures*, 64–5). Thus Lawrence concluded that "the main springs of the animal functions, the original moving forces, cannot be explained" in mechanical or chemical terms (Lawrence, *Lectures*, 68).

However, Lawrence did not take this conclusion as a reason to be a transcendentalist about life. Invoking a separable, immaterial soul or principle would be to enter the realm of "speculations and fancies" (Lawrence, *Lectures*, 58). Our understanding of nature should be based on "observation and experiment, the only sources of our knowledge of life" (Lawrence, *Lectures*, 57), but, in Lawrence's memorable terms, "an immaterial and spiritual being could not have been discovered amid the blood and filth of the dissecting room" (Lawrence, *Lectures*, 7).

Lawrence's solution, then, was for physiologists, anatomists, and chemists to limit themselves to the observation that "certain vital manifestations are connected with certain organic structures" (Lawrence, *Lectures*, 68). In other words, Lawrence said that it is enough to identify certain *constant conjunctions* of processes with structures in living entities. And this is where Hume comes into the picture: in a long footnote, Lawrence approvingly quotes from Thomas Brown's Humean account of causation (Lawrence, *Lectures*, 68–70). For example, regarding the muscles and nerves in particular, Lawrence insisted that all the physiologist can say is that living muscular fibres are irritable and living nervous fibres are sensible. As he put it:

> To say that irritability is a property of living muscular fibres, is merely equivalent to the assertion, that such fibres have in all cases possessed the power of contraction. What then is the cause of irritability? I do not know, and cannot conjecture.
>
> In physiology, as in the physical sciences, we quickly reach the boundaries of knowledge whenever we attempt to penetrate the first causes of the phenomena …
>
> (Lawrence, *Lectures*, 71)

One might think that Lawrence has misunderstood Hume, for according to Hume, to identify a constant conjunction between two types of entities or events *is* to identify the cause. But when Lawrence says he does not know, and "cannot conjecture" about, the cause of irritability, he means that we cannot know anything about the cause understood in a *non*-Humean way; we cannot know *why* irritability is always found with living muscular fibres. We must, he thinks, be content with identifying constant conjunctions.

3. Lawrence's "dangerous" error

Lawrence's reliance on a Humean theory of causation prompted Shepherd to address his views. Her criticisms fall into two groups. In Chapter Five of her *Essay*, she accuses Lawrence of committing the "dangerous mistake" of not seeing that "a real efficient cause is necessary to be assigned for *life*" (Shepherd, *Essay*, 175). In Chapter Six, she quotes six passages from Lawrence's lectures, alleging that Lawrence contradicted himself in three ways. While her charges of contradiction may not be entirely fair, space constraints preclude examining those arguments here. However, even if one or more of those particular arguments fails, that does not affect Shepherd's main objection to Lawrence, the "dangerous" mistake identified in Chapter Five, on which my discussion will focus.

Before considering this objection, it is worth noting one point on which Shepherd claims to agree with Lawrence. She identifies as Lawrence's "only clear and valuable definition" of life his view that "life is a constant internal motion, which enables a body to assimilate new and separate old particles, and prevents it from yielding to the chemical affinities of the surrounding elements" (Shepherd, *Essay*, 181; see also 183).[6] Shepherd praises this definition for being both comprehensive (inclusive of plants as well as animals) and exclusive (not applicable to anything that we would not want to say is alive). Mentioning her own "notion of life", she suggests that the Biblical description of God's breathing life into man can be read as God "giving [the organs] that internal vigour and motion, capable of enabling them to act afterwards for themselves, upon the objects which surrounded them" (Shepherd, *Essay*, 183).

Yet this agreement between Shepherd and Lawrence is only superficial. The "definition" Shepherd finds acceptable in Lawrence's text is simply a *description* of 'being alive' or 'living'. She agrees with Lawrence that all and only living entities have a certain kind of motion such that they can, on their own, assimilate new particles and separate old particles, and not succumb entirely to the environment. But this account is, to use a term Shepherd favours, an account only of the *quality* of being alive. As we shall see, for Shepherd, a quality is an *effect* that requires a cause. To say that an entity has life insofar as it has a certain kind of internal motion is only to say it has life as a quality, but is not yet to explain *why* it has that quality, or what cause *gave* it that quality. We can mark this distinction between life in the sense of 'being alive' as an *effect or quality* and life as the *cause* of a thing's having that quality

---

[6]Shepherd paraphrases Lawrence. The exact quotation is this: "Living bodies exhibit a constant internal motion, in which we observe an uninterrupted admission and assimilation of new, and a correspondent separation and expulsion of old particles. The form remains the same, the component particles are continually changing. While this motion lasts, the body is said to be alive; when it has irrecoverably ceased, to be dead. The organic structure then yields to the chemical affinities of the surrounding agents, and is speedily destroyed" (Lawrence, *Lectures*, 81).

using the labels *life$_e$* and *life$_c$*, where life$_c$ is the productive factor that explains *why* an entity has life$_e$ and is not merely a factor constantly correlated with entities that have certain structures and functions.[7] So Shepherd agrees with Lawrence only about what constitutes life$_e$, not life$_c$.

However, as we have seen, Lawrence was not interested in trying to identify the cause (understood in a non-Humean way) of life, or life$_c$. Thus Shepherd accuses Lawrence of not seeing that "a real efficient cause is necessary to be assigned for *life*" (Shepherd, *Essay*, 175). Since his resistance to identifying such a cause is due to his endorsement of a Humean account of causation in terms of constant conjunction, Shepherd starts by tackling this aspect of Lawrence's views.

She notes, first, that irritability and sensibility are not, as Lawrence had claimed, *simply* found always to be correlated with living muscles and nerves (Shepherd, *Essay*, 153). Rather, she argues, since irritability and sensibility are not found in dead bodies, but only in living ones, "it must be by a *truly necessary connexion*, between life and these qualities" (Shepherd, *Essay*, 162). That is, the relationship between life and the bodily processes of muscles and nerves is deeper than mere constant conjunction.

Second, she chastises Lawrence for *denying* that a cause can be found for qualities such as irritability and sensibility, and, in this denial, thereby assigning a "false cause" (Shepherd, *Essay*, 165–68). She writes, "Of all philosophical errors, the substitution of false, partial, or insufficient causes for the production of an end or object, is the most dangerous, because so liable to escape detection" (Shepherd, *Essay*, 167). Shepherd holds that since living entities have qualities that non-living entities lack, there must be some truly productive, efficient cause for that difference, and she thinks Lawrence's primary error is in suggesting that we cannot and do not need to know that cause. We should *not* be content with identifying constant conjunctions; we should seek to find the necessary cause of the characteristics displayed by living entities.

At this point, we need to consider Shepherd's own account of causation. This is the topic of Section 4.

4. Shepherd's account of causation

Four features of Shepherd's account of causation are especially important for our purposes: that we can know certain causal principles through reason

---

[7]Shepherd herself suggests in her discussion of Lawrence that the word 'gold' can be understood in two ways. It can be "a *name* for certain enumerated *qualities, en masse*", such as ductility, being yellow, etc.; in this case we have arbitrarily assigned the name to the effects that arise together when we perceive a certain kind of object (Shepherd, *Essay*, 155). But it can also be used to refer to the *cause* of those effects, the external object that necessarily produces certain perceived qualities when it interacts with our senses (Shepherd, *Essay*, 155). Using the terminology I have introduced, the former is gold$_e$; the latter, gold$_c$. While Shepherd does not use this terminology, I think it captures her distinctions.

alone; that causal connections are necessary connections; that causes and effects are not separable but must occur synchronously; and that all causation involves at least two causal factors.

First, Shepherd argues that we can know through reason two principles regarding causation:

The Causal Principle (CP): "A Being cannot begin its existence of itself".

(Shepherd, *Essay*, 39)

The Causal Likeness Principle (CLP): "Like causes necessarily have like effects".

(Shepherd, *Essay*, 43–44)

Briefly, her argument for CP goes like this: Suppose that CP is not true, and that an object can come into existence without an external cause. This object which allegedly has no cause itself "START[S] FORTH into existence, and make[s] the first breach on the wide nonentity around" (Shepherd, *Essay*, 35). This "starting forth", or coming into existence, is an *action*, and an action is a *quality* of an object; but the object that supposedly has the quality of coming into existence cannot have that quality until *after* it has come into existence (Shepherd, *Essays*, 290). Since denying CP requires asserting the "absurdity" both that an object does not exist and that it does exist, "we must conclude *that there is no object which begins to exist, but must owe its existence to some cause*" (Shepherd, *Essay*, 36–7). Martha Bolton has argued that Shepherd begs the question by "characterizing a beginning of existence as an act of an object other than it" (Bolton, "Mary Shepherd"), but space constraints preclude discussing the strength of Shepherd's argument here; let us grant her that principle.

With CP in place, Shepherd says that we can know CLP through a thought experiment that she calls "reasoning upon experiment" (Shepherd, *Essay*, 45). Admit "by supposition" (Shepherd, *Essay*, 55) that there are two identical causes (call them X1 and X2) in exactly similar circumstances. Since CP is true, any difference in the effects of X1 and X2 would require some cause. But the only causes posited are X1 and X2, and the situations in which they act are, by supposition, exactly the same. Thus "they must have like effects, or qualities, because there is nothing else given that can be supposed to make a difference" (Shepherd, *Essay*, 56). Shepherd concludes that this thought experiment establishes the truth of the Causal Likeness Principle. Contrary to Hume, we know CLP through reason; we do not merely accept it through custom.

Moreover, we can know that causal relationships are necessary connections. Imagine that we can control all factors in the environment in which, say, a piece of wood is put into a fire. CP tells us that no quality or difference can occur without a cause other than itself. Since wood's burning is a case of a difference occurring, it cannot have arisen without a cause. But since (by hypothesis) all circumstances remained the same other than the piece of wood being put into the fire, we know that the *only possible* cause of this difference was the wood being put into the fire; in other words, we can infer that putting the wood in the fire *necessarily caused* it to burn (Shepherd, *Essay*, 47–9 and 73). And since the connection is a necessary one, then the next time wood is put in the fire (assuming circumstances are exactly the same as before), we can know that it, too, will burn. So reason also establishes the necessity of causal connections.

Third, for Shepherd, the necessary connection between causes and effects means that causes and effects are never really separable. Contrary to Hume's account of causation, Shepherd holds that an event being antecedent to another is irrelevant to whether or not it is a cause of that event (Shepherd, *Essay*, 49 and 67). In fact, as Martha Bolton has pointed out, Shepherd's view is that an event that precedes another in time *cannot* be a proximate cause of the second. Suppose Y normally follows X. Since X and the appearance of Y are (to use Bolton's terms) 'temporally discrete', it is possible for there to be a case where X occurs, but where something else intervenes before Y occurs, thereby preventing Y from occurring. In this case, there is no necessary connection between X and Y. And, if there is no necessary connection, then X cannot be the cause of Y (Bolton, "Causality", 244).

Thus, according to Shepherd, effects do not *follow* their causes; causes and effects are synchronous, and it is misleading to express a causal relationship between A and B as 'A followed by B'. We should say, rather, that 'A x B = C', where that means that when two items A and B 'mix' or conjoin, item C arises (Shepherd, *Essay*, 141). Indeed, Shepherd says we should think of a mixture of causes as already containing their effect: "C [the effect] *is* INCLUDED *in the* MIXTURE OF THE OBJECTS CALLED CAUSE" (Shepherd, *Essay*, 141). Shepherd means us to take seriously the suggestion that a causal relationship can be represented by an *equation,* as 'A x B = C'; A and B are, literally, factors, entities that produce something else when multiplied together, and the very combining of those factors *is* the effect, just as "the results of all arithmetical combinations are included in their statements" (Shepherd, *Essay*, 142). So Shepherd defines a 'cause' as "such action of an object as shall enable it, in conjunction with another, to form a new nature, capable of exhibiting qualities varying from those of either of the objects unconjoined" (Shepherd, *Essay*, 63).

Finally, the production of any effect will involve at least two causal factors 'mixing'. Indeed, Shepherd notes, "sometimes a *vast multitude of objects are wanted,* before their *mutual bearings* and *mixtures* with each other operate so as to *produce* any peculiar existence" (Shepherd, *Essay*, 166–7). Take making cake batter, for example, which requires that flour, eggs, butter, and other ingredients be combined. Shepherd would say that the ingredients are among the causes of the batter: when the ingredients 'mix', the batter is the result. But the ingredients are only some of the batter's causes; strictly speaking, the ingredients *plus* the action of a spoon or electric mixer are the causes. While the existence of the ingredients does precede the existence of the batter, the mixing of the ingredients with the action of the spoon does not precede the existence of the batter: the coalescence of the ingredients and the mixing action synchronously produce the batter. The causes are synchronous with the effect.

Shepherd's account of causation plays a key role in her 1827 book, where she develops a causal account of sensation that provides the basis for her argument for the existence of external, continuously existing objects. Human sensory perceptions arise when those external objects interact with components in the human perceiver: the mind, sense-organs, and nervous system and brain (Shepherd, *Essay*, 170–1 and Shepherd, *Essays*, 53–7). These various components are causes that 'mix', giving rise to sensations as effects. Sensory perceptions do not *copy* the external objects that are their partial causes, Shepherd argues; if a sensory perception were *just like* the external object that helped cause it, then the interaction of the external object with the sense-organs, mind, and brain would not result in a modification or change (Shepherd, *Essays*, 184–5). Thus we cannot infer that the external objects, when unperceived, actually resemble the sensations that they cause. However, Shepherd maintains that we can know "by *reason*" that external objects bear the same "proportions" to each other that our perceptions of them bear to each other (Shepherd, *Essays*, 205). That is, the variety in our sensory perceptions must result from correlative variety in the causes, and the variety in the causes must exist in the same "proportions" as the variety in the effects (Shepherd, *Essays*, 205, 240). As Bolton puts it, "there is a structural identity between the sensory effects and the external world which enables us to know relational properties of causes" (Bolton, "Causality", 246).

Thus, according to Shepherd's account of perception, we do not actually sense or perceive the external objects themselves; rather, we infer that they must exist, as the causes of our sensations (Shepherd, *Essays*, 133–4). External objects "in relation to us" are "nothing but masses of certain qualities, affecting certain of our senses" – but in themselves, "when independent of our senses, are *unknown* powers or qualities in nature" (Shepherd, *Essay*, 46). External objects can themselves "externally intermix, and in different ways mutually affect each other" (Shepherd, "Lady Mary", 703); however, since those external objects themselves are not sensed, causal interactions among them can only be inferred, not sensed.

To see how this account differs from Hume's account of causation, consider Hume's example of one billiard ball hitting another. Hume considers the motion in the first ball to be the cause of the motion of the second ball, but notes that "Motion in the second Billiard-ball is a quite distinct event from motion in the first; nor is there anything in the one to suggest the smallest hint of the other" (Hume, *Enquiry*, 26–7). The first ball's motion is the cause of the second ball's motion because other motions like the first ball's motion have been observed to be correlated with motions like the second ball's motion, and because perceivers typically infer an instance of the second upon perceiving an instance of the first; however, on Hume's account, there is no necessary connection (as traditionally understood) between the two successive events. Shepherd actually *agrees* with Hume that there is no necessary connection between the two events, because she does not see *events* as causally related. Rather, the causal connection is between the interaction of the two balls (the causes) and the new quality (the effect) of motion in the second ball that simultaneously comes into existence as they interact. There is also a causal connection between the interaction of the external objects, senses, and mind (the causes) and the *simultaneous* sensations of the objects in a perceiver's mind (the effect). Perhaps surprisingly, in this regard Shepherd agrees with Hume: we have successions of sensations that we take to be causally connected but which are not, in fact, so connected.

In sum, when Shepherd writes about the cause of some event, she is making no claims about what precedes that event. Rather, to identify the cause of some event is to identify the factors that, when combined, result synchronously in a new quality beginning to exist. So, when Shepherd criticizes Lawrence for not identifying the cause of life, she is *not* asking what action, event, or state of affairs precedes the motions of vital processes. That might be of some interest to know, but it would not tell us the cause of an entity having the quality of life. Rather, she is seeking the *factors* that, when combined, synchronously produce that "constant internal motion, which enables a body to assimilate new and separate old particles, and prevents it from yielding to the chemical affinities of the surrounding elements" (Shepherd, *Essay*, 181). This is what Lawrence has refused to provide.

5. Vital principles and Newtonian attraction

Shepherd frames her discussion as a critique specifically of Lawrence, but she does have the resources to defend a transcendentalist theory of life more broadly against an objection implied by other immanentists as well as Lawrence. Several immanentists appealed to an analogy with Newtonian gravitational attraction, suggesting that gravity gives us a model for understanding life as inherent. Shepherd agreed that vital processes are analogous to gravitation, but she also thought that the immanentists were reading Newton incorrectly. Had they read Newton as she did, they would see (she might have argued) that the analogy with gravity actually supports the transcendentalist view.

Lawrence invoked the analogy with Newtonian gravity to argue against positing a superadded force or principle to explain life. He pointed out that *other* scientific theories explain the behaviour of matter without invoking such separable principles: "What should we think of abstracting elasticity, cohesion, gravity, and bestowing on them a separate existence from the bodies in which those properties are seen?" (Lawrence, *Lectures*, 53). Those who "think it impossible that the living organic structures should have vital properties without some extrinsic aid" nonetheless (and, he implies, inconsistently) "require no such assistance for the equally wonderful affinities of chemistry, for gravity, elasticity, or the other properties of matter" (Lawrence, *Lectures*, 72).

Indeed, others involved in the debates over the nature of life also compared vital properties to Newtonian attraction. As Timothy Lenoir notes, Blumenbach's account of *Bildungstrieb* used language that echoed Newton's language in the General Scholium; just as gravity is a force inherent in matter, life is, as Lenoir puts it, a kind of "organic version of a Newtonian force" (Lenoir, "Kant", 77 and 84). Likewise, Bichat saw physiology and anatomy as comparable to Newtonian physics; all seek to provide accurate *descriptions* of the *properties* of living organisms and to treat these properties as "*primitive principles*" for which no further cause can be found. As he put it, his account of vital powers "is a theory like that which shows in the physical sciences, gravity, elasticity, affinity, &c. as the primitive principles of the facts observed in these sciences" (Bichat, *General Anatomy*, viii).[8]

In her 1827 book, Shepherd discusses Newtonian gravitational attraction between objects, but she rejects her contemporaries' understanding of it. She allows that 'attraction' "is a word as well suited as any other to express the *effect*, the direction of the motion of *bodies towards each other*, according to those laws of velocity which given densities observe" (Shepherd, *Essays*, 362). In other words, 'attraction' can describe certain motions of bodies. But she maintains that it is a mistake to understand gravity as a "quality, an attribute of all matter as matter", that causes bodies to move (Shepherd, *Essays*, 364). To do so is "to invest matter by the deceptious use of a metaphor with a mental quality, while yet *no consciousness* is supposed" (Shepherd, *Essays*, 362). She argues that we have no reason to think that such an inherent quality of matter exists: "no organ of sense ever detected it; no experiment ever found it; no reasoning ever deduced it from admitted premises; the laboratory of the chymist never elicited it from any convincing trial" (Shepherd,

---

[8] L. S. Jacyna also notes that the English physician Thomas Charles Morgan (1783–1843) held that "a strong similarity existed between vital properties and such phenomena found in inanimate nature as chemical affinity and gravitational attraction" (Jacyna, "Immanence or Transcendence", 314).

Essays, 364; see also 365). She also offers a thought experiment in support of her claim that gravity is not an immanent force:

> Let two balls be supposed, of the relative sizes and densities of the sun and moon; – and to be placed at the same relative distance in a state of *complete rest* in an exhausted receiver, with *empty space* alone between them; is it imagined for a moment they would ever begin to move, and direct their motions towards each other after any *law of attraction* whatever? They could not, – for the causes being efficient to *rest*, they could not be also efficient to motion. And if it be said the bodies were not or could not be *at rest,* then they were in motion – but motion is not *attraction,* and the motion supposed, still lies in need of being accounted for, both in its beginning and direction.

(Shepherd, Essays, 362)

If gravity were an immanent force, it would *always* be actually present in matter, and thus should always be acting as a cause of motions that draw matter together. Yet to imagine that two balls at rest in an empty receiver begin to move towards each other requires positing some *other* cause, *extrinsic* to the matter of the balls, to initiate such motion. Since this cause would be extrinsic, Shepherd takes this to show that matter does not contain any inherent force of gravity.

To immanentists about life who invoked analogies with gravity to argue that life is inherent in certain material structures such as muscle tissue, Shepherd might have turned the analogy on its head. If we have no reason to posit that gravity is an inherent attractive power in matter (and indeed have a thought experiment to show that it is not), she might have argued that analogical reasoning would suggest that *life* is similarly not an inherent force. Indeed, her claim regarding gravity that it has never been detected by the senses, experiments, or reasoning "from admitted premises" (Shepherd, *Essays*, 364) might also apply to the "vital properties" allegedly inherent in some parts of the physical world. The thought-experiment of the two balls has an analogue, too. As Shepherd notes, "the muscle and nerve can and do exist as organized beings, without irritability and sentiency when under death" (Shepherd, *Essay*, 162); more poignantly, she observes that "many a beautiful and youthful set of organs are perfect, without animation" (Shepherd, *Essay*, 180). Just as two balls at rest in an empty receiver would require the addition of a new, extrinsic cause to make them move, an inanimate human body would require the addition of a new, extrinsic cause to bring it to life. Shepherd could thus conclude that life must be something separable from matter, an exogenous cause that, when 'mixed' with other necessary causes, results in a living organism.

6. Shepherd's account of 'life'

As we have seen, for Shepherd, a cause is a factor that mixes with another object in order to bring about (synchronously) an effect, where an effect is a new quality of an object. Being alive – that is, possessing life$_e$ – means a body has certain kinds of motions that sustain it over time without allowing it to fall prey to external forces. What causal factors did Shepherd think were required for an animal body to have this quality, life$_e$? One requirement, obviously, is the existence of a physical being organized in a certain way. Shepherd, like Lawrence, focused on muscles and nerves as the most characteristic structural features of animal bodies:

> Now as the muscle and nerve can and do exist as organized beings, without irritability and sentiency when under death, so when as substances, they are placed under that condition called *life*, and are then only capable of putting on these qualities of irritability and sentiency, it must be by *a truly necessary connexion*, between life and these qualities. Irritability and sentiency are verily new powers and beings *created* by efficient, *creating* circumstances. Sensation and all its variety, is not an effect without a cause; and *life* is that object without which it will not exist in the *nerve*; and therefore according to the doctrine laid down in this Essay, is a true cause for it: being *one* of the objects *absolutely necessary* and efficient to *that* result in *certain circumstances*; – although what the WHOLE of those conditions may be, the combination of which is needful, may possibly ever remain beyond the scrutiny of man.

(Shepherd, *Essay*, 163)

When Shepherd refers to the 'sentiency' of nerves in this passage, she means what Lawrence meant by 'sensibility'. Shepherd was actually more careful than Lawrence in distinguishing *sentience* from life; as she notes elsewhere, a living being can have nerves without being sentient, for "in sound sleep there seems no inherent *sentiency*, though there be animation" (Shepherd, *Essays*, 311). And, of course, there are living entities that lack sentience altogether. For sensation to occur, Shepherd held that an already-living nerve must be 'mixed' with something else, a further, separate principle that enables it to sense (Shepherd, *Essays*, 241). That is, she stresses that the cause of being alive is distinct from the cause of being sentient.[9]

But what *sort of thing* is this causal factor, life$_c$, that when mixed with an organized body, makes it living? Shepherd does not say much about it. In one passage she compares life$_c$ to a spark that starts a fire burning, which, in turn, can ignite further objects and set them aflame:

---

[9] Shepherd says almost nothing about what might cause muscles to be irritable, but in several passages she makes a tripartite distinction, referring to "sensation, life, or action" (Shepherd, *Essays*, 394–5). Evidently she thought muscular motion (action) is due to yet another distinct causal factor.

> Thus combustible matters may be heaped upon each other, yet neither warmth or light succeed; but let an "extra cause" kindle the pile, then the flame may be kept alive for ever, by the constant addition of such substances. – In like manner life as we find it, as a perpetual flame, must be kept up and transmitted, whilst the proper objects for its support are administered: but for its original *Cause* we must go back, until some extraneous power is referred to as its first parent.
>
> (Shepherd, *Essay*, 182)

Fire is both a cause and an effect: an initial spark of fire is needed to set a pile of combustible materials burning, to produce fire as an effect, which can then cause something else to burn. Thus fire can be passed from one entity to another, retaining a causal connection with an original source. Shepherd suggests that life is like this: the state of being alive, life$_e$, is passed from parents to offspring, and then the living offspring cause life in the next generation: as she puts it, life is "continually propagated through the species" (Shepherd, *Essay*, 183). But, like fire, there must be some initial, extraneous power that sets the causal chain in motion.

Since Shepherd says so little about this 'extraneous' power that is life$_c$, I suggest considering another causal factor, about which she has more to say, which is *mind*. I mentioned earlier that Shepherd held that for sentience to occur, an already-living nerve must be 'mixed' with something else. This additional "sentient principle and capacity" (Shepherd, *Essays*, 217), or "capacity for sensation in general" (Shepherd, *Essays*, 163 and 310) is what Shepherd calls mind. She also says mind is a "power", "the power of thought and feeling" (Shepherd, *Essays*, 40) and that it is a *cause*:

> Body is the *continually exciting cause*, for the exhibition of the perception of *extension* and *solidity* on the mind in particular; and mind is the CAPACITY or CAUSE, for *sensation in general*.
>
> (Shepherd, *Essays*, 155)

As we saw earlier, she defines a cause as "such action of an object, as shall enable it, in conjunction with another, to form a new nature, capable of exhibiting qualities varying from those of either of the objects unconjoined" (Shepherd, *Essay*, 63). And she has no objection to characterizing mind, the capacity, as an "object" (Shepherd, *Essays*, 14, 15, 17, 50). In sense-perception, mind works with, or "intermixes with", other factors – namely, the sense-organs, the nervous system and brain, and external objects – in order to produce sensations. In reasoning, sensations of sensible qualities and sensations of ideas 'mix', thereby generating new sensations (Shepherd, *Essay*, 46).

Thus Shepherd characterizes mind as a general capacity or power that, when combined with other factors, causes specific conscious sensations.

Those conscious sensations can then combine with others to produce more conscious sensations; that is, the effects can also become causes. Shepherd may conceive of life analogously: life$_c$ is a general capacity or power that, when combined with other factors, causes a body to have specific types of environment-resisting motions (life$_e$). An entity with the quality of life$_e$ can then, under the right conditions, produce another entity with life$_e$; life$_e$ can serve as a cause of life$_c$. Ultimately, Shepherd traces both life and sentience – indeed, all existing beings, with all their qualities and capacities – back to the divine cause, God: "the wide universe, with all its gradations of wonderful beings, with all its powers of life and heat, and motion, must have come out from him according to the laws with which they were endowed" (Shepherd, *Essays*, 97).

The following passage supports the suggestion that Shepherd's account of life is analogous to her account of mind. Her point here is about mind[10]; she is arguing that merely being alive is not enough for an entity to be sentient, that we must infer that there is a further cause of sentience, namely mind. But the passage is striking for the way it treats both mind and life as capacities *and* causes *and* as qualities or effects:

> If indeed the powers of matter in general, (whatever matter may be,) were sufficient to elicit sentiency when placed under *arrangement* and mixed with life, then the true causes for it [i.e. sentiency] are assigned, and found. But we cannot *prove* this. If on the contrary, the essential qualities of matter arranged and in motion be not thought sufficient to account for so extraordinary a difference as that between conscious and unconscious being, then there must be a *particular* cause for it: which cause must be considered an immaterial cause, that is, a *principle, power, being*, an unknown quality *denied* to exist in matter. – This must have a name, and may be called *soul,* or *spirit*.
>
> (Shepherd, *Essay*, 169)

Analogously, life$_c$ is a principle, a power, a cause, that when mixed with a certain kind of organized body produces the 'extraordinary' difference between living and non-living entities. That is, life$_c$ is a capacity that, under the right conditions, brings about life$_e$. Entities with life$_e$ possess the capacity (life$_c$) and thus can pass along this state of being alive to other entities of the right sort.

This conclusion may be a disappointment. To say that life$_c$ is a capacity that, under the right conditions, brings about life$_e$ seems reminiscent of Molière's satire of Aristotelian philosophers in his 1673 play *The Imaginary Invalid*; when asked why opium makes people sleepy, the explanation is that it possesses a *"vertus dormitiva"*, a "dormitive virtue" (Molière, *Imaginary*, 134). But

---

[10]She uses the term 'soul', but this is for her equivalent to mind. See Shepherd, *Essays*, 310 and Shepherd, *Essay*, 171. For further discussion of Shepherd's account of soul/mind, see Boyle, "Mary Shepherd".

this is circular; to say that the cause of being sleepy is simply the power of producing sleepiness is to explain the cause in terms of the effect. Likewise, on the interpretation offered above, Shepherd explains the cause of being alive in terms of a power of making an entity be alive. But this seems to be no explanation at all.

However, such an explanation is perhaps just what we should expect from a causal theory in which effects are 'contained in' their causes. If the effect were completely different from the cause, then cause and effect would be separable, and thus not necessarily connected – and thus not really cause and effect at all, by Shepherd's lights. Suppose we suggest that the cause of the special kind of motion in an organism that constitutes its $life_e$ is the motion of some *other* physical entity that preceded it; suppose, for example, we suggest that an embryo is alive because of the precedent motions of sperm and egg. According to Shepherd's account of causation, this suggestion would amount simply to identifying a contingent state of affairs that preceded the existence of the living embryo. To correctly identify the cause of that special kind of motion in an organism that constitutes its $life_e$ would be to identify the *various* factors that must combine for that motion to exist, and one such factor is the capacity for such motion to be produced. Such a capacity is *not*, as Molière's satire would have it, the only required factor. But it does seem reasonable for Shepherd to insist that the existence of a quality requires, among other things, a capacity or power for that quality to exist.

Acknowledgements

An earlier version of this paper was presented at San Francisco State University in May 2019. I am grateful to the members of the audience for their helpful questions, as well as to two anonymous referees for this journal who offered useful suggestions for improving the paper.

Bibliography

Abernethy, John. *An Inquiry into the Probability and Rationality of Mr. Hunter's Theory of Life*. London: Printed for Longman, Hurst, Rees, Orme, and Brown, 1814.

Barclay, John. *An Inquiry into the Opinions, Ancient and Modern, Concerning Life and Organization*. Edinburgh: Printed for Bell and Bradfute, 1822.

Benton, E. "Vitalism in Nineteenth-Century Scientific Thought: A Typology and Reassessment". *Studies in the History and Philosophy of Science* 5, no. 1 (1974): 17–48.

Bichat, Xavier. *Physiological Researches upon Life and Death*. Translated by Tobias Watkins. Philadelphia: Smith and Maxwell, 1809.

Bichat, Xavier. *Vol. 1 of General Anatomy, Applied to Physiology and Medicine*. Translated by George Hayward. Boston: Richardson and Lord, 1822. Accessed May 12, 2019. http://www.gutenberg.org/ebooks/56118.

Blumenbach, Johann Friedrich. *Handbuch der Naturgeschichte*. 5th ed. Göttingen: Dietrich, 1797.

Bolton, Martha. "Causality and Causal Induction: The Necessitarian Theory of Lady Mary Shepherd". In *Causation and Modern Philosophy*, edited by Keith Allen and Tom Stoneham, 242–61. New York: Routledge, 2011.

Bolton, Martha. "Mary Shepherd". *Stanford Encyclopedia of Philosophy*. 2017. https://plato.stanford.edu/entries/mary-shepherd/.

Boyle, Deborah. "Mary Shepherd on Mind, Soul, and Self". *Journal of the History of Philosophy* 58, no. 1 (2020): 93–112.

Hume, David. *An Enquiry Concerning Human Understanding: A Critical Edition*. Edited by Tom L. Beauchamp. Oxford: Clarendon Press, 2000.

Jacyna, L. S. "Immanence or Transcendence: Theories of Life and Organization in Britain, 1790–1825". *Isis* 74 (1983): 311–29.

Lawrence, William. *Lectures on Physiology, Zoology, and the Natural History of Man*. London: Printed for J. Callow, 1819.

Lawrence, William. *Lectures on Physiology, Zoology, and the Natural History of Man*. 3rd ed. London: Printed for James Smith, 1823.

Lenoir, Timothy. "Kant, Blumenbach, and Vital Materialism in German Biology". *Isis* 71, no. 1 (1980): 77–108.

Molière. *The Imaginary Invalid: Le Malade Imaginaire*. Translated by Charles Heron Wall. US: The Floating Press, 2009.

Newton, Isaac. "General Scholium". In Vol. 2 of *The Mathematical Principles of Natural Philosophy*. Translated by Andrew Motte. London, 1729. Accessed May 6, 2019. http://www.newtonproject.ox.ac.uk/view/texts/normalized/NATP00056.

Shelley, Mary. *Frankenstein*. 3rd ed. Edited by D.L. Macdonald and Kathleen Scherf. Peterborough: Broadview Press, 2012.

Shepherd, Mary. *An Essay upon the Relation of Cause and Effect*. London: Printed for T. Hookham, 1824.

Shepherd, Mary. *Essays on the Perception of an External Universe, and Other Subjects Connected with the Doctrine of Causation*. London: John Hatchard and Son, 1827.

Shepherd, Mary. "Lady Mary Shepherd's Metaphysics". *Fraser's Magazine* 5 (1832): 697–708.

Temkin, Owsei. "Basic Science, Medicine, and the Romantic Era". *Bulletin of the History of Medicine* 37, no. 2 (1963): 97–129.

Young, Robert M. *Mind, Brain and Adaptation in the Nineteenth Century*. New York: Oxford University Press, 1990.

"Political … civil and domestic slavery": Harriet Taylor Mill and Anna Doyle Wheeler on marriage, servitude, and socialism

Helen McCabe

ABSTRACT
Harriet Taylor Mill and Anna Wheeler are two nineteenth-century British feminists generally over-shadowed by the fame of the men with whom they co-authored. Yet both made important and interesting contributions to political thought, particularly regarding deconstruction of (i) the patriarchal institution of marriage; and (ii) the current property regime which, in dominating workers, unfairly distributing the product of labour, and encouraging 'individualism', they believed did little to maximize the general happiness. Both were feminists, utilitarians, and socialists. How they link these elements is both interestingly similar, and interestingly different. This article has four aims. Firstly, to make a strong claim concerning their authorial hand in works often considered to be solely the work of their male co-author. Secondly, to sketch those co-authoring relationships, and consider whether Taylor and Mill may even have consciously constructed their early letters 'On Marriage' based upon what they knew of Thompson and Wheeler's relationship. Thirdly, to map out their shared (though not identical) claim that marriage was a form of slavery, and the proposals they offered to free women from the domination of patriarchal relationships. Fourthly, to explore the way in which both thought female emancipation would be most truly realized via cooperative socialism.

Harriet Taylor Mill (1807–58) and Anna Doyle Wheeler (1780–1848) are philosophers overshadowed by the men with whom they co-authored – John Stuart Mill (1806–73) and William Thompson (1785–1833). Although Taylor and Wheeler both achieved brief notoriety in the nineteenth century, they did not (unlike Mary Wollstonecraft) establish themselves, particularly to posthumous memory, as figures with their own claim to be included in the canon, though interest in them has increased in recent years.[1] However, both made

---

[1] See McCabe, "Harriet Taylor Mill"; "Harriet Taylor"; Cory, "Rhetorical Re-Visioning"; Jose, "Without Apology"; and Philips, "Beloved and Deplored".

important and interesting contributions to political thought, particularly regarding deconstruction of the patriarchal institution of marriage and the current property regime. They were part of a radical utilitarian milieu surrounding Jeremy Bentham, and were also involved with utopian socialism, though it is unlikely that Taylor and Wheeler ever met. Both were feminists, utilitarians, and socialists, and contributed new ideas to these schools of thought. Interesting differences and similarities in their ideas make them worthy of comparison; and the insightfulness of their critiques makes them worthy of contemporary study.

In this article, I outline the reasons why we should consider both as the co-authors of their more famous male counterparts, and briefly explore the possibility that Wheeler and Thompson were a 'model' for Taylor and Mill. My main focus is on comparing and contrasting their claim that marriage was a form of slavery, and the proposals they offered to free women from the domination of patriarchal relationships, in particular how they thought female emancipation would be most truly realized via cooperative socialism.

1. Co-authoring, contribution, and conscious modelling

In 1825, Thompson published *Appeal of the One Half of the Human Race, Women, Against the Pretentions of the Other Half, Men, to Retain them in Political, and thence in Civil, and Domestic Servitude: in reply to a paragraph of Mr. [James] Mill's celebrated "Article on Government"*. It starts with a lengthy "Introductory Letter to Mrs Wheeler" written "to perform … a debt of justice; to show myself possessed of that sincerity which I profess to admire" and not be guilty of literary 'piracy'.[2] Thompson explains that he has "endeavoured to arrange the expression of those feelings, sentiments, and reasonings, which have emanated from your mind". The *Appeal* contains "on paper, what you have so often discussed in conversation' regarding 'the condition of women … in what is called civilised society". "[T]hanks to the chance of being born a man", Thompson does not have the same life-experience from which to write, "yet can I not be inaccessible to the plain facts and reason of the case". He is 'indebted' to Wheeler "for those bolder and more comprehensive views" which are now so much his that "to separate your thoughts from mine were now to me impossible". Thus, *Appeal* is presented as an "arrangeme[nt] [of] our common ideas" (Thompson, "Introductory Letter", v–vii).

Thompson admits Wheeler had no hand in penning the manuscript of *Appeal*, as "leisure and resolution to undertake the drudgery of the task were wanting" on her part.[3] "A few only therefore of the following pages

---

[2] I follow Cory ("Rhetorical Re-Visoning", 114) in treating Thompson as the Letter's sole author.
[3] Though see Dooley (*Equality in Community*, 79–80) for why these might not have been Wheeler's *only* reasons.

are the exclusive produce of your mind and pen, and written with your own hand. The remainder are our joint property, I being your interpreter and the scribe of your sentiments" (Thompson, "Introductory Letter", vii).[4]

In a similar vein, though detailing a longer relationship, Mill (*Autobiography*, 247) recalls a long-standing "partnership of thought, feeling, and writing" with Taylor, which began in 1830.[5] In 1833, Mill and Taylor penned matching essays *On Marriage* (Mill, *Marriage*, 35–49; Taylor, *Complete Works*, 17–24).[6] Taylor also published (anonymously, but her authorship seems to have been an open secret) *Enfranchisement of Women* (1851) – the notes for it, along with other notes which bear more resemblance to *Subjection of Women* are in both her and Mill's hand (Taylor and Mill, *Papers on Women's Rights*).

Taylor played a variety of roles in co-authoring Mill's work. He says, when two people have "their thoughts and speculations completely in common ... all subject of intellectual or moral interest are discussed between them in daily life, and probed to much greater depths than ... usually or conventionally"; when they "set out from the same principles", and "arrive at their conclusions by processes jointly pursued", then:

> [I]t is of little consequences in respect to the question of originality which of them holds the pen; the one who contributes least to the composition may contribute most to the thought; the writings which result are the joint product of both, and it must often be impossible to disentangle their respective parts and affirm that this belongs to one and that to another.
> (Mill, *Autobiography*, 251)

"In this wide sense", he adds, "all my published writings were as much her work as mine", with many of "the most valuable ideas ... in these joint productions ... originat[ing] with her" (*Autobiography*, 251). Some more specific cases of co-authoring include: "working together" on "every sentence" of *On Liberty*; influencing the "tone", or fundamental ontology, of *Principles of Political Economy* as well as dictating some key passages; and co-authoring a series of articles on domestic violence (Mill, *Autobiography*, 249 and 255; Taylor (and Mill), *Complete Works*, 77–131).

Despite Thompson's "Introductory Letter", Wheeler's role as co-author has been underplayed historically, though now generally acknowledged. Much less has Taylor been recognized as Mill's co-author, Mill's claims about

---

[4] The concluding "Address to Women" is generally seen as being more by Wheeler than Thompson, though her authorship should not be limited to that section, – see Cory, "Rhetorical Revisioning", 113–9; Jose, "Without Apology", 831–2; and Dooley, *Equality in Community*, 69–70 for analysis of Wheeler's distinctive style, and evidence of it in *Appeal*.

[5] For more on their relationship, see McCabe, "Harriet Taylor Mill"; Rossi, "Sentiment and Intellect"; and Miller, "Harriet Taylor Mill".

[6] The various drafts of both essays are undated. Taylor's is written on paper watermarked 1831 and 1832, and Jacobs ("Chronology", xlii) gives an 1832 date as does Hayek for Mill's piece. However, for plausible text-based reasons, Robson ("Textual Introduction", lix–lx) suggests summer 1833 for Mill's piece because of which, and because she quotes Tennyson's *Eleanore*, first published in 1833, I give this date for Taylor's piece, too.

which have been denied and denigrated (see Jabobs, "Gifted Ladies"; Philips, "Beloved and Deplored", 627 and 639–40; and McCabe, "Harriet Taylor Mill", 121–3). But if we accept the arguments put forward for Wheeler's co-authorship of *Appeal*, then we ought also to accept those made about Taylor, and begin to reapprise both women's position in the 'canon' of political thought.

That the *Appeal* was so openly credited as being co-authored was radical and – at the time – unique.[7] Mill's one public attempt during their lifetimes to acknowledge Taylor's input – a dedicatory passage for first edition of *Principles* (1848)[8] – was scotched by Taylor's (or perhaps her husband's – see Rossi, "Sentiment and Intellect", 39–41) "dislike of publicity" (Mill, *Autobiography*, 257). However, Mill and Taylor left a meticulous account of the different ways in which they collaborated in the *Autobiography* (in which Taylor had a significant editorial hand). Many elements of this account bear striking resemblance to Thompson's description of working with Wheeler, giving weight to the suggestion that they may have provided a model for Mill and Taylor's own complicated relationship.

This possibility seems to have been first mooted by Terence Ball who "conjecture[s] ... that Thompson's chaste and cerebral relationship with Mrs Wheeler provided a model for ... Mill's subsequent relationship with ... Taylor" (Ball, "Utilitarianism", 206). Jose ("Without Apology", 844–5) also sees the younger pair taking the elder as "a model", in a similarly Platonic way. Noting that all four thinkers share the idea of marriage as "sympathetic association", he praises Wheeler and Thompson for "recognis[ing] that mutual and respectful shared sensual gratification was an important, indeed necessary, part of egalitarian, loving relationships" (though not suggesting it was any part of their own egalitarian relationship), but reads Mill and Taylor as "remain[ing] much more closely in tune with the sexual stereotypes of [the] Victorian era". Rossi ("Sentiment and Intellect", 10) also "surmises that 'passion' in the lives of both ... Mill and Harriet [Taylor] was a sublimated and highly intellectualised emotion". However, though Taylor certainly linked sexual pleasure with the imagination, and contrasted this 'higher pleasure' with 'sensuality', this is not to say she 'intellectualized' it. Similarly, she thought people could assert rational control over sexual impulses, but this does not mean she 'subliminated' passion. (For more on this, see McCabe, "Harriet Taylor". Also note Dooley, *Equality in Community*, 81–2 for whether Ball and Jose read Thompson and Wheeler's relationship correctly.)

---

[7] See also Jose ("Without Apology", 833–4) for discussion of why Wheeler was not more formally acknowledged as the co-author; and Cory ("Rhetorical Re-Visioning", 106) for discussion of the implications of a portrait of Wheeler being the frontispiece and (111–3) how Thompson reverses the usual gendered authorial roles in his "Introductory Letter".

[8] The dedication read: "To Mrs. John Taylor. as the most eminently qualified of all persons known to the author either to originate or to appreciate speculations on social improvement, this attempt to explain and diffuse ideas many of which were first learned from herself, is with the highest respect and regard, dedicated."

More important than whether or not both pairs had 'chaste', 'intellectual' relationships is the thought that Thompson and Wheeler modelled equality for Mill and Taylor, personally and professionally. Jose ("Without Apology", 841) says Mill's account of co-authoring with Taylor "eerlier echoes" Thompson's account of co-authoring with Wheeler: my suggestion is that there is nothing uncanny about it.

The similarity *might* be a coincidence. Perhaps what Mill and Thompson say could be said of any co-authoring relationship – but it is striking that they are rare (perhaps unique) among men in writing about themselves as "scribes" and "interpreters" of a woman's thought (see Cory, "Rhetorical Re-Visioning", many of whose arguments also apply to Mill). Perhaps Thompson/Mill and Wheeler/Taylor were quite similar, so their co-authoring relationships was also similar. There may be some truth in this, but – though as Ball ("Utilitarianism", 206) notes there is no direct testamentary evidence – we do see potentially deliberate echoes of Thompson's account in Mill.

Like Thompson calling himself a "scribe", "interpreter" and one who "arrange[d] ... expression" of ideas "which ... emanated from" Wheeler (Thompson, "Introductory Letter", v), Mill writes, "[d]uring the greater part of my literary life I have performed the office in relation to her ... of an interpreter of original thinkers, and mediator between them and the public" (Mill, *Autobiography*, 251). Similarly, Mill (*Autobiography*, 251-61) recalls writing down for publication what had been "so often discussed" (Thompson, "Introductory Letter", v) between him and Taylor, and describes his *Marriage* (37) as "a written exposition of ... opinions" prompted by Taylor, following conversations between them on the topic.

Mill (*Autobiography*, 256) also expresses gratitude to his female co-author for "those bolder and more comprehensive views" (Thompson, "Introductory Letter", vi): "I was her pupil, alike in boldness of speculation and cautiousness of practical judgment ... she was much more courageous and farsighted than without her I should have been, in anticipations of things to come". Again, like Thompson ("Introductory Letter", vi–vii) noting that "to separate your thoughts from mine were now to me impossible" and that *Appeal* is an "arrangeme[nt] [of] our common ideas", Mill (*Autobiography*, 259) writes of *Liberty* being a "conjunction of her mind with mine", and that:

> [I]t is difficult to identify any particular part or element as being more hers than all the rest. The whole mode of thinking of which the book was the expression, was emphatically hers. But I also was so thoroughly imbued with it that the same thought naturally occurred to us both.
> (Mill, *Autobiography*, 259)

Lastly, just as Thompson notes "can I not be inaccessible to the plain facts and reason of the case" (Thompson, "Introductory Letter", v–vi) for women's equality, Mill (*Autobiography*, 251) rejects what he suspects most will think

– that Taylor's influence over his "mental growth" would be solely around "equality ... between men and women"[9] – and insists "those convictions were among the earliest results of the application of my mind to political subjects", though, "until I knew her, the opinion was, in my mind, little more than an abstract principle".[10] Taylor made this less 'abstract'. Philips ("Beloved and Deplored", 633–4) argues that Taylor was more concerned with the 'everyday' nature of women's oppression, and their joint works are filled with 'practicalities' and details which are missing from Mill's single-authored feminist pieces. Her analysis is generally excellent, and helps flesh out Mill's (*Autobiography*, 251) account "that perception of the vast practical bearing of women's disabilities which found expression in ... *Subjection* ... was acquired mainly through her teaching", without which he "should have had a very insufficient perception of the mode in which the consequences of the inferior position of women intertwine themselves with all the evils of existing society and with all the difficulties of human improvement".[11]

It seems plausible – and indeed Mill himself seems to say – that Taylor's lived experience and recognition of the importance of the everyday in women's oppression informed her feminism, and also enriched his. Mill does not make exactly the same claim as Thompson ("Introductory Letter", v–vi), that being "born a man" he cannot see these things, but – by extension – because she was "born a woman", Wheeler can. In part, this is because Mill wants to make a more general claim for Taylor's unique genius, marrying imagination and great practical sagacity (Mill, *Autobiography*, 195 and 256), and also because both he and Taylor were chary of anything which seemed to suggest that women 'innately' understood things better than men (Mill, *Subjection*, 304-6), or that they were 'innately' 'higher' or 'better' beings (Mill, "Letter 261", 509–10). However, Mill's description of Taylor's contribution to their joint feminism links to Thompson's idea that his experiences as a man blinded him to some problems which were much more evident to his female co-author.

2. Marriage and slavery

Leaving aside the question of conscious modelling by Taylor/Mill, I turn now to the second part of this article: mapping Taylor and Wheeler's shared,

---

[9] See Philips ("Beloved and Deplored", 632–3) for an interesting analysis of why Mill might have made this assertion in the *Autobiography*.

[10] Rossi ("Sentiment and Intellect", 20–22 and 24–6) gives a good account of the feminist Utilitarian/Unitarian background of both Taylor and Mill when they met.

[11] However, though Mill does often give 'exalted' rather than everyday examples in *Subjection*, sometimes this is because he is referring to specific arguments about women-as-rulers (Philips, "Beloved and Deplored", 633; Mill, *Subjection*, 299–322). It is true, though, that there is no corresponding passage to that probably authored by Taylor (though the surviving copy is in Mill's hand) where she charts how women's practical involvement in politics (e.g. Abolition and prison reform) has had a beneficial effect, making people more capable of acting in the common good (Mill and Taylor, *Papers on Women's Rights*, 385).

though not identical, claim that marriage was a form of slavery, and the proposals they offered to free women from the domination of patriarchal relationships. Jose ("Without Apology", 843–4) also charts similarities between the analysis of marriage-as-slavery in *Appeal* and *Subjection*.[12] In this article, I seek to tease out this analogy in Taylor's writing, which is subtly different to Mill's, as well as to Wheeler's. That is, I am particularly interested in how two women who had experienced marriage formulated, and used, the marriage-as-slavery analogy (even though having to piece together their thought, on occasion, via words written by their male co-authors describing their views).

Thompson and Wheeler call "the existing system of marriage", an institution "under which, for the mere faculty of eating, breathing and living, in whatever degree of comfort husbands may think fit, women are reduced to domestic slavery, without a will of their own, or power of locomotion, otherwise than as permitted by their respected masters" (Thompson, "Introductory Letter", xi). The whole title of their book makes plain the connection they saw between women's lack of voting (and other political) rights; women's lack of economic and educational opportunities; marriage; and slavery.

Women's exclusion from political rights, legal protections, and educational and economic opportunities which allow for independence without marrying leaves them in the position of 'slaves', because someone can legally exercise almost absolute power over them (Thompson and Wheeler, *Appeal*, 41–2). This involves control over where they live; whether, when and with whom they leave the house; over their property and income (if any); over their sexual lives; over their friendships; over their children; over what they learn and their ambitions for life; and, ultimately, over all their interests, and everything that contributes to their happiness. Marriage merely allows women to swap the despotism of a father for that of a husband. Wives and daughters might not be subjected – in Europe – to the kind of brutal treatment experienced by slaves as we generally imagine them, but regarding their rights, they are in the same position.

---

[12] Jose ("Without Apology", 843) notes that, when *Subjection* was published "slavery had been abolished in the British Empire". We might also add that 13th Amendment had been passed in the USA. *Appeal*, however, was written eight years before the British Slavery Abolition Act. Thus, he argues Mill "could not presuppose, as could Wheeler and Thompson, an energised antislavery discourse" in the audience of his work. Arguably, though, Mill is attempting (as with other feminists) to extend the energy of the Abolitionist movement to what they saw as female slavery, rather than letting its momentum fade. Moreover, the fact that the American Civil War (1861–65) was so recent a memory, and had ended in victory for the North and the passing of the 13th Amendment, adds rhetorical weight to Mill's claim about women's slavery: slavery was now abolished in countries which considered themselves 'advanced' everywhere but in the home. Slavery was legal in more places when *Appeal* was published, it is true, but slavery was still politically salient in Mill's day. (Though increased knowledge of the conditions experienced in the Southern States of America may underly Taylor's caution regarding claiming marriage *is* slavery, and wives *are* slaves.)

Moreover, Wheeler argues, all the vices usually considered 'natural' to, and irremediable in, women, "are the vices of slaves", caused by tyranny, and curable by equality (Wheeler, *Rights of Women*, 35 qtd. in McFadden, "Wheeler", 96). Women are made to fawn, be sycophantic, think only about narrow interests, be 'irrational', live only for their looks, for love, for their families etc., because their unequal position means they *must* secure a husband, and this is what they are told (probably rightly) that a husband wants (very few men appreciating the 'higher pleasures' of intercourse with an equal) (Thompson, "Introductory Letter", xi). For these reasons, giving a lecture in in 1829, entitled *Rights of Women*, Wheeler even introduced herself as speaking "in my capacity as slave and woman" (Wheeler, *Rights of Women*, qtd in McFadden, "Wheeler", 96).[13]

Taylor's claim is never quite as strident. In *Papers on Women's Rights* (380) she does say that because "the disabilities of women" being "disabilities by birth" which a woman "cannot by any exertion get rid of", "[t]his makes her case ... like that of the negro in America", her disabilities being "indelible ones". However, she is not likening women's position to slavery, but saying that women's exclusion from equality of opportunity on the basis of a biological and social construct (sex/gender) is as permanent as exclusions on the grounds of race in America.

Similarly, she traces a history of society from a Hobbesian state of nature where "the races and tribes which are vanquished in war are made slaves, the absolute property of their conquerors" through a "gradual progress" whereby "[m]orality recommended kind treatment of slaves by their masters, and just rule by despots over their subjects, but it never justified or tolerated either slaves or subjects in throwing off the yoke", a case about which she says "[i]t is needless to point out how exactly the parallel holds in the case of women and men" (Taylor and Mill, *Papers on Women's Rights*, 387).

Similarly, she emphasizes the "domestic subjection" of women, which she says will "will be acknowledged to be as monstrous an infraction of the rights and dignity of humanity, as slavery is at last" (Taylor and Mill, *Papers on Women's Rights*, 387). She also notes that there are 'practical' differences in the treatment of 'subjected' women, "as ... in the case of slaves" through history, "from being slowly murdered by continued bodily torture, to being only subdued in spirit and thwarted of all those higher and finer developments of individual character of which personal liberty has in all ages been felt to be the indispensable condition". That is, in several places Taylor

---

[13] I am very aware that this way of speaking – and the *Appeal*'s appeal to the position of enslaved people in the Caribbean – might cause offence to the modern reader, perhaps more aware of – or more sensitive towards – the horrors and injustice of trans-Atlantic slavery, and the vast gulf in experience between even a woman in Wheeler's position (white and wealthy, though married to an abusive husband with no legal, political or economic rights as a single woman) and that of any enslaved African. I am not endorsing Wheeler's claim (or, later, Taylor's and/or Mill's), just laying it out.

makes a comparison between marriage and slavery, or using slavery (as the exemplar of the worst form of despotism) as an analogy to marriage, but this is subtly different to claiming marriage is *the same as* slavery, or is a form of slavery.

This said, she does say "[t]he exclusion of women from the suffrage becomes a greater offence and degradation in proportion as the suffrage is opened widely to all men. When the only privileged class is the aristocracy of sex the slavery of the excluded sex is more marked and complete" (Taylor and Mill, *Papers on Women's Rights*, 390). She also asserts that when humanity was "in a primitive condition", "women were and are the slaves of men for the purposes of toil", and that in a slightly further stage of human progress, "women were and are the slaves of men for the purposes of sensuality". Passing through a "third and milder dominion", beginning in Ancient Greece, whereby "[t]he wife was part of the furniture of home", subject to "a patriarch and a despot", but recognized as someone to whom men might owe "kindness, and ... duty", in modern times she identifies "a sense of correlative obligation": "The power of husbands has reached the stage which the power of kings had arrived at, when opinion did not yet question the rightfulness of arbitrary power, but in theory, and to a certain extent in practice, condemned the selfish use of it". This position, "that women should be, not slaves, nor servants, but companions" is, she thinks, the position of "moderate reformers of the education of women" (Taylor, *Enfranchisement of Women*, 406–8). Taylor herself argues for much more equality.

In the main, then, we see in Taylor a more nuanced argument – though similar to Wheeler's – that the underlying justifications given for slavery (that 'might is right', or that greater power or strength is a normative justification for rule; that there are natural, justifiable hierarchies of power and status; and that 'dependence' is some people's 'natural' and 'right' state) are those also given for women's inequality. Similarly, that historical relationships which allowed men to tyrannise over women (and, often, other men) are still prevalent today, and persist in marriages; in women's education; in the lack of opportunities afforded women outside of marriage; their lack of legal, political, social and economic rights; and in fathers' control over their daughters. Moreover, that as society progresses, we move more and more towards equality. This is happening, "very tardily" as she puts it, with race (and particularly with justifications for slavery) but not changing at all for women, the only caste – at least in Europe and America – where people think it is completely natural for there to be irremediable inequality: women, in the view of almost everyone alive, just are not equal to men.[14]

---

[14]Interestingly, the 'marriage as slavery/women as slaves' trope is more visible in Mill's work (see particularly *Subjection of Women*, 264–7 and 271). He even added a footnote to the 1859 reprint of *Enfranchisement* which called working-class women, in particular, "household slave[s]" (Mill, footnote to Taylor, *Enfranchisement*, 404. See also editor's notes to the publication history of this work on 393.)

3. Socialism as the means to emancipation and equality

Having charted their similar – but not identical – arguments about marriage, women's oppression, and slavery, I turn in the last part of this article to considering Wheeler and Taylor's suggested solutions to the issue. Both, at root, suggest this has to be equality – that is meaningful equality, not mere equality of legal rights (though these are an important first step). Both argue that this kind of equality is a "higher pleasure" (Thompson, "Introductory Letter", xi; Taylor, *Marriage*, 17–24). Both also endorse socialism as the ideal future for humans. Wheeler is more definite in saying female equality is impossible without socialism; a position which is also discernible in Taylor's views, though never stated overtly.

Wheeler was very involved with contemporary socialism, particularly Owenism, Saint-Simonism, and Fourierism. Thompson describes Wheeler as look[ing] forward to

> a ... society, where the principle of benevolence shall supersede that of fear; where restless and anxious individual competition shall give place to mutual co-operation and joint possession; where individuals in large numbers, male and female, forming voluntary associations, shall become a mutual guarantee to each other for the supply of all useful wants, and form an unsalaried and uninsolvent insurance company against all insurable casualties; where perfect freedom of opinion and perfect equality[15] will reign amongst the co-operators; and where the children of all will be equally educated and provided for by the whole.
>
> (Thompson, "Introductory Letter", ix–x)

Thompson and Wheeler thought "the principle of individual competition" being "the master-key and moving principle of the whole social organisation" and "*individual* wealth the great object sought after", "it seems impossible – even where all unequal legal and unequal moral restraints removed ... – that women should attain equal happiness with men": biological factors "must eternally render the average exertions of women in the race of the competition for wealth less successful than those of men" (Thompson, "Introductory Letter", x). Thompson adds that they thought:

> Were all partial restraints, were unequal laws and unequal morals removed, were all the means and careers of all species of knowledge and exertion equally open to both sexes; still the barriers of physical organisation must, under the system of individual competition, keep depressed the average station of women beneath that of men. Though in point of knowledge, talent, and virtue, they might become their equals; in point of independence *arising from wealth* they must, under the present principle of social arrangements, remain inferior.
>
> (Thompson, "Introductory Letter", xi)

---

[15] Jose ("Without Apology", 842) highlights how this phrase also links Thompson, Wheeler, Taylor and Mill.

That is, what might be thought of as 'liberal feminist' reforms would be useful, but could never be sufficient for female equality. The whole system of competition needs to be replaced with cooperation for equality to occur. This is both because competition systematically discriminates against women (and the social structures of gender and women's education though exacerbating this, also flow naturally from this structural iniquity), and because only in cooperation will both men and women's characters be changed sufficiently for them to experience the 'higher pleasure' of life among equals.

Speaking of his and Taylor's ideal view (and in a text which Taylor had chance to edit), Mill says they saw the "social problem of the future" being "how to unite the greatest individual liberty of action, with a common ownership in the raw material of the globe, and an equal participation of all in the benefits of combined labour". Their ideal "society will no longer be divided into the idle and the industrious" and "the division of the produce of labour, instead of depending... on the accident of birth, will be made by concert, on an acknowledged principle of justice" with "human beings... exert[ing] themselves" for benefits which would be "shared with the society they belong to" (Mill, *Autobiography*, 239).

They thought 'cooperative societies' might be the best way of achieving this ideal society (Mill and Taylor, *Principles*, 793–4). "Associations of the labourers with themselves", spreading gradually throughout society until almost all industry (including agriculture) was organized on cooperative lines (with some additional state provision), "in perhaps a less remote future than may be supposed", "may" effect "a change in society, which would combine the freedom and independence of the individual, with the moral, intellectual, and economical advantages of aggregate production" without needing a violent revolution.

> [This] would realise, at least in the industrial department, the best aspirations of the democratic spirit, by putting an end to the division of society into the industrious and the idle, and effacing all social distinctions but those fairly earned by personal services and exertions... a transformation... thus effected, (and assuming of course that both sexes participate equally in the rights and in the government of the association) would be the nearest approach to social justice, and the most beneficial ordering of industrial affairs for the universal good, which it is possible at present to foresee.
> (Mill and Taylor, *Principles*, 793–4)

Taylor may also have been more open to communism than Mill, though the evidence for this is scanty, relying solely on part of Mill's half of their correspondence on the issue (Mill, *Mill-Taylor Correspondence*, 1026–7). She seems to have thought there was much to be gained for happiness from the guarantee of subsistence made under communism (which Mill thought might be over-exaggerated by those who had never experienced it). She also thought that society might adopt communism within fewer generations than Mill did (who thought there might be something of a chicken-and-the-egg problem: certainly, communist teachers could raise communist children, but who would have made these communist teachers in the first place?). In this, she may have been endorsing more communal schemes than Mill in general advocated (though arguing that those who wanted to make these experiments in living should take the chance), or she may only have been advocating 'equal shares' (the core principle of communist distribution as they saw it) as a more feasible and desirable principle of justice within cooperative associations than Mill. (In *Principles*, they advocate an initial adoption of principles akin to Fourierism, "allowing to every one a fixed minimum, sufficient for subsistence, the[n] apportion[ing] all further remuneration according to the work done" – which, interestingly, meets Taylor's endorsement of the importance of securing subsistence without needing to endorse full-blown communism – and endorse 'equal shares' as a 'higher' principle of justice than securing for the labourer the fruits of their own labours, and the Blancian principle of "from each according to their capacities, to each according to their needs" as a 'still higher' principle (Mill and Taylor, *Principles*, 203 and 782-4).)

There are several similarities between this view and that of Thompson and Wheeler in *Appeal* (and with Thompson in *Inquiry*). There are also interesting links with Owenite ideas and Fourierism regarding small-scale communities, inter-relations between members, distributive justice, and the transition to socialism, as well as a shared feminism (see McCabe, "Mill and Fourierism", 35-61). Given Wheeler's links to the Saint-Simonians, it is also worth noting that Mill describes Taylor's most-significant contribution to *Principles* being the setting of its 'tone'. This may sound slight, but it refers to the foundational ontology of the book, and its view of the difference between laws of production (which are laws of nature) and laws of distribution (which are human constructs), the recognition of which opens up the space for consideration of a more just socialist future. Mill (*Autobiography*, 253-7) acknowledges that this is a Saint-Simonian idea, but says Taylor "made [it] a living principle pervading and animating the book".

Mill/Taylor and Thompson/Wheeler envisage a transformation of both economic organization and individual human character – both being inextricably linked to, and influencing, the other. Men and women will be capable of equal relationships and 'benevolent' feelings,[16] as well as being able to tolerate freedom of speech and action (and eccentricity of personality) among their fellow citizens. There will be meaningfully equal participation in work and government in these associations, with women no longer being

---

[16] See Cory ("Rhetorical Re-Visioning", 120) for an interesting analysis of Wheeler's view of gender power-relations in socialism.

confined to the entirely domestic sphere where, if they are not domestic 'drudges', they live lives of enforced idleness. (It is worth considering a feminist angle on the commitment that *all* shall work, as well as recognizing that Wheeler/Thompson and Taylor/Mill recognized domestic labour *as* work, and the necessity for society to recognize it as such). (Mill, *Autobiography*, 239; McCabe, "'Good Housekeeping'?", 135–55.)

Mill and Taylor saw as the greatest difference between their views and those of socialists like Thompson and Wheeler, their inability to share the socialist antipathy to competition. As noted, Thompson and Wheeler see a system of individual property, based on and necessitating, individual competition to be innately biased against women, and one of the core causes of their inequality. Taylor and Mill (*Principles*, 794–6) do not take on this feminist critique of competition, instead offering arguments *for* competition based on considerations of efficiency (of production); and increased quality and lower prices (for consumers), reminding socialists that "wherever competition is not, monopoly is; and that monopoly, in all its forms, is the taxation of the industrious for the support of indolence, if not plunder". They recognize many of the ills associated with competition, but insist that it is not, in itself, the root cause of all social evils.

This said, their commitment to competition can be over-stressed. As they point out (*Principles*, 795), "if association were universal, there would be no competition between labourer and labourer; and that between association and association would be for the benefit of the consumers, that is, of the associations; of the industrious classes". They acknowledge the moral case against competition put forward by socialists, preferring a society characterized by fraternity. But they also think associations would stagnate, and people's faculties "rust", "unless their knowledge of the existence of rival associations made them apprehend ... that they would be left behind in the race".

We should, however, ask what kind of race. Elsewhere in *Principles* (754) – and even more strongly in *Chapters on Socialism* (which may have some input from Taylor, despite being published after both her and Mill's death, as they discuss a separate work on socialism in correspondence). Taylor and Mill

> confess [they are] not charmed with the ideal of life held out by those who think that the normal state of human beings is that of struggling to get on; that the trampling, crushing, elbowing, and treading on each other's heels, which form the existing type of social life, are the most desirable lot of human kind, or anything but the disagreeable symptoms of one of the phases of industrial progress.

Similarly, they claim:

> the power ... of emulation, in exciting the most strenuous exertions for the sake of the approbation and admiration of others, is borne witness to be experience in every situation in which human beings publicly compete with one another,

even if it be in things frivolous ... A contest, who can do most for the common good, is not the kind of competition which Socialists repudiate.

(*Principles*, 205)[17]

They describe competition between cooperative associations as being conducted in a spirit of "friendly rivalry in the pursuit of a good common to all" (*Principles*, 792).

It is important, then, to note that the 'race' in which associations might be left behind is not like the 'race' described by Mill in *Chapters* (713) – that is, the contemporary 'race' for existence created by the current system of private property in which those who "come hindermost" are "put to death" for no other fault than being slower than their competitors. Instead, it is more like an Olympic race; run for medals and public acclaim. In Taylor and Mill's preferred institutions, no one would be allowed to suffer privation (never mind death) through poverty or lack of employment; there would be no competitive labour market; and feminist reforms and better education would keep the supply of labour under control (a primary cause, in their view, of low wages). If associations went out of business, then, through stagnation, inefficiency, or simple ineptitude, social safety nets and the chance of re-employment in other cooperatives would protect workers from penury.

Thompson – in *Inquiry* – envisaged a series of self-sufficient communities, though Wheeler's interest in Saint-Simonism (a system organized at the national level, with everyone being an employee of the state, contributing, and rewarded, according to his or her abilities) means she may have not been wedded solely to small-scale socialism. Similarly, Fourier (whom Wheeler translated into English), also pictured small-scale, self-sufficient communities, made harmonious via a range of competing 'series' of workers, all emulating each other and striving to out-do one another in excellence. In what has been called his 'second-best' utopia (Stafford, "Paradigmatic Liberal", 330), Thompson also envisaged competition between mainly self-sufficient 'villages' for goods and services, though not in the labour market (Thompson, *Inquiry*, 156–7, 168–70 and 274–80).

There are, then, two main differences between the Wheeler/Thompson view and the Taylor/Mill one. Taylor and Mill envisaged cooperative associations, rather than self-sufficient communities. That is, rather than the population being re-distributed to roughly equally sized villages throughout the country, we might live in the contemporary mix of urban and rural settings, whichever best suited the industry in which we were engaged, and our home lives could be separate from our place of work. Similarly, where Wheeler and Thompson see villages 'trading' (in some sense), Taylor and Mill envisage producer-cooperatives producing goods which are distributed by consumer cooperatives. Under the Rochdale model, goods are sold to

---

[17] Again, this has strong echoes of Fourier: see McCabe, "Mill and Fourierism", 35–61.

members of the cooperative, and any profits made distributed among those members (with a portion reserved for mutual insurance, and often other services such as libraries). So something approximating cost price is actually paid, in the end, by the consumer. The same could be applied to sale of goods by producer coops, redistributing profits to buyers and thus trading at something like cost price, while retaining the advantages for quality, efficiency and innovation provided by competition between rival producers all motivated by emulation rather than profit.

Socialists like Wheeler and Thompson would no doubt have concerns that Taylor and Mill do not eradicate enough of the individual property system to properly free women from domestic servitude, even if they would free them from political and civil 'slavery' through their preferred reforms. That is, in not embracing the communal living elements of many socialist schemes, and retaining more nuclear family structures in individual houses (*Principles*, 209), Taylor and Mill do not succeed in freeing women. These charges are not without merit.

On the other hand, Taylor and Mill's preferred institutions *do* do away with many of the evils of competition which Wheeler and Thompson thought lay at the root of women's inequality. In Taylor and Mill's ideal society, we are no longer motivated by a desire for individual wealth, but communal well-being, and so individualistic competition is no longer "the master-key and moving principle of the whole social organisation" – instead, fraternal concern with one another's well-being is, aided, in terms of social mechanisms, by human psychology's urge for emulation and desire for praise. In itself, the idea of "a contest, who can do most for the common good" (Mill and Taylor, *Principles*, 205), is not innately gendered. Female biology, that is, need not "eternally render the average exertions of women" in this 'race' "less successful than those of men" (Thompson, "Introductory Letter", x). Women's enforced absence from the labour market to have children, that is, might always be a disadvantage in a race for individual wealth, but given the importance of parenting to the common good, this does not immediately disadvantage women in a socialist society (even without the hope that parenting, too, would be more equal, and that domestic work which might conceivably be linked to female biology (such as breast-feeding) would *also* be recognized as socially important work).

Certainly, if a sort of 'masculine' ideal still permeates cooperative society – if *only* work done outside the home in producer-cooperatives (and perhaps at traditionally masculine work, be that hard physical labour, engineering/manufacturing or the professions) is recognized as contributing to the social good, then women will be disadvantaged in terms of rewards in the same sort of ways, though the rewards would be very different. However, though no longer a matter of life and death, they would have serious consequences of equality, and allow the notion that women are just worth less than men to persist. This said, the same fear might be raised over Thompson and Wheeler's idea of self-sufficient villages, if there was also a gendered division of labour within them.

Overall, then, Wheeler is more strident in her claim that the system of individual property and particularly competition for individual wealth needs to be dismantled if women are to be freed from 'slavery', and men and women made equal. Taylor supports *both* equality for women *and* a radical restructuring of the economy towards communal property and cooperative associations. Her insistence on securing minimum subsistence may have feminist roots – after all, it secures women from dependence on fathers, brothers and husbands (at least if they work, and/or want to separate from the husbands or live independently from their families – something which was, at the time, almost impossible for women to do without finance and approval from a male relative). This, however, is not stated forthrightly in her work, and – in the main – she treats of feminism and socialism separately (while noting both that it is to the socialists credit that they are, in the main, feminists, and that her preferred socialist institutions must allow women an equal role). Given her insight into how the patriarchy affects *all* elements of progress, however, and her evident belief that socialism was a key part of human progress, it might be the case that this separation in published works is a political decision more than seeing the issues as not really related. That is, like Wheeler, she may well have believed that 'liberal' feminist reforms (i.e. equal rights) would not be sufficient to end women's subjection, but still have thought there were a necessary first step, and one which was more easily to be accomplished by advocating a single argument (i.e. regarding the vote), rather than also bringing in claims about economic justice. (She may also have desired to make the demand for women's votes seem less radical and dangerous than working-class demands for a mixture of political and economic reforms, and thus be more likely to win her case.)

This said, both women are alike in their analysis of women's subjection, marriage, and individual property relations. Wheeler goes further than Taylor, being more willing to call marriage slavery; and firmly labelling eradication of individual property, and a social system based on competition as necessary for female emancipation. They both had strong interests in the work of Owen, Thompson, Saint-Simon and Fourier, and in the events of 1848 in Paris (which Wheeler was invited to participate in, though declining due to ill health, and from which Taylor learned a great deal regarding the possibilities of 'association'). They both saw themselves as socialists, and had similar, though not identical, preferred institutions, in which the achievement of emancipation, social justice, fraternity and equality was not just a question of redistribution of economic assets, but also a question of fundamentally changing human nature such that meaningful equality between the sexes was not only realizable, but recognized to be a core element of happiness.

Acknowledgements

I would like to extend my thanks to Alison Stone, Charlotte Alderwick and two anonymous reviewers for comments on this piece, as well as the organisers and attendees of "Wollapolooza!" at APSA 2018 and 2019; ISUS 2018; CSiW conference (Johannesburg, 2018); "Bridging the Gender Gap Through Time" workshop (Kings College, London, 2018); Workshop on Mill (Lancaster, 2017) and Symposium on J.S. Mill's *Subjection of Women* at 150 (Cyprus, 2019) where some of these ideas were first tried out in public. I also want to thank the AHRC for the award of a Leadership Fellowship, for which project this piece forms an initial part.

Funding

This work was supported by Arts and Humanities Research Council [AH/S012788/1].

ORCID

Helen McCabe http://orcid.org/0000-0002-7625-7916

Bibliography

Ball, Terence. "Utilitarianism, Feminism and the Franchise". In *Reappraising Political Theory: Revisionist Studies in the History of Political Thought*, 175–212. Oxford: Oxford University Press, 1995.

Cory, Abbie L. "Wheeler and Thompson's *Appeal*: The Rhetorical Re-Visioning of Gender". *New Hibernia Review* 8, no. 2 (2004): 106–20.

Jacobs, Jo Ellen. "The Lot of Gifted Ladies is Hard: A Study of Harriet Taylor Mill Criticism". *Hypatia* 9, no. 3 (1994): 132–62.

Jacobs, Jo Ellen. "Chronology". In *Complete Works of Harriet Taylor Mill*, edited by Jo Ellen Jacobs, xli–xliii. Bloomington: Indiana State University Press, 1998.

Gardner, Catherine Villanueva. *Empowerment and Interconnectivity: Toward a Feminist History of Utilitarian Philosophy*. University Park: University of Pennsylvania Press, 2013.

McCabe, Helen. "Harriet Taylor Mill". In *A Companion to Mill*, edited by Christopher MacLeod and Dale E. Miller, 112–25. Chichester: Wiley-Blackwell, 2017.

McCabe, Helen. "'Good Housekeeping'? Re-Assessing John Stuart Mill's Position on the Gendered Division of Labour". *History of Political Thought* 39, no. 1 (2018): 135–55.

McCabe, Helen. "John Stuart Mill and Fourierism: 'Association', 'Friendly Rivalry' and Distributive Justice". *Global Intellectual History* 4, no. 1 (2019): 35–61.

McCabe, Helen. "Harriet Taylor". In *The Wollstonecraftian Mind*, edited by Sandrine Bergès Eileen Hunt Botting and Alan Coffee. Abingdon: Routledge, 2019.

McFadden, Margaret. "Anna Doyle Wheeler (1785–1848): Philosophy, Socialist, Feminist". *Hypatia* 4, no. 1 (1989): 91–101.

Mill, James. "Government". In *Encyclopaedia Britannica: Supplement*. Edinburgh: Archibald Constable and Company, 1820.

Mill, John Stuart. *John Stuart Mill – Harriet Taylor Mill Correspondence Concerning the Principles, Collected Works III*. Toronto: University of Toronto Press, 1965.

Mill, John Stuart. *Chapters on Socialism, Collected Works V*. Toronto: University of Toronto Press, 1967.

Mill, John Stuart. Letter 261, to George Jacob Holyoake, 21 September, 1856, *Collected Works* XV. Toronto. University of Toronto Press, 1972.
Mill, John Stuart. *Autobiography, Collected Works I*. Toronto: University of Toronto Press, 1981.
Mill, John Stuart. *On Marriage, Collected Works XXI*. Toronto: University of Toronto Press, 1984.
Mill, John Stuart. *The Subjection of Women, Collected Works XXI*. Toronto: University of Toronto Press, 1984.
Mill, John Stuart, and Harriet Taylor. *Principles of Political Economy, Collected Works II and III*. Toronto: Toronto University Press, 1965.
Mill, John Stuart, and Harriet Taylor. *Papers on Women's Rights, CW XXI*. Toronto: University of Toronto Press, 1984.
Miller, Dale E. "Harriet Taylor Mill". *Stanford Encyclopedia of Philosophy* (2002; revised 2018), https://plato.stanford.edu/archives/spr2019/entries/harriet-mill/.
Pankhurst, Richard. "Anna Wheeler: A Pioneer Socialist and Feminist". *Political Quarterly* 25, no. 2 (1945): 132–43.
Philips, Menaka. "The 'Beloved and Deplored' Memory of Harriet Taylor Mill: Rethinking Gender and Intellectual Labor in the Canon". *Hypatia* 33, no. 4 (2018): 626–42.
Robson, John. "Textual Introduction". In *Collected Works XXI*, edited by John Robson. Toronto: University of Toronto Press, 1984.
Rossi, Alice S. "Sentiment and Intellect: The Story of John Stuart Mill and Harriet Taylor Mill". In *John Stuart Mill and Harriet Taylor Mill: Essays on Sex Equality*, edited by Alice S. Rossi, 1–64. Chicago, IL: University of Chicago Press, 1970.
Stafford, William. "How can a Paradigmatic Liberal Call Himself a Socialist? The Case of John Stuart Mill". *Journal of Political Ideologies* 3, no. 3 (1998): 325–45.
Taylor, Harriet. *Enfranchisement of Women, Collected Works XXI*. Toronto: University of Toronto Press, 1984.
Taylor, Harriet. *Life of William Caxton, Complete Works*. Edited by Jo Ellen Jacobs. Bloomington: Indiana State University Press, 1998.
Taylor, Harriet. *On Marriage, Complete Works of Harriet Taylor Mill*. Edited by Jo Ellen Jacobs. Bloomington: Indiana State University Press, 1998.
Thompson, William. *An Inquiry Into the Distribution of Wealth Most Conducive to Human Happiness*. London: Longman, Hurst, Rees, Orme, Brown and Green, 1824.
Thompson, William. "Introductory Letter to Mrs Wheeler". In *Appeal of the One Half of the Human Race, Women, Against the Pretentions of the Other Half, Men, to Retain Them in Political, and Thence in Civil, and Domestic Servitude*. London: Longman, Hurst, Rees, Orme, Brown and Green, 1825.
Thompson, William, and Anna Wheeler. *Appeal of the One Half of the Human Race, Women, Against the Pretentions of the Other Half, Men, to Retain Them in Political, and Thence in Civil, and Domestic Servitude*. London: Longman, Hurst, Rees, Orme, Brown and Green, 1825.

Elizabeth Cady Stanton and Lucretia Mott: radical 'co-adjutors' in the American women's rights movement

Lisa Pace Vetter

ABSTRACT
Elizabeth Cady Stanton is widely considered to be the founder of the early women's rights movement in America. She convened the first convention dedicated specifically to women's rights in America, at Seneca Falls, New York, and she is credited with authoring the Declaration of Sentiments, arguably the founding document of the American women's rights movement. Stanton's unwavering insistence on women's enfranchisement drove much of her efforts. *The History of Woman Suffrage* (1881–1922), which Stanton initiated and coedited, is considered the definitive account of the early movement. For many commentators, the radicalism of Stanton's claims sets her apart from other reformers. However, I argue that another women's rights advocate, Lucretia Mott, is as radical as Stanton and, in some respects, perhaps more so. Mott held a comprehensive view of women's rights that included, but was not limited to, women's suffrage. Whereas Stanton sought to establish an organized reform movement and craft the official account of its origins, Mott resisted these efforts, instead preferring informal networks of activism and a more inclusive historical understanding. Whereas Stanton has been criticized for her elitist and racist views, Mott's lifelong commitment to abolitionism and human rights never wavered.

Introduction

Elizabeth Cady Stanton is widely considered to be the revolutionary founder of the early women's rights movement in America. She convened the first convention dedicated specifically to women's rights in America, at Seneca Falls, New York, and she is credited with authoring the Declaration of Sentiments, arguably the founding document of the American women's rights movement. Stanton's unwavering insistence on women's enfranchisement drove much of her efforts. *The History of Woman Suffrage* (1881–1922), which Stanton initiated and coedited, is considered the definitive account of the early movement. Her later work, *The Woman's Bible* (1895–98), offers innovative scriptural interpretations stripped of patriarchal influence. Stanton's radicalism fundamentally challenged American ideals and began one of the most powerful social movements in history.

I use the term radical here in several ways: first, to characterize the comprehensive worldview that served as the foundation for Stanton's philosophy; second, to frame Stanton's call for fundamental change, offering innovative and unorthodox views on women; third, to capture the zeal of Stanton's single-minded focus on women's rights, especially suffrage.

Often referred to as the 'philosopher' of the early women's rights movement, Stanton is credited with synthesizing various schools of thought into a new theory of women's rights. Drawing from Rogers Smith's 'multiple traditions' of political theory, Sue Davis argues that Stanton's thought reflected a combination of 'liberalism', 'civic republicanism', racial, ethnic, and socioeconomic 'ascriptivism', and a new category, 'radicalism'. Lockean liberalism focused on the role of limited government in protecting individual rights. Republicanism emphasized the common good and the importance of collective self-government. As the term suggests, "ascriptive forms of Americanism" attribute "particular moral, intellectual, and physical qualities to people on the basis of their sex, race, or nationality" and view these qualities as "natural and unchangeable" (Davis, *Political Thought*, 11–13). Stanton's 'radicalism' is seen through her fundamental transformation of the institution of marriage into an "equal partnership" that extended beyond the "liberal boundary between public and private" (Davis, *Political Thought*, 11–13). Davis concludes that Stanton's most radical contribution is a "conception of women" as a class that transcended liberal individualism, civic republicanism, and the "ascriptive rhetoric of women's superiority" (Davis, *Political Thought*, 22–3). Stanton transformed American law by collectivizing women as a new 'gender class', and she developed a new kind of 'experiential' or pragmatic philosophizing that is based on "shared values rather than essentialist truths" because it relied on "experiential narratives" (Thomas, "Elizabeth Cady Stanton", 150). Her reinterpretation of Christian doctrine purged of its patriarchal history "challenged a deeply ingrained facet of American culture" that for her was "thoroughly entwined with women's subordination" (Davis, *Political Thought*, 22).

Stanton was influenced by other reformers such as Sarah and Angelina Grimke, Lucretia Mott, Abby Kelley Foster, and Lucy Stone. And yet "Stanton was the first person to devote her considerable intellect solely to developing the philosophy and promoting the cause of women's rights" (Ginzberg, *Elizabeth Cady Stanton*, 11). Unlike the Grimkés, who retreated to private life in the face of relentless controversy, Stanton dedicated herself "to challenging the ways that ideas about gender shaped women's place in society, politics, law, and marriage" and "elaborating the nature of women's subordination and providing the verbal ammunition to anyone who wanted to join her to change it" (Ginzberg, *Elizabeth Cady Stanton*, 11). Whereas other reformers were equally committed to abolitionism and women's rights – some prioritizing the former over the latter when thought necessary – Stanton did not share her husband Henry's fervent support for ending enslavement, nor were her loyalties torn between two causes. Rather, Stanton distinguished herself among other activists with her single-minded focus on ending the oppression of women.

Although Stanton combined aspects of classical liberalism and republicanism in novel ways, the legal category of woman she sought to create still operated within the confines of the established system. In other words, Stanton sought to grant women essentially the same rights held by (white) men. It is unclear to what extent her concept of woman as a (legal) individual avoided the shortcomings of Lockean liberalism, namely, the fact that "individual autonomy" would always take precedence over "substantive equality", thereby allowing "economic, social, and even political inequalities" to persist (Davis, *Political Thought*, 12). Stanton devoted her entire life to the struggle for women's rights, but her zeal was alienating. Stanton believed that the "Jeffersonian individual" applied to all men and women, yet the "particular battle" she waged over women's rights "set her apart from, and sometimes at odds with, her putative allies" (Gordon, "Stanton and the Right to Vote", 112). Her drive to establish an reform movement with formal organizations such as the National Woman Suffrage Association (NWSA), founded in 1869, sowed divisions among supporters of abolitionism and women's rights, and sidelined reformers who preferred informal networks and pursued other varieties of activism. After the American Civil War, the early women's rights movement split over the proposed Fifteenth Amendment to the Constitution, which would grant freed Black men the vote without extending enfranchisement to women. Several months later, in response to Stanton and Susan B. Anthony's opposition to the amendment, Lucy Stone and Julia Ward Howe formed the American Women Suffrage Association (AWSA), supporting the amendment while lobbying individual states to enfranchise women. The so-called 'split narrative' was ill-suited to the more complex positions held by Black women advocates such as Frances Watkins Harper and Sojourner Truth, both of whom supported greater rights for women as well as African American men (McDaneld, "Harper, Historiography"). Stanton's efforts to literally rewrite history in her formal account of the early women's rights movement further sidelined those who did not fit comfortably into her narrative. Perhaps ironically, Stanton made many of the same mistakes for which she criticized men.

The comprehensiveness of Stanton's transformative worldview was limited by inconsistencies in her thought, arguing for universal suffrage while relying on racist and elitist rhetoric.[1] Throughout her career Stanton had mocked the hypocrisy of the white male American ruling elite who opposed the enfranchisement of educated white women like herself while allowing uneducated white and immigrant men to vote. Stanton's rhetoric intensified when faced with the prospect that freed Black men would be granted a fundamental right that would forever be deprived of women. Although Stanton's racist comments were likely designed to persuade her audience to accept universal suffrage by expressing shared values, she effectively "reified the social hierarchy her speech was intended to undermine". By appealing to whites, Stanton "subtly (and probably inadvertently) casts Black people as the Other" and, as a result, "asked not for revolution so much as for help in redistributing class privilege" (Skinnell, "Elizabeth Cady Stanton's 1854 'Address'", 131, 138, 141).[2]

If we were to look for a comparably radical activist to Stanton, we would most likely choose her close associate, Susan B. Anthony. For it was Anthony who continued to engage in organizational work even when Stanton's attentions turned to lecturing and writing (Tetrault, *Myth of Seneca Falls*, 50–1). And of course, it was Anthony, not Stanton, who had herself arrested and tried before a federal court for daring to cast a ballot in New York state in 1873.

Perhaps the least likely candidate for the title 'radical reformer' in the American early women's rights movement would be the Quaker abolitionist Lucretia Mott. The diminutive, plainly dressed woman hardly resembles the imposing, forceful combatant for women's rights. Unlike Stanton, who produced a voluminous body of work that laid the theoretical groundwork for women's equality, Mott left no formal writings or extended theoretical reflections behind. Instead, we are left with second-hand transcriptions of speeches she delivered primarily at Quaker meetings, and with volumes of personal correspondence about a dizzying array of topics that even Mott described as 'kaleidoscopic'. However, there are important, though neglected, radical elements of her thought.

I argue that a closer look at Mott's works reveals a far more complex thinker whose own radicalism was at least on par with her 'co-adjutor', Stanton, in several important respects. Like Stanton, Mott had a comprehensive worldview that advocated for universal equality. Stanton and Mott emphasized the importance of natural rights and equality of individuals, but for Mott, these principles ultimately originated from the Hicksite

---

[1] See, for instance, Mitchell, "'Lower Orders'"; Stansell, "Missed Connections"; Caraway, *Segregated Sisterhood*; and Newman, *White Women's Rights*.
[2] See also Southard, "A Rhetoric of Epistemic Privilege".

Quaker view of human beings as creations of God who were guided by an inner light. Mott understood the individual holistically, created by a non-sectarian God to engage in reflective action and thereby honour her duties and obligations to others. Human beings should take active responsibility for discerning the inner light and constructing a world that allowed all people to function as moral beings. Only in such a fundamentally transformed world would enfranchisement be truly effective. Thus for Mott, women's rights and abolitionism were truly inseparable.

As a prominent Quaker preacher, Mott's own egalitarian reinterpretation of Scripture predates Stanton's by over fifty years. She supported Stanton's efforts to promote deeply controversial reforms of marriage and divorce, and she deplored the Quaker tradition of disowning those who had formed interfaith marriages or who had divorced. Yet Mott criticized as 'extravagant' Stanton's divisive characterizations of marriage as a legal contract, itself a vestige of classical liberalism. Consistent with her progressive Quaker world view, Mott believed that marriage was a spiritual bond made voluntarily by equal parties and should only be dissolved in the most dire of circumstances.

Whereas Stanton sought to establish an organized reform movement and craft the official account of its origins, Mott resisted these efforts, instead preferring informal networks of activism that connected diverse groups of people with a wide variety of interests. Mott's inclusiveness extended to her own account of the early women's rights movement. Whereas Stanton sought to repress the more revolutionary and unorthodox aspects of the movement in order to appeal to a mainstream audience, Mott's effort to retain the unconventional viewpoints of more radical thinkers sought to honour the true diversity of women's rights advocates.

Mott's role in (Stanton's) history reconsidered

Many of our preconceptions about Mott originate in Stanton's own account of the movement. Mott's position among abolitionists and early women's rights advocates was established in the early volumes of the *History of Woman Suffrage* that were edited by Stanton, along with Anthony and Matilda Joslyn Gage. Stanton sought to craft an "origins story" to help "unify activists" who found themselves among disputes "over the direction of a postwar women's rights agenda, and larger battles among Americans over the memory of the Civil War" (Tetrault, *Myth of Seneca Falls*, 6–7). By placing themselves front and centre of the 'Seneca Falls mythology' as radical reformers, Stanton and Anthony used their political acumen to "market their particular agenda for women's rights and also to insist upon women's place in national memory" (Tetrault, *Myth of Seneca Falls*, 9). While giving Mott and others "the status of foremothers of the woman's rights movement", Stanton and Anthony "effectively removed them as active participants by claiming 1848 as the moment of its conception and relegating all that came before to prehistory" (Hewitt, "From Seneca Falls to Suffrage", 21).[3]

In the *History*, Stanton duly acknowledged Mott's influence. Indeed, Stanton pinpointed the beginning of her own commitment to women's rights to her encounter with Mott at the 1840 World Anti-Slavery Convention in London, where male officers prevented the women from speaking or actively participating. Whereas Mott characterized the exclusion of women speakers at the 1840 meeting as a regrettable setback for abolitionism, Stanton chose to frame the event as a personal turning point and the beginning of a new movement.

Stanton's choice to present the 1848 Seneca Falls Convention as the official starting-point for the women's rights movement further established her own position as the founder. Stanton had taken a leading role in the event and was likely the main contributor the Declaration of Sentiments. Stanton's bold proposal for including a resolution for woman's suffrage was met with Mott's oft-quoted response: 'Why Lizzie, thee will make us ridiculous'. In her correspondence, Mott referred to the Convention not as a momentous historical event, but rather as one of a number of undertakings on an extended journey with her husband James that summer. The couple attended the Yearly Meeting of Quakers in Genesee, New York, visited the Cattaragus Seneca Indian reservation near Buffalo, and met with fugitive slaves near the Canadian border. Mott's correspondence reflected her deep preoccupation with tensions within the Quaker community and her abolitionist commitments, with comparably fewer references to women's rights. As the Declaration of Sentiments was drafted, Mott was away visiting close friends. Mott had asked Stanton if she planned to address any additional causes at Seneca Falls, such as abolitionism, but received no response (Faulkner, *Lucretia Mott's Heresy*, 130–9).

By placing herself at the centre of the narrative, as founder of the movement, Stanton inevitably portrayed herself as ultimately surpassing her elder predecessor. Stanton "presents a clear contrast to prominent abolitionist women" like Mott because Stanton ultimately moves beyond their religious strivings for human rights by establishing a comprehensive (and largely secular) political theory of women's rights and a concrete plan for legal and political reform (Davis, *Political Thought*, 44, 47). Stanton transcends

---

[3]The *History of Woman Suffrage* has understated and obscured other women's rights advocates such as Hannah Mather Crocker as well (Botting and Houser, "'Drawing the Line of Equality'", 266). The tensions within the traditional narrative of the movement were not wholly lost on Stanton or Anthony, however. Anthony lamented the tendency among younger advocates to regard their predecessors such as Mott in terms of "something less than a 'usable past'". She was appalled when Carrie Chapman Catt's suffrage calendar placed Mott at the bottom, calling it an "inversion of the 'natural order'" and a violation of "the proper rank of old soldiers" within the movement (Kern, *Mrs. Stanton's Bible*, 94).

women's rights advocates who also supported abolitionist William Lloyd Garrison, including Mott, by developing a "notion of women as a class with the potential to develop consciousness of itself as such and to organize for radical political change" (Davis, *Political Thought*, 23). On this view, Mott's moral and spiritual influence gives way to Stanton's theoretical and pragmatic contributions. Whereas Mott, like other abolitionists, saw women's rights and the end of slavery as mutually complementary causes, admirers of Stanton's single-minded commitment to the cause of women saw split loyalties.

Thus it is not surprising that Mott has been characterized as a mythic, prophetic figure whose role was "to initiate the movement" rather than to lead it (Isenberg, *Sex and Citizenship*, 3). On this view, Mott is "the voice of inspiration rather than causation", a matriarchal, mystical, religious figure who had to be superseded by more driven activists such as Stanton (Isenberg, *Sex and Citizenship*, 3). It served Stanton's purposes to preserve Mott's memory while downplaying the sharper, more radical edges of her worldview. As Stanton and her allies faced increasing criticism for their racism and divisiveness, Mott lent legitimacy to their efforts because her anti-slavery bona fides were unimpeachable. In this way, Stanton could present herself as the true path breaker for women's rights (Faulkner, *Lucretia Mott's Heresy*, 217).

Mott's Quaker radicalism

The origins of Mott's unique brand of radicalism can be traced to her early encounter with Elias Hicks, whose influence led to the 1827 Schism of the Society of Friends. Hicks opposed what he perceived as an overreliance by worshippers on the scriptural interpretations of Quaker elites and an undue reverence for the written word at the expense of good works. Instead, Hicks sought to reassert the importance of direct, individual encounters with scriptural teachings and the necessity of actively applying religious principles to everyday life. Concurrent with the Hicksite emphasis on practice over principle was a downplaying, and in more radical circles an outright denial, of the divinity of Christ. Hicks also strove to reestablish the prominence of the 'inner light' in Quaker practice, a kind of internal voice possessed by all human beings regardless of religious persuasion which nevertheless provides a direct connection to the divine. The Hicksite understanding required active engagement and reasoning, not passive obedience to the word of God. Hicksites discouraged formal worship of the Sabbath in favour of encouraging, as Jesus did, good works at every opportunity, not just on high days and holy days.

Although many of its tenets have become more widely accepted in mainstream circles today, the radical nature of Hicksite Quakerism cannot be overstated. Not all Quakers supported abolitionism, immediate or gradual, and not all wanted to expand women's rights. Opponents, who would be labelled

'Orthodox', balked at the anarchic implications of Hicks' ideas and his apparent denial of the divinity of Christ, "or at least the Christian notion that it is Christ alone who makes salvation possible" (Jordan, *Slavery and the Meetinghouse*, 10). Much like the French Revolution, "Hicks's preaching would further rend the social fabric of early America and generate a false faith in the human ability to change sinful human nature" (Jordan, *Slavery and the Meetinghouse*, 10). Efforts to expand women's role in Quaker leadership met with particularly strong resistance. For opponents, Mott "believed that religious liberty often included efforts to infuse religious worship with 'political' or even potentially seditious discussions concerning movements like abolitionism, or, later, women's rights". Some even accused Mott and other women's rights advocates of attempting to establish a kind of utopian community unmoored from Christian doctrine (Jordan, *Slavery and the Meetinghouse*, 82).

Mott on suffrage, participation, and political power

Mott once described herself as a "belligerent Non-Resistant" because she would never contemplate "submitting tamely to injustice" of any kind; instead, she would "oppose it with all the moral powers with which I am endowed" (Densmore et al., *Lucretia Mott Speaks*, 141). Mott embraced pacifism, but she did not reject political engagement – belligerent or otherwise – as did many abolitionists who followed William Lloyd Garrison. Referred to as 'no-governmentalism' was Garrison's belief that any form of direct political participation in a government which permitted enslavement represented collusion with his opponents. Garrison focused his efforts on influencing politics indirectly through 'moral suasion', by petitioning, writing, participating in antislavery societies, and supporting antislavery conventions.

Closer examination of Mott's speeches and writings, I argue, reveals a view of political power and citizenship as radically egalitarian and democratic. Oppression emerged when dogmas are accepted at face value. Mott claimed that by adopting a sceptical stance, individuals would realize the systemic nature of oppression that relied on doctrines that justified enslavement, women's inequality, economic injustice, intemperance, and political violence. All people, including herself, must reflect on their complicity in systems of oppression. Because power for Mott was located within every individual, radical change would not rely on traditional authorities. Instead, individual men and women empowered with self-knowledge would work to reconstruct a pluralistic society in accordance with true freedom, equality, and justice.

Virtually every speech Mott delivered after returning from the 1840 World's Antislavery Convention in London, where she first encountered Stanton, and leading up to the 1848 Convention at Seneca Falls began with a systematic condemnation of mindless acceptance of religious dogma and unreflective observance of rituals and practices. Although Stanton's narrative observed little notable activity among early women's rights activists before she emerged on the scene in 1848, my examination of Mott's speeches leading up to this time period challenges this observation by revealing that Mott was in fact formulating a comprehensive worldview that contributed to the movement's progress.[4]

Delivered a year after the Seneca Falls Convention, Mott's speech "Discourse on Woman" was a culmination of her earlier efforts. It articulated an understanding of 'superior law' that is not only informed by God but also developed through the transformative process of self-reflection and self-examination. This 'law' required direct and indirect political participation by women and men alike.

Mott began her discussion of suffrage in the "Discourse" by explaining that woman "asks nothing as favor, but as right. ... She is seeking not to be governed by laws, in the making of which she has no voice". Women were "cypher[s] in the nation" because their views and opinions about political matters could not be expressed openly. Women were denied status as "moral" and "responsible" human beings because they were deprived of the full range of opportunities to reflect on political options, express their preferences openly, and exercise informed consent in obeying laws (Densmore et al., *Lucretia Mott Speaks*, 75).

If the right to vote were granted to women, Mott was convinced that it would emerge in a deeply hostile environment. It was not because suffrage was distasteful to her personally that Mott was reluctant to endorse it, but rather because it was so controversial to others. Along similar lines, for Mott, women avoided political involvement not because they were incapable or unwilling but rather because they feared the inevitable backlash that would result. For this reason, Mott stated, "Far be it from me to encourage woman to vote, or to take an active part in politics, in the present state of our government" that relies on violence to enforce its laws. However, a woman's "right to the elective franchise ... is the same, and should be yielded to her, whether she exercise that right or not" (Densmore et al., *Lucretia Mott Speaks*, 76). Although Mott supported women's suffrage, she did not demand that women vote. To do so would effectively replace one dogmatic teaching for another in a way that contradicted her fundamental principles. Instead, Mott proposed that women be given the opportunity to choose to participate with the hope of improving political life and society generally. Upon closer inspection, what appeared to be ambivalence toward political action was a principled stance fully consistent with her worldview: Even in

---

[4] This section draws from my previous work on Mott. See Vetter, "Lucretia Mott" and Vetter, *Political Thought*.

an extremely corrupt society, women should without question be granted the opportunity to vote and participate in politics if they wish, with the ultimate hope of transforming it. Considering that it would take another seventy years to ratify the Nineteenth Constitutional Amendment, Mott's recognition of the deeply entrenched injustice in American society that would keep women from enfranchisement was far from naïve.

While the right of suffrage was essential, Mott had a still broader understanding of female political action in mind. Indeed, "when, in the diffusion of light and intelligence, a convention shall be called to make regulations for self-government on Christian, non-resistant principles", Mott argued, "I can see no good reason, why woman should not participate in such an assemblage, taking part equally with man". Mott speculated, "who knows, but that if woman acted her part in governmental affairs, there might be an entire change in the turmoil of political life", and "if a woman's judgment were exercised, why might she not aid in making the laws by which she is governed?" (Densmore et al., *Lucretia Mott Speaks*, 76). Mott was vague about the structure and implementation of such a founding gathering. Nevertheless, she did not minimize political involvement for women, but rather insisted that they participate in the (re)founding of their community. Woman suffrage should be exercised within a larger context of reform efforts in religion, philosophy, economics, and culture.

Mott's Hicksite Quakerism helps explain her deep ambivalence about partisan organizations generally, which by their very nature encouraged conformity and effectively discouraged free thinking among participants. Partisan organizations, according to Mott, were supported by dogmas and empowered by unreflective followers. For this reason, sectarian societies "encroach far too much on individual rights". By contrast, "associations ... if properly conducted", namely, by encouraging diversity and independent thought, "need not destroy individuality" (Palmer, *Selected Letters*, 122). Mott's aversion to formal organizations extended to the women's rights movement as well. After the Civil War, she lamented that "it was a great mistake to ... organize a Soc[iet]y For Wom[en's] Rig[hts]" because the "several Conventions held were far more effective" (Palmer, *Selected Letters*, 399). To encourage reform on specific issues such as women's rights, Mott preferred the relatively informal, decentralized, non-hierarchical nature of the conventions over the more rigid and bureaucratic organizations and societies that emerged from them.

Moreover, for Mott, unity should never be secured by suppressing dissent within a group: harmony would never be 'absolute'. Instead, true pluralism required the sort of constructive conflict that arose when individuals confronted injustice and oppression by questioning traditional beliefs and practices, and translated true equality, freedom, and justice into action. Mott's rejection of coercion was unconditional, and she believed that she and other women's rights activists should "wish to avoid all angry opposition or ridicule". But she nevertheless maintained that women "must at the same time enter the ranks, prepared to 'endure hardness as good soldiers'; – and not disclaim the needful antagonism which a faithful presentation of Womans wrongs imposes upon us" (Palmer, *Selected Letters*, 211, emphasis added).

Although African American women were deprived of the franchise even after the Civil War, they nevertheless participated in political life on many levels, by attending mass meetings, church assemblies, and formal state constitutional conventions, and by mobilizing African American men to exercise their newfound right to vote – not as autonomous individuals per se, but rather as representatives who shouldered responsibility for a much larger community (Ginzberg, *Elizabeth Cady Stanton*, 129). Whereas Stanton viewed such a compromise as unacceptable, as her opposition to the Fifteenth Amendment would attest, Mott would more likely accept this sort of indirect enfranchisement as one of many valuable forms of political participation.

Mott stood apart from Stanton and other women's rights advocates because her commitment to abolitionism and human rights never wavered in her lifetime. In 1833 Mott founded and actively participated in the longest-lasting interracial abolitionist organization in the United States, the Philadelphia Female Anti-Slavery Society (PFASS), and she established enduring associations with African American men and women. Mott's insistence on immediate emancipation predates Garrison's commitment by several years, and she never entertained the possibility of colonization or similar compromises. When many abolitionists, including Garrison, turned away from antislavery societies to focus on aiding freedmen after the Civil War, Mott, like Frederick Douglass, continued to support both efforts because she knew the detrimental effects of slavery on freed blacks did not end after the conflict and subsequent constitutional reforms. Well into her sixties, Mott also fought for equal access to streetcars in Philadelphia and forcefully advocated for better treatment of Black soldiers after the Civil War (Faulkner, *Lucretia Mott's Heresy*, 4). Mott's belief that political reform alone was insufficient in implementing fundamental social change proved correct, as brutal racial oppression reemerged in the form of Jim Crow laws and persisted well beyond the Reconstruction era. Mott's words and deeds did not reflect the sort of ascriptive inegalitarianism that diminished elements of Stanton's thought.

Mott's radically revisionist history of women's rights

A newfound appreciation for the truly radical nature of Mott's thought is able to emerge when freed from Stanton's perspective and examined on its own terms. Mott's own account of the early women's rights movement merits reexamination as well. Mott and Stanton corresponded extensively about the *History of Woman Suffrage* project, and it became clear that the two had very different understandings of the movement itself and how its story should be told. Throughout her career, Mott sought to acknowledge the important contributions of controversial women's rights advocates such as Mary Wollstonecraft, Frances Wright, and Ernestine Rose. In fact, Mott took particular pride in defending Wollstonecraft from detractors, offering to lend her personal copy of *A Vindication of the Rights of Woman* (1792) to friends and allies. For critics, Wollstonecraft represented the excesses of the French Revolution and its bloody aftermath, in which sacred political, religious, and social institutions were trampled under an uncontrollable surge of populism. The scandal surrounding Wollstonecraft's personal life further added to the controversy. To invoke her was a risky endeavour in respectable social circles. And yet, Mott consistently advocated for Wollstonecraft throughout her lifetime.

Mott urged Stanton to acknowledge the important contributions of fellow radicals like Wollstonecraft, and to reach further back in history while tracing the origins of the women's rights movement to include Sarah Grimke's *Epistle to the Clergy of the Southern States* (1836) and *Letters on the Equality of the Sexes* (1838). Mott's repeated insistence that Stanton 'give honor where honor is due' to revolutionary thinkers such as Wollstonecraft was, I argue, an extension of her own radicalism.[5] For Mott, expanding the emerging popular narrative of the early women's rights movement was crucial in preserving the revolutionary nature of the cause and offering a reminder of the transnational roots of the struggle for women's rights. But if Stanton were to heed Mott's advice, her own historical position in the movement would be compromised. Stanton would appear as one among many radical reformers who waged a protracted battle for women's rights on a number of fronts. The Seneca Falls meeting would be rendered a "mere footnote" in history (Tetrault, *Myth of Seneca Falls*, 3).

Mott's recollections have been criticized because, unlike Stanton's motivational account, she "drew no casual connection between" the 1840 convention and the 1848 meeting in Seneca Falls. Mott's understanding "followed no particular sequence", and offered few "memories to hold onto – no story at all, in the sense of a linear, unified narrative". Indeed, Mott offered an "incoherent" historical account "without causality or even chronology and without any overarching sense of design" (Tetrault, *Myth of Seneca Falls*, 3). Mott's more fluid historical understanding seemed ill-suited to the times and hence ripe for replacement.

---

[5] For an extended discussion, see Vetter, "Lucretia Mott".

Mott repeatedly urged Stanton to revise her overly selective account of the movement not from muddled thinking or naivete, but rather as a natural outgrowth of her commitment to free thinking and inclusivity. As early as 1848 Mott pointed out to Stanton that "the early Quakers still earlier 1660 & 70 asserted & carried out ... reciprocal vows in the Marriage covenant" (Palmer, *Selected Letters*, 172–3). Perhaps it is not surprising that Stanton would resist attempts to credit the progressive views on marriage that she would herself promote to a far earlier, religious, source. Mott had also encouraged Stanton to acknowledge the importance of the early Anti-Slavery societies and the role of clerical opposition to women serving in leadership roles in laying the groundwork for the movement. Stanton's opposition could be explained by her preference for formal associations, aversion to organized religion, and her relatively weak commitment to abolitionism.

In another important example, Mott emphasized the importance of providing a comprehensive account of the women's rights movement that included earlier reformers such as Wollstonecraft in her 1866 speech at the National Woman's Rights Convention in New York, where Stanton and Anthony sought to merge the causes of enfranchisement for freed Black men and (all) women. In this account, Mott references the French Revolution as the beginning of the movement, and continues with the 1840 World Anti-Slavery Convention in London, where she and Stanton were prevented from speaking or serving as officers (Densmore et al., *Lucretia Mott Speaks*, 151–3). Not only did Mott resist Stanton's (and Anthony's) efforts to craft an overly selective narrative to suit their purposes. Mott was equally reluctant to embrace Stanton's and Anthony's forceful efforts to conflate the plight of the two oppressed groups, explaining that "I have never liked to use the word 'slavery', as applied to the oppression of women, while we had a legalized slavery in this country", but she concedes that "the oppression of woman has been such, and continues to be such, by law, by custom, by a perverted Christianity, by church influence" (Densmore et al., *Lucretia Mott Speaks*, 151–3). Thus in many respects, Mott's history of early feminism is "more complicated" and "racially egalitarian" than Stanton's (Faulkner, *Lucretia Mott's Heresy*, 216).

Conclusion

Stanton and Mott remain radical 'co-adjutors' in the struggle for women's rights, but for very different reasons. Mott's radicalism was fundamentally rooted in her Hicksite Quaker worldview, and was clearly manifested in her life and work. Mott aimed for inclusivity, whether it be in the diverse activist networks she preferred, the multiracial coalitions she forged with others, the democratic and egalitarian view of political life she articulated, and in the complex narrative of the history of early women's rights she sought to promote. Mott's underappreciated contributions to early women's rights help us better understand how later "antiracist, global, and multicultural coalitions" could and eventually would emerge in the ongoing struggle for gender, racial, and economic justice (Hewitt, "From Seneca Falls", 33).

ORCID

Lisa Pace Vetter http://orcid.org/0000-0002-1048-5959

Bibliography

Botting, Eileen Hunt, and Sarah L. Houser. "'Drawing the Line of Equality': Hannah Mather Crocker on Women's Rights". *The American Political Science Review* 100, no. 2 (2006): 265-78.
Caraway, Nancie. *Segregated Sisterhood: Racism and the Politics of American Feminism*. 1st ed. Knoxville: University of Tennessee Press, 1991.
Davis, Sue. *The Political Thought of Elizabeth Cady Stanton: Women's Rights and the American Political Tradition*. New York: New York University Press, 2008.
Densmore, Christopher, Carol Faulkner, Nancy A. Hewitt, and Beverly Wilson Palmer, eds. *Lucretia Mott Speaks: The Essential Speeches and Sermons*. Urbana: University of Illinois Press, 2017.
Faulkner, Carol. *Lucretia Mott's Heresy: Abolition and Women's Rights in Nineteenth-Century America*. Philadelphia: University of Pennsylvania Press, 2011.
Ginzberg, Lori D. *Elizabeth Cady Stanton: An American Life*. 1st ed. New York: Hill and Wang, 2009.
Gordon, Ann D. "Stanton and the Right to Vote: On Account of Race and Sex". In *Elizabeth Cady Stanton, Feminist as Thinker: A Reader in Documents and Essays*, edited by Ellen Carol DuBois and Richard Candida Smith, 111-27. New York: New York University Press, 2007.
Hewitt, Nancy A. "From Seneca Falls to Suffrage? Reimagining a 'Master' Narrative in U.S. Women's History". In *No Permanent Waves: Recasting Histories of U.S. Feminism*, edited by Nancy A. Hewitt, 15-38. New Brunswick, NJ: Rutgers University Press, 2010.
Isenberg, Nancy. *Sex and Citizenship in Antebellum America*. Chapel Hill: University of North Carolina Press, 1998.
Jordan, Ryan P. *Slavery and the Meetinghouse: The Quakers and the Abolitionist Dilemma, 1820-1865*. Bloomington: Indiana University Press, 2007.
Kern, Kathi. *Mrs. Stanton's Bible*. Ithaca, NY: Cornell University Press, 2001.
McDaneld, Jen. "Harper, Historiography, and the Race/Gender Opposition in Feminism". *Signs: Journal of Women in Culture & Society* 40, no. 2 (2015): 393-415.
Mitchell, Michele. "'Lower Orders,' Racial Hierarchies, and Rights Rhetoric: Evolutionary Echoes in Elizabeth Cady Stanton's Thought During the Late 1860s". In *Elizabeth Cady Stanton, Feminist as Thinker: A Reader in Documents and Essays*, edited by Ellen Carol DuBois and Richard Candida Smith, 128-54. New York: New York University Press, 2007.
Newman, Louise Michele. *White Women's Rights: The Racial Origins of Feminism in the United States*. New York: Oxford University Press, 1999.
Palmer, Beverly Wilson, ed. *Selected Letters of Lucretia Coffin Mott*. Urbana: University of Illinois Press, 2002.

Skinnell, Ryan. "Elizabeth Cady Stanton's 1854 'Address to the Legislature of New York' and the Paradox of Social Reform Rhetoric". *Rhetoric Review* 29, no. 2 (2010): 129–44. doi:10.1080/07350191003613419.

Southard, Belinda A. Stillion. "A Rhetoric of Epistemic Privilege: Elizabeth Cady Stanton, Harriot Stanton Blatch, and the Educated Vote". *Advances in the History of Rhetoric* 17, no. 2 (2014): 157–78. doi:10.1080/15362426.2014.890962.

Stansell, Christine. "Missed Connections: Abolitionist Feminism in the Nineteenth Century". In *Elizabeth Cady Stanton, Feminist as Thinker: A Reader in Documents and Essays*, edited by Ellen Carol DuBois and Richard Candida Smith, 32–49. New York: New York University Press, 2007.

Tetrault, Lisa. *The Myth of Seneca Falls: Memory and the Women's Suffrage Movement, 1848–1898*. Chapel Hill: University of North Carolina Press, 2014.

Thomas, Tracy A. "Elizabeth Cady Stanton and the Notion of a Legal Class of Gender". In *Feminist Legal History: Essays on Women and Law*, edited by Tracy A. Thomas and Tracey Jean Boisseau, 153–55. New York: New York University Press, 2011.

Vetter, Lisa Pace. "'The Most Belligerent non-Resistant': Lucretia Mott on Women's Rights". *Political Theory* 43, no. 5 (2014): 600–30. doi:10.1177/0090591714522043.

Vetter, Lisa Pace. *The Political Thought of America's Founding Feminists*. New York: New York University Press, 2017.

Vetter, Lisa Pace. "Lucretia Mott". In *The Wollstonecraftian Mind*, edited by Sandrine Bergès, Eileen Hunt Botting, and Alan Coffee, 236–47. Abingdon: Routledge, 2019.

Lydia Maria Child on German philosophy and American slavery

Lydia Moland

ABSTRACT
As editor of the *National Anti-Slavery Standard* in the early 1840s, Lydia Maria Child was responsible for keeping the abolitionist movement in the United States informed of relevant news. She also used her editorial position to philosophize. Her column entitled "Letters from New York" is particularly philosophical, including considerations of infinity, free will, time, nature, art, and history. She especially turned to German philosophers and intellectuals such as Kant, Schiller, Bettina von Arnim, Karoline von Günderrode, Jean Paul, Herder, and Hegel in an attempt to guide her readers to a rejection of slavery for the right philosophical reasons. I consider the influence of German philosophy on three particular themes in her writings: a Romantic-Spinozistic view of humans and nature; a Kantian conception of conscience; and a Hegelian description of the philosophy of history.

In the early 1840s, the American Anti-Slavery Society founded a newspaper called the *National Anti-Slavery Standard*. Published weekly from New York, the *Standard* promised its nation-wide readership a full account of the abolitionist movement and its activities. Here abolitionists could find reports of congressional debates about slavery's expansion, detailed descriptions of atrocities against slaves in the South, and stories of anti-slavery speakers attacked by pro-slavery mobs. They could also find the movement's more practical news: which local abolitionist society had met when, how much money the most recent Anti-Slavery Christmas Fair had raised, and which abolitionist speaker was lecturing in Boston, or Providence, or Philadelphia.

But amidst these political realities and practical facts, readers of the *Standard* encountered something less expected: they encountered German philosophy. This unlikely inclusion was due to the paper's editor, a forty-year-old woman named Lydia Maria Child. Child had been chosen by the newspaper's executive committee because of her national literary reputation and her extraordinary record as an early abolitionist. In her twenties, Child had authored two acclaimed novels, edited the nation's first periodical for children, and written popular self-help books. In her early thirties, she had sacrificed her popularity by writing the first book-length condemnation of slavery in the United States, entitled *An Appeal for that Class of Americans Called Africans* (1833). The book was so radical in its call for immediate emancipation, with no compensation to slaveholders, that she had found herself ostracized by an elite Boston society with enduring and substantial economic ties to the South.

In addition to these literary credentials, Child was also a deeply philosophical thinker. She was convinced that eradicating an evil as egregious and deeply rooted as American slavery required an understanding of greater truths about humans and the world they inhabit. Soon after assuming editorship of the *National Anti-Slavery Standard*, she began to introduce her readers to themes from German philosophy in particular that she hoped would help accomplish the goal of emancipation. These themes appear in her writing, both public and private, after she left the *Standard*, and they informed the life of activism she lived. In what follows, I will suggest three such themes: a Romantic-Spinozistic belief in wholeness and unity; a Kantian emphasis on conscience and duty in moral life; and an understanding of progress in history that echoes German philosophers from Herder to Hegel. I will also suggest how these themes illuminate Child's lifelong activism and her response to key moments in the anti-slavery struggle.

1. Gems from the German

Child was born in 1802 in Medford, Massachusetts to a working-class family that did not value education for girls. But her older brother, who was enrolled at Harvard, lent her books and encouraged her intellectual development. Her interest in things German began in her early twenties when she and Margaret Fuller convened an informal study group that included the writings of French-Swiss intellectual Germaine de Staël. Staël's work probably came to Child's attention through George Ticknor, then a professor of literature at Harvard who had helped Child publish her first novel in 1824. Ticknor had been so inspired by Staël's work entitled *Germany*, and by the German intellectuals described there, that he had travelled to Europe to meet her and continued his education in German universities. Indeed, Staël's book – a wide-ranging treatise on German history, culture, religion, and geography – was widely credited with inspiring early American enthusiasm for German philosophy and literature. It included discussions of Herder, Jacobi and Kant, as well as Goethe, Schiller, Fichte, and Schelling.[1]

---

[1] For details on Ticknor's influence in Child's life, see Karcher, *First Woman*, 147. On Ticknor and Staël, see Staël, *Politics*, 21. For Staël's discussion of German philosophy, see *Germany* vol. 3, Chapters 6 and 7.

Child herself was so inspired by Staël's life and works that she wrote a biography of her in 1832. But she was also converted to Staël's Germans. She wrote later in life of an early romantic interest that faded after a period of separation: "I, in the meantime", she wrote, had "dwelt in friendly companionship with Herder, Schiller, and Jean Paul. Strangely, like some meagre, foreign tongue, [my former suitor's] words fell upon my ear" (Child, *Letters from New York*, 204). "I think I was made for a German", she wrote at another point, "and that my soul in coming down to earth, got drifted away by some side-wind, and so was wafted into the United States, to take up its abode in New-York" (Child, *Letters from New York*, 178).[2]

Shortly after beginning as the *Standard*'s editor, and apparently with the goal of anchoring both her own and others' activism in philosophical thought, Child initiated a series in the editorial section called "Letters from New York".[3] Here she gave free rein to her most speculative impulses. Surprised readers looking for updates on anti-slavery legislation instead found themselves confronted by deeply philosophical questions. What is the relation between the finite and the infinite? Between past, present, and future? Between necessity and free will? How are colours related to music? What great interconnected truths might unite the disparate strands of humans' confused, fragmentary experience? "I have lost the power of looking merely on the surface", she confessed to her readers. "Every thing seems to me to come from the Infinite, to be filled with the Infinite, to be tending toward the Infinite" (Child, *Letters from New York*, 10).

Her writing in these epistolary columns is exploratory, exuberant, and mystical, sometimes bordering on the ecstatic. In one letter, she speculates about "invisible radii, inaudible language, [that] go forth from the souls of all things. Nature ever sees and hears [this language]; as man would, were it not for his *self-listening*". "Minerals, flowers, and birds", she writes, "among a thousand other tri-une ideas, ever speak to me of the Past, the Present, and the Future". "The same soul pervades them all", she continued: "they are but higher and higher types of the self-same Ideas; spirally they rise, one out of the other" (Child, *Letters from New York*, 112). She explicitly associated these speculative moods with German philosophy. "I strove *not* to speak in mysticism", she wrote to her readers after one particularly lofty flight, "and lo, here I am, as the Germans would say, 'up in the blue' again" (Child, *Letters from New York*, 115).[4]

---

[2] Child was not alone in this feeling: the *North American Review* reported in 1840 that a "German mania" prevailed in nineteenth-century American poetry, literature, and philosophy (Kaag and Jensen, "The American Reception of Hegel", 672).
[3] These letters were later published as a stand-alone book.
[4] For these passages, see: on the infinite, 10; on the future, 152; on music and light, 112–13; on free will, 133.

Which Germans did she have in mind? Scattered references throughout the *Standard* give us some clues. Early in her editorship, she included a column entitled "Gems from the German", comprised of aphorisms by Lessing, August Wilhelm Schlegel, Jean Paul, and Beethoven on topics including beauty, honesty, and the value of hard work. She was drawn, she wrote in another column, to Herder's idea that "matter is only the time-garment of the spirit" (Child, *Letters from New York*, 165). In one particularly mystical passage in "Letters from New York", she describes an imagined spiritual journey in which she "met Herder", who, she quotes Jean Paul as saying, "'dwelt with the great of all ages, yet with a divine Spinozism of the heart, loved the humblest reptile, the meanest insect, and every blossom in the woods'" (Child, *Letters from New York*, 204).[5] In a more cynical mood, she agreed with Jacobi, who, she wrote, "spoke true words, when he said 'All governments are, more or less, a contract with the Devil'" (Child, *Collected Correspondence*, 1107).

In Novalis, she loved the suggestion that in places where ancient peoples lived, nature has become "more human, more rational", allowing us to enjoy a "two-fold world" that includes "the magic [of] poetry and fable of the mind. Who knows whether also an indefinable influence of the former inhabitants, now departed, does not conspire to this end?' The solemn impression", Child concluded, "so eloquently described by Novalis, is what I have desired above all things to experience" (Child, *Letters from New York,* 109).[6] Another German of this period who appears in her private letters is Rahel von Varnhagen, keeper of a Berlin salon in which Schelling, Friedrich Schlegel, the Humboldt brothers, and Hegel were participants. She quotes Varnhagen as saying "[W]e only love those whom we *know*; and we *must* love all whom we *really* know. That which is hateful always continues unfamiliar to us. Dislike and fault-finding are only an unlove" (Child, *Collected Correspondence*, 1102).

She felt an exuberant connection with Bettina von Arnim, the author of two genre-defying novels, *Goethes Briefwechsel mit einem Kinde* and *Die Günderode*, both of which are highly philosophical and portray von Arnim herself as a free, eccentric spirit – or, as Child put it, "wild as a savage, graceful as a child, bright as the sunshine, free as the wind" (Child, *National Anti-Slavery Standard*, 14 April 1842). Von Arnim was herself a kind of embodiment of the state of German philosophy and literature in the early nineteenth century. She was the sister of the Romantic poet Clemens Brentano and the wife of poet and novelist Achim von Arnim. She had intense and complicated friendships with Goethe and Beethoven. *Die Günderode* is an epistolary novel

---

[5]The original quote is a description of Herder by Jean Paul, reported in Sarah Austin's 1833 *Characteristics of Goethe, from the German of Falk, von Müller, etc.*
[6]Child may have read this quotation in an 1842 translation of Novalis' *Heinrich von Ofterdingen*, 81.

based on von Arnim's friendship with Karoline von Günderrode, herself the author of intense philosophizing inspired by Fichte and Schelling.[7] Von Arnim's *Die Günderode* was a literary sensation in Germany and had been translated into English by Margaret Fuller in 1842.

Child especially loved *Günderode*, reporting that it was among the possessions she seized when fleeing a fire that had broken out in her neighbourhood. "It gave my mind elasticity and vigor, like the mountain breeze or the forest ramble", she reported (Child, *National Anti-Slavery Standard*, 14 April 1842). References to von Arnim are woven throughout her 'Letters from New York'. "Whoever quarrels with his fate, does not understand it, says Bettine", Child for instance declared (Child, *Letters from New York*, 174).[8] She sympathetically mentions von Arnim's belief that she was surrounded by spirits – that "there was something living near me, in whose protection I trusted" – suggesting a dimension of reality that we sometimes sense but cannot confirm. "What a great mystery is life, so closely embracing the soul, as the chrysalis the butterfly!" she quotes von Arnim as saying (Child, *Letters from New York*, 174). As an unconventional woman, von Arnim had been subjected to much censure, which Child – herself an unconventional woman – resented on her behalf. "Bettine is a perpetual refreshment to my soul", she wrote to her brother. "Nothing disturbs me so much as the Philistine remarks made about her" (Child, *Collected Correspondence*, 336).

While Child did much of this philosophizing in her official "Letters from New York" that continued to appear in the *National Anti-Slavery Standard*, she confirmed her interest in von Arnim in her letters. She cites von Arnim's assertion that "music is the *soul* of [all?] Art", adding only that music, in her own opinion, is the soul of *all* science (Child, *Collected Correspondence*, 1081).[9] To her brother, she quotes von Arnim's suggestion that some thoughts are imparted, not created: "There were thoughts shaped within me", Child quotes von Arnim as saying. "I did not perpend them; I *believed* in them. They had this peculiarity that I felt them not as *self thought* but as *imparted*".[10] "I dare say this all sounds very crude to you", Child continues to her brother, by then a theology professor at Harvard:

> for I never had any faculty at metaphysics. I can only say that things *reasoned* about seem to me like the visible, tangible objects of *this* world; and things imparted to the *imaginative faculty* seem like the *divine realities*, the Creative

---
[7]Günderrode's posthumously published essays include "Idea of the Earth", "The Manes" and "An Apocalyptic Fragment". See Günderrode, *Sämtliche Werke* and Nassar, forthcoming.
[8]Child follows literary convention by referring to von Arnim as 'Bettine', which was von Arnim's way of fictionalizing the name by which she was known, namely 'Bettina'. Von Arnim appears to have done the same thing with Günderrode's name, which she spells with only one 'r'.
[9]The manuscript is obscured here.
[10]Child's handwriting here is obscured, but the quotation is from von Arnim's *Goethe's Correspondence with a Child*, vol. 2, 19.

Ideas, in Plato's ethereal world of intelligences. *All* the very highest truths are not cognizable by *reason*; are they?
(Child, *Collected Correspondence*, 892, emphases in original)

She also sympathized deeply with von Arnim's description of nature. She quotes von Arnim's complaint that "Nature seems to wail, as if begging to be released from prison. And *is* the soul of man to set nature free?" "Oh, how full Nature is of meaning!", Child exclaims in agreement, "and how she *tries* to utter it to our unapprehensive souls!" "[W]hen the sun shines on the moss and makes it *golden*", she continues, "I opine it means the natural affections raised into the spiritual in some degree, or, in transcendental phrase, 'linked with the infinite'". Someday, Child asserts, all will be clear, and von Arnim's longing for nature's liberation will be realized: "The beams that will melt the prison bars are even now shining brightly; though the darkness comprehendeth them not" (Child, *Collected Correspondence*, 200, emphases in original).

Another of Child's favourite Germans was Jean Paul Richter. Jean Paul, as he called himself, was the antic author of sprawling novels inspired by Laurence Sterne's *Tristram Shandy* and of a work on theoretical aesthetics. He had been the subject of a biography, translated into English in 1842, that Child and many of her friends had loved (Child, *Collected Correspondence*, 419, 422). In her "Letters from New York", she promises her reader that "whosoever reads [Jean Paul], with an earnest thoughtfulness, will see heavenly features perpetually shining through the golden mists or rolling vapour" (Child, *Letters from New York*, 173). Interpreting an engraving of Jean Paul surrounded by clouds in which the faces of angels were dimly visible, she wrote:

> If man looked at his being as a whole, or had faith that all things were intended to bring him into harmony with the divine will, he would gratefully acknowledge that spiritual dew and rain, wind and lightning, cold and sunshine, all help his growth, as their natural forms bring to maturity the flowers and the grain.
> (Child, *Letters from New York*, 173)

Jean Paul's pithy aphorisms so impressed her that she published three separate columns in the *National Anti-Slavery Standard* entitled "Gems from Jean Paul" disseminating his short comments on poetry, suffering, and hope (Child, *National Anti-Slavery Standard*, 31 March 1842, 19 January 1843, 13 April 1843).

What were these reflections on nature, spiritualism, and poetry doing in an anti-slavery newsletter? "Strange material this for a reformer!" Child herself conceded in one column (Child, *Letters from New York*, 134). There is evidence that some of her readers, as well as the executive committee who had hired her, were thinking the same thing. But Child clearly believed that this kind of philosophical foundation would equip her readers for sustained, right-minded reform. A sense of wholeness with the universe; a connection with nature; a belief in the spiritual; an acceptance of fate; an awareness of oneness among humans: Child hoped that these ideas would prompt Americans to oppose slavery not for economic, political, or explicitly religious reasons but because of a conviction that all humans, including Africans and their descendants, were part of a great interconnected whole. All of these themes are traceable to Germans she revered: Herder, Novalis, von Arnim, Günderrode, Jean Paul.[11] Her exuberant, sometimes mystical style is traceable to them as well, as is her conviction that poetic grace in philosophical writing could best communicate important truths. In a letter to a young poet who feared Child would disapprove of his poetry because it was not explicitly anti-slavery, Child responded that his poetry "*is* akin to anti-slavery" because it presented an image of love and unity. "Do you not remember", she wrote to him:

> that Jean Paul says, 'Love *one* human being, purely and warmly, and you will love *all*. The heart in this heaven, like the wandering sun, sees nothing from the dewdrop to the ocean, but a mirror which it warms and fills'.
> (Child, *Collected Correspondence*, 300)

This constellation of ideas also informed Child's attitude towards reform. "Place not tempest against tempest", she quotes Jean Paul as saying, "but set the Æolian harp of the poet against the storm, and perhaps it will answer thee with sweet accord". This image was undoubtedly meaningful to Child because of her and other abolitionists' commitment to two positions as regards activism: moral suasion and non-resistance.[12] Moral suasion was the belief that social change would only happen through moral influence: through patient argument, emotional appeal, and moral example, not through politics or physical force. Moral suasion paired easily with non-resistance, or the belief that force of any kind was antithetical to moral improvement. Child's dedication to these principles was undoubtedly bolstered by the philosophical vision I have tried to sketch above. Better to believe in an underlying spiritual unity that can be disclosed by love, as several of the Germans she was reading suggested; better to set an example of a soft and soothing instrument that, when confronted by the violent gales of a tempest, produces not more force but calming, ethereal music. Better, in short, to embrace the unity and harmony that characterizes the vision of the Germans she admired, and to hope that this vision could prompt the change so desperately needed.

---

[11] It is possible that Child was aware of Herder's arguments against slavery as found for instance in his *This, Too, a Philosophy of History*. See Gjesdal, *Herder's Hermeneutics*, 152–3, 166–9 and Solbrig, "American Slavery in Eighteenth-Century German Literature". Staël had also written against slavery in two novels, *Mirza ou Lettre d'un voyageur*, and *Historie de Pauline*. See Moland, forthcoming.

[12] These positions characterized what is often called Garrisonian abolitionism, named for William Lloyd Garrison. Garrison's non-resistance was firmly based in Christianity; Child's, as I see it, was based more in a philosophical approach to Christianity and in philosophy itself. Other abolitionists, both black and white, soon began rejecting non-resistance as a principle of reform, turning instead to more violent resistance. See Jackson, *Force and Freedom*, 43ff.

How would these reformist principles play out in practice? A wrenching test came when John Brown conducted a raid on the federal armoury at Harpers Ferry, Virginia, in October 1859. Brown, a white veteran of early anti-slavery conflict in Kansas, had concluded that a system of violence like slavery had to be met by violence, and that enslavers had forfeited their right to life by enslaving their fellow humans. He had attacked the armoury with the aim of stealing weapons, arming enslaved Virginians, and beginning an insurrection. Several people were killed; the raid failed; Brown and his co-conspirators were captured and ultimately executed.

Brown's martyrdom put non-resistant abolitionists, Child acknowledged, in a "perplexing corner". She herself was enormously energized by Brown's actions despite their violence. Against those who condemned him, she argued that *if* we endorse violence in *any* situation, we should endorse it in the case of freeing enslaved humans. It was, she insisted, inconsistent to praise Revolutionary War heroes for using violence to gain independence and then blame Brown "for going to the rescue of those who are a thousand times more oppressed than we ever were" (Child, *Selected Letters*, 336). To glorify the violence of the American Revolution and condemn Brown was thoughtless at best and self-serving hypocrisy at worst.

In addition to this argument from hypocrisy, Child made an argument of shared responsibility that resonates with Jean Paul's image of the harp in the storm and the philosophical beliefs supporting it. "Instead of blaming [Brown] for carrying out his own convictions by means we cannot sanction", she wrote, "it would be more profitable for us to inquire of ourselves whether we, who believe in a 'more excellent way,' have carried our convictions into practice, as faithfully as he did *his*". And what, again, were those convictions? "*We* believe in *moral influence* as a cure in the diseases of society", Child reminded those who, like her, were committed to non-resistance; then she called them to consider whether they were in fact practicing what they preached. "Have we exerted [moral influence] as constantly and as strenuously as we ought?" she asked.

> Do we bear our testimony against it at the parlour and the store, the caucus and the conference, on the highway and in the cars? ... Do we brand with ignominy the statesmen, who make compromises with the foul sin, for their own emolument?
>
> (Child, *Selected Letters*, 336–7)

The answer, all too often, was no. Child then laid responsibility for Brown's violence at her own and her readers' feet. "And because *we* have thus failed to perform our duty in the 'more excellent way,'" she predicted, "the end cometh by violence; because come it *must*" (Child, *Selected Letters*, 336). The philosophical commitment to wholeness and harmony here reveals a darker edge. It is not just that non-resistance will lead to a harmonious world. It is that a failure to live by that commitment guarantees its opposite: a world where injustice is met with violence rather than remedied by love.

2. A Kantian conscience

In her moral life, Child was a deontologist. She never uses this word, to my knowledge, and insofar as she discusses Kant's theories, she focuses on his theoretical philosophy. In a November 1841 editorial in the *Standard* in which she again, probably to her readers' surprise, takes up explicitly philosophical themes, she describes him as the "celebrated" head of a "German school of metaphysics" which "denies that all knowledge is received through the senses; and maintains that all the highest, and therefore most universal, truths are revealed within the soul, to a faculty *transcending* the understanding. This faculty they call pure Reason". But she then connects this metaphysical position to something with moral potential: "To this pure Reason, which some of their writers call 'The God within,'" she informs her readers, "they believe that all perceptions of the True, the Good, and the Beautiful are revealed, in its unconscious quietude; and that the province of the Understanding, with its five handmaids, the Senses, is confined merely to external things".[13]

"The God within" is certainly a reference to another of Child's deepest moral commitments, namely to the centrality of conscience in moral life. The word conscience pervades her reformist writings. She reports herself, for instance, willing to "sell comfort, repose, taste, everything but conscience" in the cause of abolitionism (Child, *Selected Letters*, 263).[14] To no less a luminary in the abolitionist cause than John Brown, she writes "I care not who frowns, or who smiles upon me, if power is given me to be faithful to my own conscience" (Child, *Selected Letters*, 327). When she looks back in regret at a period in which infighting among abolitionists forced her to withdraw from activism for several years, she writes: "Conscience twinges me now and then, that I ever turned aside from this duty, to dally in primrose paths" (Child, *Selected Letters*, 377). And Child certainly understood conscience as entailing a kind of necessity reminiscent of Kant's categorical imperative. "[R]eforming work lies around me like 'the ring of Necessity,'" she wrote in the *Standard*, "and ever and anon Freewill bites at the circle. But this necessity is only another name for conscience; and that is the voice of God" (Child, *Letters from New York*, 133).

---

[13] Child's deontological convictions probably also explain her enthusiasm for a book called *An Essay on Intuitive Morals* by Francis Power Cobbe, which she describes as "an attempt to adapt the system of Kant to popular comprehension", (Child, *Collected Correspondence*, 1116). Child also sometimes took a dim view of Kant's metaphysics: see Child, *Collected Correspondence*, 1447.

[14] *Selected Letters*, 263. It is worth noting that Staël's chapter on Kant includes a vigorous description of the place of conscience in his moral theory. See Staël, *Germany*, 98. Child does not reference this discussion explicitly, but she certainly read it.

What that voice communicated corresponds to another central Kantian concept: duty. Acting from duty, Kant had claimed, is acting out of respect for the law, not out of inclination or because of an assessment of an action's probable outcomes. "Duties are ours; events are God's" had, by the 1830s, become an abolitionist mantra, and it, too, was meant to warn Americans away from consequentialist arguments claiming that ending slavery was too difficult, too costly, or would result in formerly enslaved people revenging themselves on their enslavers. Child uses the phrase in her 1833 *Appeal*, adding that "[u]nder all circumstances, there is but one honest course; and that is to do right, and to trust the consequences to Divine Providence" (Child, *Appeal*, 213). In one of her columns for the *National Anti-Slavery Standard*, Child set this philosophical approach explicitly against utilitarianism. After describing someone reasoning his way to freeing some but not all of his slaves through calculating a complicated "balance of evils", she describes this theory as "obviously absurd, as well as slippery in its application; for none but God *can* balance evils; it requires omniscience and omnipresence to do it". She goes on to claim that this man, like all humans, had been born with a conscience that *could* have told him his duty to free all his slaves immediately. But "[w]hether this utilitarian remembers it or not, he must have stifled many convictions before he arrived at his present state of mind". Child continued to believe in "eternal and unchangeable principles of right and wrong" and that all men "inwardly know better than they act". What, then, was the duty of a reformer like Child? It was to "renew our zeal to purify public opinion". "How shall we fulfill this sacred trust, which each holds for the good of all?" she asked her readers. "Not by calculating consequences; not by balancing evils; but by reverent obedience to our own highest convictions of individual duty" (Child, *Letters from New York*, 100–1).

A challenge to this deontological principle confronted Child after John Brown's raid. In a letter published in its aftermath, the Governor of Virginia directly accused Child and other abolitionists of inspiring Brown's violence. Child fired back, also in print, claiming instead that it was the South's violation of earlier compromises and its draconian fugitive slave laws that had inspired Brown's raid (Child, *Correspondence with Gov. Wise*, 5ff.). But even if it were true that, by enumerating slavery's evils, abolitionists made violence more likely, Child would not stop doing what she saw as her duty. She could feel, she wrote to a friend, some sympathy for terrified Southerners, including mothers whose worst nightmare – being murdered in their beds by the humans they enslaved – seemed all too plausible after Brown's raid. But Child concluded that she could not let such sympathy interfere with her duty to preach the evil of slavery. "I *force* myself to remember", she wrote,

> that, terrible as an insurrection would be to *white* women and children, *black* women and children have, for many generations, been living in subjection to

things *as* horrid, with no *Union*, no *laws*, no *public sentiment* to help *them*. And so, I go steadily forward to the slave's rescue, leaving their oppressors to take care of the consequences.

(Child, *Collected Correspondence*, 1169)

"I cannot calculate the *consequences*", she continued, "but my *duty* is clear to me .... Nay, shrinking and quivering at every nerve, I would *still* do it, if I *knew* their pathway to freedom must be 'over their master's bodies'" (Child, *Collected Correspondence*, 1169, emphases in original). It was, to be sure, a fraught application of the principle of conscience for someone who believed in non-resistance. But it was rooted in a philosophical position that Child had consciously adopted and that she now sought to apply with rigour and consistency. It is unlikely that this position in Child's particular case came from reading Kant directly. But it is consistent, for instance, with Allen Guelzo's suggestion that American abolitionists were influenced by a "politics of ethical absolutism" inspired by Kant and mediated through American Romantics including Emerson and Coleridge (Guelzo, *Lincoln's Emancipation Proclamation*, 10). If Child's own appeal to conscience was not a result of reading Kant himself, it was surely strengthened by Kant's influence in the American intellectual life around her.

3. Spirit, moral feeling, and progress in history

A final topic remains on which I want to consider Child's thought in light of a German philosophical tradition: the philosophy of history. For someone who had staked her life and career on revolutionary social reform, philosophical questions about history were pressing. Was there progress in history? If so, through what? Here, too, Child was asking questions that had preoccupied German philosophers for the last generations, including Lessing, Herder, Schiller, Kant, and Hegel. Each of these theorists had written or lectured on the subject, with conclusions ranging from Kant's optimistic "Idea for a Universal History with Cosmopolitan Intent" to Schiller's appeal to art's role in human progress in his "Letters on Aesthetic Education". By the time the Civil War started, Child had herself written two works relevant to questions about history these philosophers had asked. The first was a two-volume work published in 1835, entitled *The History of the Condition of Women, in Various Ages and Nations*. Here Child collected for her readers accounts of Chinese marriage rituals, Turkish dowries, and female African warriors. She reported on civilizations as distant as the Philippines, Syria, Poland, and Sumatra. But in the end, Child did not synthesize this record of facts into an all-encompassing theory of what women's history meant. Her reviewers noticed. "[F]rom her did we anticipate somewhat more of the philosophy of history", one wrote (Hale, "History of the Condition",

588). In other words: what did all of these facts about the condition of women *mean*? Child, at least here, didn't say.

The second of Child's works relevant to the philosophy of history was a three-volume history of religion entitled *The Progress of Religious Ideas Through Successive Ages*, published in 1855, that one reader said could easily have served as the foundation of a philosophy of religion (Child, *Collected Correspondence*, 914). Here, after detailing the beliefs and histories of Hinduism, Judaism, Islam, Confucianism, and finally Christianity, Child comes to a conclusion regarding how religions and their progress should be judged: namely, by their 'practical results'. All religions, she claimed, "contain truth, all of them have produced, and are producing, greater or less degrees of good" – a progressive claim in an era which often simply denigrated other religious worldviews as heathen. "But after making due deductions, on account of the iniquitous practices of Christendom", she continued:

> we are still compelled to admit that there only do we find sympathy, benevolence, and active exertion for the improvement of all mankind. Christianity is the only form of religion which has warmed up whole nations, to sacrifice time, talent, and wealth, for the benefit of remote and degraded classes of people, from whom no return of advantages could be expected.

She connects this interpretation with the eradication of slavery:

> Where the slave trade has been abolished, it has not been done by policy of government. It has been the expansive force of Christian sympathy, compelling cold reluctant statesmen to move in obedience to the mighty pulsation of the popular heart.
>
> (Child, *Progress*, 433–4)

We should certainly be skeptical of Child's conclusions about Christianity's virtues and other religions' deficiencies. But her underlying philosophical claim about history's progress is clear. How do we measure progress in history? By humans' willingness to sacrifice for the least fortunate among them.[15]

In May 1859, Child again engaged explicitly with a question about the philosophy of history. It was then that she read Henry Thomas Buckle's *History of Civilization in England*. Child was energized by Buckle's sweeping theory and wrote about it in several letters to friends. "Buckle says truly", she wrote to one,

---

[15]Child also engaged in the kind of deeply problematic speculation about 'Ages' of history popular in both European and American thought during this time. She writes for instance that the 'Physical Age' had been followed by the 'Intellectual' age, and that the 'Spiritual Age' was still forthcoming. She associates Africans with this 'Spiritual Age' in a way that is both progressive and objectionable; it elevates Africans to a higher historical status than their "intellectual" European counterparts but justifies racialized claims that Africans are more spiritual and more musical than other races (Child, *Letters from New York*, 51). See also her claim that "the African race" is "probably most susceptible of religious feeling, and have the strongest tendency to devotion" and that "a very prominent place among the nations must be assigned to the African race, whenever the age of Moral Sentiments arrives" (Child, *Letters from New York*, 182). The pernicious effects of these kinds of claims are, unfortunately, still with us today.

"that intellect grows continually, while moral principles are precisely the same as they were thousands of years ago". Here we might sense echoes of the kind of moral universalism in Child's work that I have suggested is reminiscent of Kant. "True[,] the *principles* are the same", Child continues But "the *application* of those principles is continually growing wider. At one period, intellect applies them to the treatment of prisoners, at another to the treatment of the insane, of slaves, sailors, women" (Child, *Collected Correspondence*, 1101).

But Child objected to Buckle's use of the world "intellect" to describe the engine of that progress. In all cases of moral reform, she instead suggests, "intellect is excited to action by *moral feeling*". "A few centuries ago, what nations thought of applying [moral principles] to the condition of prisoners, of slaves, of women?" she asks. "Slavery was abolished in England by rousing the *moral feelings* of the people; and under that stimulus, they collected *facts* to convince the *intellect*". And then she makes an important philosophical distinction. "It seems to me that Hegel, in his Philosophy of History uses a better word [than intellect]. He calls the motive-power of the universe *spirit*" (Child, *Collected Correspondence*, 1101). Spirit was the superior term, she wrote to another friend, "because it includes both moral and intellectual influences, which surely always move together in human progress. It seems to me as difficult to separate them, as it is to separate light and heat" (Child, *Collected Correspondence*, 1099).[16]

The beginning of the Civil War raised even more pressing issues about the philosophy of history, specifically the question of progress. History was progressing, Child was sure: "man's history is eternal progression", she wrote. But where in history was she, and where was her country? "Thus far, the U.S. have been acting so basely towards the slaves, that it seems that God could not think us *worth* saving, as a nation", she lamented to a sister-in-law. "Perhaps we are destined to be a *warning* to future nations, having proved ourselves too wicked to be used as an *example*" (Child, *Collected Correspondence*, 1343). She mourned this possibility. "I love my country", she wrote as its future grew ever darker (Child, *Collected Correspondence*, 958). But her country's survival was not the standard by which she would measure progress.

> Whether the ship I sail in sinks rapidly, or floats tremulously for a long time, with this dreadful leak at the bow, I will still wave this banner to the last, to cheer the kindred souls who are sadly watching our experiment, With my latest breath, I will shout aloud to them, 'It is not *Freedom* that has failed, my friends. *She* faileth never. We are sinking because we have Despotism on board. Throw her over from *your* ships, my friends! Throw her over, whatever form she takes!'
> (Child, *Collected Correspondence*, 956)

---

[16] It is not clear how Child encountered Hegel's philosophy of history, but one possible source is through her friend and fellow abolitionist Theodore Parker. See Kaag and Jensen, "The American Reception", 675.

What, then, are the resonances of German philosophy in the thinking of this American reformer? Child was clearly inspired by a Romantic-Spinozistic conceptualization of the unity of the spiritual and the natural. Like some of the German Romantics she admired, she was convinced that the world was full of meaning that humans could – so far, anyway – only vaguely intuit. Society's ills – slavery foremost among them, but also prostitution, poverty, and abusive prison conditions – were caused, in Child's diagnosis, by ignorance of the deep unity suggested by this Romantic worldview: by humans' tendency to view themselves as alienated both from each other and from the natural world. If humans could be brought to recognize the underlying unity of all of reality, they would treat each other, and nature, differently: namely, to return to a Romantic-Spinozistic theme, with love. But Child's moral vision also shared central commitments with Kant's moral universalism and its emphasis on necessity and duty. In fact, Child combines what sometimes seem to be opposing impulses in early nineteenth-century philosophy: the mystical romanticism of Jean Paul, Novalis, von Arnim, and others on the one hand and Kantian deontology on the other. She adds to this constellation a Hegelian sense of the progress of history, filtered through her own understanding of moral feeling as the force that will drive that progress.

Child clearly felt a deep affinity with German culture, and she used insights from German philosophy in particular to fight the very American evil that had pitched her country into crisis.[17] Given that, in many cases, we do not know exactly which works by which German philosophers Child read, or whose summaries of which texts she would have relied on, the precise nature of this influence remains undefined. What I have tried to show is not how Child's abolitionist convictions were caused by German philosophy but how she turned to them for inspiration or noted when their insights seemed to be in harmony with her own. Child was in fact reluctant to consider herself a philosopher, likely both out of self-consciousness about her limited formal education and a distrust of the abstraction and obfuscation that sometimes – then as now – characterize the discipline.[18] An early reviewer of Child's writings in the *Southern Quarterly Review* wrote: "Mrs. Child disclaims the character of a philosopher, but she knows how to teach the art of living well, which is certainly the highest wisdom".[19] By introducing readers to philosophical themes both in the *Standard* and in her other writings, Child clearly hoped to lead others to attain this highest wisdom as well. In doing so, she provides

---

[17] Much work remains to be done detailing these influences, for instance that of von Arnim's *Günderode* on Child's thought and style; of Herder's critiques of slavery and emphasis on sympathy on her philosophy of history (see Gjesdal, *Herder's Hermeneutics*, 113ff); and Child's use of Swedenborg's doctrine of correspondences together with Swedenborg's influence on Kant.
[18] For examples of her resistance to philosophical obfuscation, see Child, *Collected Correspondence*, 1147.
[19] *Southern Quarterly Review* Vol. IX, 1846, page 539. Quoted in Karcher, *First Woman*, 148.

a compelling example of the possibility of using philosophical thought in the service of social criticism and reform.

Acknowledgements

For their insights, inspiration, and comments on previous drafts of this essay, I would like to thank Kristin Gjesdal, Dalia Nassar, and Anne Pollok. I am also grateful to Michael Rosen and the participants in Harvard University's European Philosophy Workshop for their encouragement and feedback.

Bibliography

Arnim, Bettina von. *Goethe's Correspondence with a Child*. Lowell: Daniel Bixby, 1841.
Arnim, Bettina von. *Günderode*. Translated by Margaret Fuller. Boston: E. P. Peabody, 1842.
Arnim, Bettina von. *Werke und Briefe*, Vol. 1. Edited by Walter Schmitz. Frankfurt am Main: Deutscher Klassiker Verlag, 1986.
Austin, Sarah. *Characteristics of Goethe, from the German of Falk, von Müller, etc.* Philadelphia: Lee and Blanchard, 1841.
Child, Lydia Maria. *An Appeal in Favor of that Class of Americans Called Africans*. Boston: Allen and Ticknor, 1833.
Child, Lydia Maria. *The History of the Condition of Women, in Various Ages and Nations*. Boston: John Allen, 1835.
Child, Lydia Maria. *The Progress of Religious Ideas, Through Successive Ages*. New York: C.S. Francis, 1855.
Child, Lydia Maria. *Correspondence Between Lydia Maria Child and Gov. Wise and Mrs. Mason of Virginia*. Boston: American Anti-Slavery Society, 1860.
Child, Lydia Maria. *Collected Correspondence*. Edited by Patricia G. Holland, Milton Meltzer, and Francine Krasno. Millwood, NY: Kraus Microfilm, 1980.
Child, Lydia Maria. *Selected Letters, 1817–1880*. Edited by Milton Meltzer, Patricia G. Holland, and Francine Krasno. Amherst, MA: University of Massachusetts Press, 1982.
Child, Lydia Maria. *Letters from New York*. Edited by Bruce Mills. Athens: University of Georgia Press, 1998.
Gjesdal, Kristin. *Herder's Hermeneutics*. Cambridge: Cambridge University Press, 2017.
Guelzo, Allen C. *Lincoln's Emancipation Proclamation: The End of Slavery in America*. New York: Simon & Schuster, 2004.
Günderrode, Karoline von. *Sämtliche Werke und ausgewählte Schriften*. Frankfurt: Stroemfeld/Roter Stern, 1990–91.
Hale, Sarah Josepha. "The History of the Condition of Women, in Various Ages and Nations, by Mrs. D. L. Child". *American Ladies' Magazine* 8 (1835): 588.
Jackson, Kellie Carter. *Force and Freedom: Black Abolitionists and the Politics of Violence*. Philadelphia: Pennsylvania University Press, 2019.
Kaag, John, and Kipton E. Jensen. "The American Reception of Hegel (1830–1930)". In *The Oxford Handbook of Hegel*, edited by Dean Moyar, 670–96. New York: Oxford University Press, 2017.
Karcher, Carolyn. *The First Woman of the Republic: A Cultural Biography of Lydia Maria Child*. North Carolina: Duke University Press, 1994.
Moland, Lydia. "Is She Not an Unusual Woman? Say More: Germaine de Staël and Lydia Maria Child on Progress, Art, and Abolition". In *Women in Philosophy in Eighteenth-Century Germany*, edited by Corey Dyck. Oxford: Oxford University Press, forthcoming.

Nassar, Dalia. "The Human Vocation and the Question of the Earth: Karoline von Günderrode's Philosophy of Nature". *Archiv für Geschichte der Philosophie*, forthcoming.

Novalis (Friedrich von Hardenberg). *Henry of Ofterdingen: A Romance*. Cambridge: John Owen, 1842. https://archive.org/details/henryofterdinge00schlgoog.

Solbrig, Ingeborg H. 1990. "American Slavery in Eighteenth-Century German Literature: The Case of Herder's 'Neger-Idyllen'". *Monatshefte* 82, no. 1 (1990): 38–49.

Staël, Germaine de. *Germany*. London: John Murray, 1813. https://archive.org/details/dli.bengal.10689.7366.

Staël, Germaine de. *Politics, Literature and National Character*. Edited by Morroe Berger. New Brunswick: Transaction Publishers, 2000.

The fragility of rationality: George Eliot on akrasia and the law of consequences

Patrick Fessenbecker

ABSTRACT
George Eliot often uses the language of determinism in her novels, but we do not understand her view very well by treating such phrasing as addressing debates about the freedom of will directly. Instead she uses seemingly deterministic terms, like the 'law of consequences', to depict and analyse a particular problem in moral psychology: those instances where we ourselves make it impossible to act on our own best judgements. When we fail to act on our best judgement, this has downstream effects, since it can produce a gap between prudential rationality and one's all-things-considered judgement. Surveying depictions of this problem in Silas Marner, Adam Bede, and Romola, I argue that it's a revealing problem for Eliot's larger view, bringing together her objections to consequentialism, her recognition of the fragility of virtue, and her account of the role of sympathy in practical deliberation.

Much of the scholarship on George Eliot over the last two generations has investigated with subtlety and care her attention to the tension between freedom and determinism. Taking its departure from George Levine's landmark 1962 article "Determinism and Responsibility in George Eliot" and more directly from Eliot's famous phrase from the end of *Middlemarch*, "there is no creature whose inward being is so strong that it is not greatly determined by what lies outside it", a variety of scholars have seen in Eliot nuanced analyses of the threats to a pre-reflective notion of free will by discoveries in the nascent social sciences and evolutionary biology (*Middlemarch*, 872).[1] Attentive in particular to the way social norms constrained and produced women's behaviour in Victorian England, critics have

---
[1] Levine's diagnosis is that Eliot is a compatibilist: she believes in a 'rigidly determined' world but that moral responsibility is compatible with that fact when properly understood (269). That claim has generally been accepted; see for instance Beer, *Darwin's Plots*; Stone, "Chance and Ego", and Forrester, "Aiming to Hit". For a revisionary response, see Newton, "George Eliot, Kant, and Free Will".

uncovered an Eliot who recognizes the determinative force of such norms but seeks ways of exerting meaningful human agency in spite of them.[2]

To a significant extent, attention to this philosophical problem is licensed by a consideration of her key terms and their sources in Eliot's reading during her formative period in the 1840s. Charles Bray's 1841 work *The Philosophy of Necessity; or, The Law of Consequences* explicitly sets out to debunk intuitive notions of freedom and show how seemingly free acts are the result of inevitable processes; as he puts it, "Motive is to voluntary action what cause is to effect in the physical, and the order of nature is as fixed in the world of mind as of matter" (*Philosophy of Necessity*, 171). Similarly, Robert William Mackay's 1850 *The Progress of the Intellect* – a review of which was Eliot's first contribution to the *Westminster Review*, when she was thirty-one – argues for the importance of scientific conceptions of law for social and cultural study. "The master key", Eliot writes,

> is the recognition of the presence of undying law in the material and moral world – of that invariability of sequence which is acknowledged to be the basis of physical science, but which is still perversely ignored in our social organization, our ethics, and our religion.
>
> (*Essays*, 31)

Human history is a series of experiments in the effects of the 'inexorable law of consequences,' and social improvement depends above all on comprehending that law.

But we do not grasp the nature of Eliot's philosophical project very clearly by putting it only in the light of her sources.[3] When her narrators speak of the role of necessity in human actions and occasionally of their regulation by a 'law of consequences, the phrase denotes something quite different than a social or a biological structure constraining or producing human agency. In Eliot's hands, it names a specific problem in moral psychology: a particular species of akrasia, or action against one's intentions and judgements. While there is an inexorability to the law of consequences, it appears insofar as our previous actions constrain our present deliberations in ways we regret. A path dependency appears when – to pick a pattern Eliot returns to several times – I tell a lie, and then discover that despite my desire to be honest I must tell more lies in order for the first lie to have its intended effect.

There is certainly a sense in which the law of consequences interferes with my freedom, then, but it is not the freedom of choice unconstrained by social custom or biological impulse. Rather, the law of consequences prevents me from acting on the basis of the person I want to be, and is thus a threat to

---

[2] This tension is particularly complex with regards to Eliot's feminism, which was by no means straightforward. For a recent entry in the debate, see June Szirotny, *The Right to Rebellion*.

[3] This is a point Elizabeth Ermarth has brought out. She writes: "When she speaks of invariability of sequence George Eliot is usually making an analogy, not an identification between natural law and cultural law" ("Incarnations 277").

something like my autonomy. But its force isn't anything external: it's just a past version of me, a version whose actions I regret. So Eliot's use of the language of metaphysical freedom ultimately is connected to what philosophers might now think of as the weakness of practical rationality. While it may be possible for agents to act on the basis of their best judgements, that capacity is fragile, and depends on maintaining one's character in such a way that one's interests don't become aligned with actions that violate those judgements. When they do become aligned – in other words, when one has to lie to keep a secret hidden – the law of consequences obtains, and the need to pursue a goal overcomes any principled commitment to honesty.

Eliot seems to have been particularly interested in this problem at the beginning of her novelistic career: *Adam Bede* (1859), *Silas Marner* (1861), and *Romola* (1862–3) all contain versions of it. The problem is presented in its simplest form in *Silas Marner*: in the character of Godfrey Cass, Eliot shows us one key akratic action, a second akratic action made necessary by the first, and the life-changing consequences that follow. Both *Adam Bede* and *Romola* expand significantly on this basic model: *Adam Bede* shows how the rational capacity in question is really the ability to sympathize with other people, and *Romola* shows how consequentialist deliberation without sympathy makes this kind of akrasia particularly likely. In other words, Eliot's thinking about akrasia and its causes is not an isolated project, but part of a broader analysis of the structure of the self closely connected to her overall thinking about the nature of sympathy and the process of moral deliberation. Elsewhere I have argued that Eliot's interpreters have significantly overstated the opposition between sympathetic impulse and rational deliberation, and that Eliot in fact views sympathy as an essential part of the self-mastery that makes it possible to overcome momentary impulses and act on the basis of a reason.[4] What the akratic agents who suffer from the law of consequences ultimately demonstrate, then, is the kind of irrational heteronomy that comes with a selfish failure to sympathize with others.

Although the problem of akrasia has been recognized by many writers going back to Plato, the analysis of the problem in contemporary moral philosophy takes its departure from a key 1970 paper by Donald Davidson.[5] Perhaps the major debates in recent years have taken place along three lines. First, whether akrasia is better understood as action against

---

[4] See my essay "Sympathy, Vocation, and Moral Deliberation in George Eliot", and particularly "The Scourge of the Unwilling: George Eliot on the Sources of Normativity", Chapter 4 of my book *Reading Ideas in Victorian Literature: Literary Content as Artistic Experience*.

[5] For an excellent review of the scholarship, see Stroud and Svirsky, "Weakness of Will". I discuss this scholarship as well in "Anthony Trollope on Akrasia, Self-Deception, and Ethical Confusion," Chapter 2 of *Reading Ideas in Victorian Literature*.

one's best judgement or as action against a prior intention; to use the terms of the debate, whether akrasia and weakness of will are essentially the same or whether there is a significant difference between them (Holton, "Intention and Weakness of Will"; Mele, "Weakness of Will and Akrasia"). Second, whether and under what conditions akrasia can be rational – that is, whether there are moments in which one's best judgement is so mistaken about one's real interests that action against the best judgement is more rational than action in accord with it (Arpaly, *Unprincipled Virtue*). And perhaps the largest and most fundamental question stems from what's often called Davidson's internalism – the idea that judgements carry at least some motivational force (Stroud and Svirsky, "Weakness of Will").

George Eliot is not very interested in what one might call cases of classic, synchronic akrasia, where an agent acts against a judgement she consciously holds at the moment of its violation. She is slightly more interested in action against an intention, as we'll see in a moment, but what really draws Eliot's attention are the downstream effects of akrasia. Via such depictions she suggests that while it may be possible for judgements to carry motivational force, they do not do so of themselves. A self-constitution where one is motivated by principled judgements is surprisingly fragile, and does not happen accidentally or automatically. Correspondingly both rationality and akrasia are better understood as characteristics of the narrative history of individual lives, in which agents either succeed or fail at making it possible to act on the basis of their most important commitments.

To see this, let me briefly summarize the problem as it appears in *Silas Marner*. When Godfrey Cass appears in the novel's third chapter, it is with a significant backstory. Godfrey's brother Dunstan is successfully blackmailing him, and we quickly learn that Godfrey has secretly married and had a child with a poor opium addict named Molly Farren. He dares not let the secret emerge, however, because he dreams of marrying the principled Nancy Lammeter and still hopes that somehow it will be possible for him to do so. Thus he regards his marriage as a profound mistake:

> A movement of compunction [...] had urged him into a secret marriage, which was a blight on his life. It was an ugly story of low passion, delusion, and waking from delusion, which needs not to be dragged from the privacy of Godfrey's bitter memory [...] And if Godfrey could have felt himself simply a victim, the iron bit that destiny had put into his mouth would have chafed him less intolerably. If the curses he muttered half aloud when he was alone had had no other object than Dunstan's diabolical cunning, he might have shrunk less from the consequences of avowal. But he had something else to curse – his own vicious folly, which now seemed as mad and unaccountable to him as almost all our follies and vices do when their promptings have long passed away.
>
> (*Silas Marner*, 31. Henceforth SM)

We see in this passage first of all a clear example of Eliot's subtle alteration to the language of metaphysical determinism. 'Destiny' has indeed placed an 'iron bit' in Godfrey's mouth, but what Eliot means by this is that Godfrey himself has given Dunstan the means of controlling him. And that's what Godfrey finds so maddening; had Dunstan found some other way to extract money it would have been less painful, because less dependent on and therefore less reminiscent of Godfrey's own mistakes. Sleeping with Molly was a momentary failure in which sexual desire deluded him, but that moment of akrasia has made more such moments inevitable. The narrator continues: "The yoke a man creates for himself by wrong-doing will breed hate in the kindliest nature; and the good-humoured, affectionate-hearted Godfrey Cass was fast becoming a bitter man, visited by cruel wishes" (SM, 31). The need to continually lie to keep his marriage secret is a burden that is changing Godfrey's character, reducing his kindness and introducing 'cruel wishes'.

Those wishes become clear later on, when Molly dies walking through the snow and her body is discovered outside Silas's cottage while her baby daughter Eppie is found inside. Godfrey, of course, is relieved – but that relief demonstrates how distanced he has become from his own principles. "There was one terror in his mind", the narrator writes; "it was, that the woman might not be dead. That was an evil terror [...] but no disposition is a security from evil wishes to a man whose happiness hangs on duplicity" (SM, 114). Because he has made dishonesty an essential virtue for the pursuit of his goals, Godfrey has correspondingly opened a place in himself for desires he would otherwise reject. Something about the way he has had to act is changing him: one way to put it is that he now cannot help but recognize the way certain events would benefit him, a fact that would ordinarily not enter into his assessment of possible futures.

A second akratic moment demonstrates this change. In lying to his uncle about why exactly he had to run through the snow to see a dead woman, Godfrey discovers he is good at deception. That by itself is indicative of his changing nature; as the narrator writes,

> The prevarication and white lies which a mind that keeps itself ambitiously pure is as uneasy under as a great artist under the false touches that no eye detects but his own, are worn as lightly as mere trimmings when once the actions have become a lie.
>
> (SM, 119)

Previously, Godfrey has had the kind of honesty that reacted to even harmless untruths, but now he is different: his 'actions' have become a lie, and so merely verbal lies are hardly noticeable as moral failures. What it means for an action to be a lie is perhaps not immediately clear, but we can think of it as a failure of self-expression. Having lied as frequently as he has,

Godfrey has lost ahold of the link between his principles and his behaviour, and thus his actions no longer express the person he wants to be.

This decision, the novel's climax, has an ironic consequence. Part of Godfrey's deception, of course, included denying that he was Eppie's father. But having married Nancy after Molly's death, he finds to his sorrow that they cannot have children. Godfrey proposes that they adopt Eppie, but discovers that his wife is adamantly opposed to adoption. Eventually circumstances compel Godfrey to admit that Eppie is in fact his child, an admission that leads Nancy to say something surprising:

> Godfrey, if you had but told me this six years ago, we could have done some of our duty by the child. Do you think I'd have refused to take her in, if I'd known she was yours?
>
> At that moment Godfrey felt all the bitterness of an error that was not simply futile, but had defeated its own end.
>
> (SM, 163)

The key phrase here is an error that 'defeated its own end'. By denying that he had a child in order to have a child with Nancy, he made it impossible to do so, precisely because he did not understand what really mattered to the woman he wanted to marry. Having found himself in a state where his moral principles and his practical rationality seemed to dictate contradictory actions, he learns too late that the conflict was merely superficial. What seemed to be a tension between doing something for himself and doing something for others turns out to be quite different: it was actually a conflict between the immediate discomfort of admitting a secret marriage and (what he sees as) the long-term dissatisfaction of a childless marriage. Correspondingly the apparent dilemma between sympathy for others and rational pursuit of his goals turns out to also be merely apparent: had he sympathized more fully with Nancy, he would not have thought he faced a dilemma between benefiting himself and benefiting others. That's part of the problem the narrator alludes to in an early passage: we learn that Godfrey longs for "some tender permanent affection" that "would make the good he preferred easy to pursue" (SM, 31). In other words we mistake Godfrey's problem if we think of it in terms of emotion overcoming reason: what has happened rather is that Godfrey lacks the kind of emotional commitment that makes self-controlled action possible.

Two additional elements of Godfrey's moral psychology are worth noting, since they echo key points in *Adam Bede* and anticipate a theme of *Romola*. First, Godfrey is the kind of person who hopes and to a large extent believes everything will turn out well, even and especially if the path to that desired consequence is unclear; the narrator portrays this attitude as fundamentally connected to his akrasia. A belief in luck is a symptom of failure throughout Eliot's fiction, which as Jesse Rosenthal has demonstrated stems from her thinking about the nature of probability; as Rosenthal describes the mistake, it's "the failure to understand that though, over long enough time spans, certain statistical certainties will hold sway, such laws are not reducible to the individual case" ("Why George Eliot Hates Gambling", 802). Godfrey's failure is not that he believes in uncertainty but that he believes it will benefit him: "Favourable Chance is the god of all men who follow their own devices instead of obeying a law they believe in", the narrator explains; "the evil principle deprecated in that religion is the orderly sequence by which the seed brings forth a crop after its kind" (SM, 73–74.) That's to say the refusal to confront the likelihood of undesirable events stems from Godfrey's own inability to believe in and act on a law: an epistemic refusal to recognize 'orderly sequence' in the world follows from a volitional failure to give his life such an order.

Arthur Donnithorne in *Adam Bede* has a similar certainty: a "sort of implicit confidence" lets him believe that because he is "really such a good fellow at bottom, Providence would not treat him harshly" (*Adam Bede*, 344. Henceforth AB). The narratorial distance and corresponding cutting irony here is made especially apparent by a later passage where the narrator contends that in "young, childish, ignorant souls there is constantly this blind trust in some unshapen chance" (AB, 396–397). Like Godfrey, Arthur hides from the likely consequences of his actions, a sign to Eliot of his naiveté and egoism. More than in Godfrey Cass's case, however, Eliot shows via Arthur how this attitude is linked to a conviction of the praiseworthiness of one's character and to the general need for self-approval.

At the beginning of *Adam Bede,* Arthur is a young man whose life promises to be both good and happy. On the brink of inheriting a large estate in the England of 1799, he also has a much better relationship with the tenants than the current squire (his grandfather), and so believes that his personal success will also benefit the world. Indeed it is vital to his self-conception that this be true, for Arthur needs to believe that he is a good person: it is "necessary" for him "to be satisfied with himself" (AB, 289). So, when he starts a relationship with Hetty Sorrel, a girl whom he does not plan to marry, he cannot openly admit to himself that this is what he's doing. His conviction of his own fundamental decency prevents him from coldly assessing the likelihood of certain events – such as pregnancy – when such conclusions threaten his positive self-evaluation.

Flirting with Hetty in her home at the novel's opening, Arthur recognizes that he is falling in love with her and resolves not to see her alone again. But somehow he finds himself walking in a place where she is likely to be, at a time when she is likely to be there. "Nothing could be more natural," he thinks to himself: "meeting Hetty was a mere circumstance of his walk, not its object" (AB, 143). After a clandestine meeting he again resolves to end the relationship, only to find himself subsequently finding, embracing, and kissing her. Yet Arthur is dissatisfied himself with himself all the while, and refuses to consider the logical consequences of letting the relationship continue: "irritated and mortified," the narrator explains, "he no sooner fixed his mind on the probable consequences of giving way to the emotions which had stolen over him to-day [...] than he refused to believe such a future possible for himself" (AB, 151). The volitional failure of meeting Hetty akratically stems from and is caused by an epistemic failure in recognizing what is likely to happen.

This is the point conveyed in a striking passage via the Reverend Irwine, an Anglican clergyman who figures as something like the novel's conscience. Arthur goes to Irwine to tell him that he is falling in love with Hetty, knowing that by saying so he will make it impossible for the affair to continue. Unable to bring it up directly, Arthur asks Irwine whether a man who succumbs to a temptation after a struggle is better than a man who acts on the temptation with no struggle. Irwine's answer is decisive:

> No, certainly; I pity him in proportion to his struggles, for they foreshadow the inward suffering which is the worst form of Nemesis. Consequences are unpitying. Our deeds carry their terrible consequences, quite apart from any fluctuations that went before – consequences that are hardly ever confined to ourselves. And it is best to fix our minds on that certainty, instead of considering what may be the elements of excuse for us.
>
> (AB, 188)

Irwine's ideas are echoed and extended by the narrator after Arthur's relationship with Hetty is discovered by Adam:

> Our deeds determine us, as much as we determine our deeds, and until we know what has been or will be the peculiar combination of outward with inward facts, which constitutes a man's critical actions, it will be better not to think ourselves wise about his character. There is a terrible coercion in our deeds, which may first turn the honest man into a deceiver and then reconcile him to the change, for this reason—that the second wrong presents itself to him in the guise of the only practicable right. The action which before commission has been seen with that blended common sense and fresh untarnished feeling which is the healthy eye of the soul, is looked at afterwards with the lens of apologetic ingenuity, through which all things that men call beautiful and ugly are seen to be made up of textures very much alike.
>
> (AB, 342)

As George Levine notes, this line of thought calls attention to the way a recognition of deterministic sequences is itself a moral belief with effects on one's actions ("Determinism and Responsibility", 277). Rather than taking the causal role of one's emotions as a mitigating excuse, far better to recognize that an action may have unintended but unavoidable consequences, what Stefanie Markovits has called Eliot's "sense of the impossibility of controlling consequences in the world" (*The Crisis of Action*, 91). Of course, one of the consequences is the effect on moral agents themselves. They lose their ability to clearly assess the ethics of their actions when once they have acted wrongly, since 'the second wrong presents itself' as 'the only practicable right'. It is particularly here, then, where it is important to grasp the idiosyncrasies in Eliot's use of the language of determinism: what determines us is us. She is skeptical of the strength of moral character, and convinced that virtues must be reinforced if they are to be continually expressed in the agent's actions. And they are maintained by keeping our capacity for self-awareness free of the need to engage in self-deception in order to maintain self-approval.

As in Godfrey Cass's case, moreover, that capacity depends as much or more on an emotional state as it does on rational capacity – or, better, the rational capacity lacking is an emotional one. What Arthur loses, according to the narrator, is the 'blend of common sense and fresh untarnished feeling', the combination of which is the 'healthy eye of the soul'. The moral objectivity at stake here is more an ability to feel a certain way when regarding an action than it is the ability to deduce certain facts about it. A key scene in the novel demonstrates the capacity that Arthur no longer has easy access to, when he finds out that his good friend Adam Bede is in love with Hetty and wants to marry her:

> The discovery that Adam loved Hetty was a shock which made him for the moment see himself in the light of Adam's indignation, and regard Adam's suffering as not merely a consequence, but an element of his error. The words of hatred and contempt – the first he had ever heard in his life – seemed like scorching missiles that were making ineffaceable scars on him. All screening self-excuse, which rarely falls quite away while others respect us, forsook him for an instant, and he stood face to face with the first great irrevocable evil he had ever committed.
>
> (AB, 328)

What's important here is the conjunction of three attitudes, which the narrator implies are interrelated and mutually constitutive. First, this moment shows Arthur seeing his action through Adam's eyes, which is to say that he sympathizes with him. That sympathy also shows Arthur the real nature of his own actions, cutting through his self-deception to show the genuine evil of his relationship with Hetty. Finally, he takes responsibility for the wrong he has done: Adam's suffering is not merely an random event that happened because of Arthur's actions but rather something that Arthur himself has brought about and for which he can be blamed. What this conjunction of attitudes implies is that Arthur's akratic pursuit of Hetty and his refusal to take responsibility for his actions stem from a more fundamental failure, albeit one not generally connected with the capacity for self-control: Arthur has failed to sympathize.

There is a massive literature parsing the philosophical influences on Eliot's thinking about sympathy, and this is not the place to review it in depth.[6] But to pick up one thread, a number of critics have seen in *Adam Bede* evidence of Eliot's encounter with Spinoza.[7] This line of thought has recently received a significant resource in the publication of Eliot's translation of Spinoza's *Ethics*, making it possible to see more exactly how she understood his thought. And certainly, her depiction of the nature of akrasia and self-control agrees with Spinozistic themes. First of all, Spinoza decisively rejects accounts that portray the body as a thing controlled by the mind: those who think this "know not what the body can do" (*Spinoza's Ethics*, 166). We believe that we are free in moments when we are 'conscious of our actions', but akrasia shows us otherwise. The moments when moral agents "struggle with contrary desires", and "see the better and follow the worse", demonstrate that we are not controlled by a "free determination of the mind" (*Spinoza's Ethics*, 167).[8]

This claim becomes more explicit in Spinoza's definition of love. In Eliot's translation, the passage reads: "I do not mean by *will* a consent of the mind, a deliberate purpose or a free decision [...] but by *will* I understand a satisfaction of the being who loves in the presence of the beloved object" (*Spinoza's Ethics*, 211). Will in this instance is not well understood as an authority that stands apart from a desire and authorizes it; rather, it is itself a certain way of experiencing the desire, a comfort with acting on the desire that augments the pleasure that comes with satisfying it. And finally self-control is not well understood as the capacity to act on the basis of moral principles even when they conflict with one's happiness. Instead, as both Godfrey and Arthur realize, acting on the basis of such principles is in fact the best way to be happy. In Spinoza's phrase according to Eliot, "To act absolutely from virtue is nothing else in us than to act, to live, to preserve our being (three things which are essentially one) according to the guidance of reason, on the basis of each seeking his own good" (*Spinoza's Ethics*, 243). To understand myself and what is good for me is also to want it, and there need be no distinction between doing what I want and doing what is good.

But one might note that there is a tension in the account of moral deliberation elaborated so far. On the one hand, Eliot seems to be insisting on the

---

[6] For a brief and clear survey of this scholarship, see Albrecht, *Ethical Vision*, 14.

[7] The scholarship here is indebted to Dorothy Atkins's 1978 book George *Eliot and Spinoza*, and has been extended by Moira Gatens in a number of ways; see "Art and Philosophy" and "Imagination and Belief". The comparison has been carried out further by a number of other critics, including James Arnett, Virgil Nemoianu, and Ted Zenzinger, and is likely to expand in the future in the wake of the recent publication of George Eliot's translation of Spinoza's *Ethics*. See Clare Carlisle's Introduction to this volume for a clear survey of the topic.

[8] In discussing Spinoza's account of akrasia I am indebted to two recent essays on the topic; see Marshall, "The Problem of Akrasia" and Lin, "Spinoza's Account of Akrasia".

importance of objective, even mathematical analysis: one has to recognize and not shy away from the likely results from a given action. On the other hand, she also gives the impression that this kind of self-effacing awareness isn't really the essential feature: what matters more than probabilistic calculations is the emotional capacity to share the perspectives of other people, and thus to recognize when one's actions don't take their intended shape. That tension is not trivial or accidental. It stems from Eliot's complex reaction to John Stuart Mill's consequentialism, and her worry that simplistic forms of consequentialist deliberation make akrasia more likely rather than less.

To briefly recall the broad strokes of this view, John Stuart Mill (1806–73) was the dominant figure in mid-Victorian moral philosophy and intellectual life, and the figure against whom Eliot developed much of her thought. He famously attempted to develop a less reductive version of Jeremy Bentham's utilitarianism, arguing that Bentham was correct to think the morality of an action ought to be assessed on the basis of whether it increased pleasure and minimized pain more than other alternatives, and that neither Bentham's reductive account of human pleasures nor his simplistic calculus for making decisions were essential to the view.[9] A major problem for consequentialist theories, both in Mill's time and subsequently, was clarifying how exactly individuals were supposed to make decisions, given that calculating the possible consequences of every alternative in every decision seems obviously impossible. In an important recent book, Dermot Coleman has surveyed Eliot's worries about such views, noting that her basic objection – consequentialism is ultimately just a self-aware selfishness – is common across the genre of the so-called industrial novel as a response to the fusion between utilitarian ethics and liberal economics in mid-Victorian England (*George Eliot and Money*, 79). But what is unique is Eliot's analysis of the moral psychology involved, in which the calculation of probable consequences actively hinders moral awareness.

Romola takes up these issues in Eliot's third sustained representation of the 'law of consequences'. In this iteration she is particularly interested in the gradualness of the descent into akrasia, showing how small detours from one's best judgement snowball and thus make larger detours rational. To briefly summarize the process, a young man named Tito Melema makes his way to Renaissance-era Florence after his ship has been attacked by Turkish pirates, and the central question in the beginning of the novel is whether Tito's companion and adoptive father Baldassare Calvo has been killed or instead captured and enslaved. The question is especially pertinent because Tito has a large set of jewels belonging to Calvo and thus enough money to find him and purchase his freedom. If, that is, he is still alive. At first, this seems like a genuine dilemma, and Tito's decision not to leave

---

[9] See Mill's essay "Bentham", in *Utilitarianism and Other Essays*.

immediately but to invest the jewels and wait for more evidence seems reasonable if perhaps unnecessarily prudent. Eliot's narrator, however, warns the reader that Tito has

> given an inevitable bent to his wishes. He had made it impossible that he should not from henceforth desire it to be the truth that his father was dead [...] The contaminating effect of deeds often lies less in the commission than in the consequent adjustment of our desires – the enlistment of our self-interest on the side of falsity.
>
> (*Romola*, 100. Henceforth R)

The way this desire threatens Tito's moral psychology becomes obvious a few weeks later, when Tito receives a note from Baldassare confirming he is alive – yet Tito refuses to go, thinking to himself: "the prospect was so vague [...] To spend months, perhaps years, in a search for which even now there was no guarantee it would not prove vain" (R, 115). The novel shows here how Tito's calculations suffer from motivated reasoning, as his analysis of the likelihood of success of a search for Baldassare depends upon an unspoken wish that such a search be unsuccessful.

When Baldassare himself appears in Florence and grabs his arm in a public square, Tito's moral psychology takes another twist. If he has been guilty of negligence before, Baldassarre's presence forces him into active wrongdoing. Tito cannot bring himself to act well – he experiences "that inexorable law of human souls, that we prepare ourselves for sudden deeds by the reiterated choice of good or evil which gradually determines character" (R, 223) – and he refuses to admit he recognizes Baldassare, calling him a madman. That's the trajectory leading to a crucial scene naming Tito's psychological state, where Baldassare confronts Tito at a party. The guests at the party try to test Baldassarre's identity and thus his accusation, but driven mad from his experience as a Turkish slave, he fails the test. Tito is of two minds about the experience:

> so distinct sometimes is the working of a double consciousness within us, that Tito himself, while he triumphed in the apparent verification of his lie, wished that he had never made the lie necessary to himself – wished he had recognised his father on the steps – wished he had gone to seek him – wished everything had been different.
>
> (R, 352)

Tito has in a practical sense succeeded: he has stolen jewels from this man and concealed the crime. But in the moment of his success he wishes that none of it had happened. Like Arthur and Godfrey, actions have been reasonable to Tito that he wishes had not been reasonable. What is especially striking about this process, however, is how Eliot represents the moral deliberation at work. Because unlike Godfrey and Arthur, Tito thinks a great deal about the possible consequences of his actions. It simply turns out this makes things worse instead of better.

One of Eliot's signature literary techniques is called 'free indirect discourse', a process of representing a character's thoughts without signalling that they are the character's.[10] Often, the narrator passes back and forth between representing such thoughts and her own, at one moment commenting on them and at another letting the character's voice through without mediation. A remarkable passage shows Tito's deliberations in this way; I quote at length:

> Certainly the gems and therefore the florins were, in a sense, Baldassarre's: in the narrow sense by which the right of possession is determined in ordinary affairs; but in that large and more radically natural view by which the world belongs to youth and strength, they were rather his who could extract the most pleasure out of them. That, he was conscious, was not the sentiment which the complicated play of human feelings had engendered in society. The men around him would expect that he should immediately apply those florins to his benefactor's rescue. But what was the sentiment of society? – a mere tangle of anomalous traditions and opinions, which no wise man would take as a guide, except so far as his own comfort was concerned. [...] Any maxims that required a man to fling away the good that was needed to make existence sweet, were only the lining of human selfishness turned outward: they were made by men who wanted others to sacrifice themselves for their sake. He would rather that Baldassarre should not suffer: he liked no one to suffer; but could any philosophy prove to him that he was bound to care for another's suffering more than for his own? To do so he must have loved Baldassarre devotedly, and he did not love him: was that his own fault? Gratitude! seen closely, it made no valid claim: his father's life would have been dreary without him: are we convicted of a debt to men for the pleasures they give themselves? Having once begun to explain away Baldassarre's claim, Tito's thought showed itself as active as a virulent acid, eating its rapid way through all the tissues of sentiment.
>
> (115–116)

What Eliot shows us here is that Tito's consideration of two possible futures – one in which he uses the money to rescue Baldassare, and one in which he keeps the money for himself – does not make the moral facts of his situation clearer to him. Instead, the act of reducing the dilemma to the bare question of who can 'extract more pleasure' from the gems serves to cut away many of the reasons he might otherwise recognize. The fact that the gems are Baldassare's does not matter; the fact that others would judge him is irrelevant; the fact that Baldassare raised him and might be thought to have some special call on his loyalty is ultimately inconsequential. After all, didn't Baldassare raise a child only for his own happiness? What matters is whose use of the gems will produce more pleasure, and Tito sees no reason to think he will enjoy them less than Baldassare. Understanding the situation in terms of a choice between possible happiness for Baldassare and possible happiness

---

[10] For an effective recent discussion of this technique and its connection to sympathy more generally, see Greiner, *Sympathetic Realism*.

for himself thus appears as a technique for lying to himself about what his duties actually are. In Eliot's vivid metaphor, such thoughts are an 'acid' that dissolves all the moral feelings he would otherwise have recognized. This disintegration appears particularly in the way Tito's deliberation undermines the various deliberative factors, anticipating Nietzsche for instance in thinking that moral principles of self-sacrifice are merely a technique the powerful use to benefit themselves. It is not enough to simply set aside a particular factor: its normative basis has to be eliminated.

As with the case of Arthur Donnithorne, Tito's selfishness is interestingly correlated with two other failures. First, Tito becomes increasingly incapable of self-control in moments where his goals are frustrated. When for instance it appears his secrets will be discovered, he cannot do anything but wander around in the city, because "he was at one of those lawless moments which come to us all if we have no guide but desire" (R, 136). His autonomy is vulnerable, one might say: lacking the firm self-command that comes with a commitment to a principle of action, he is liable to being pulled in random directions when his pursuit of a desire is interrupted. Second and correspondingly, he becomes increasingly incapable of sympathizing with others, and therefore finds it more difficult to act intelligently when doing so requires understanding how others will react. As the narrator puts it:

> it was impossible for him, shut up in the narrowness that hedges in all merely clever, unimpassioned men, not to overestimate the persuasiveness of his own arguments. His conduct did not look ugly to himself, and his imagination did not suffice to show him exactly how it would look to Romola.
>
> (R, 282)

The stupidity of egoism: consequentialist deliberation has cut off his emotional connection with others, and thus he is paradoxically less able to grasp what they will do and thus what consequences are most likely.

Thus while Tito's evolution demonstrates a different aspect of Eliot's thinking about moral psychology, ultimately his story fits with the view she developed in *Adam Bede* and *Silas Marner*. The capacity to sympathetically inhabit the perspectives of other people turns out to be an essential component of deliberative self-control. When Godfrey, Arthur, and Tito lose this emotional connection they lose the ability to act well, understood both as the ability to pursue their own interests effectively and to respect the interests of others. What Tito's narrative adds to the view developed in Eliot's earlier works is a response to a possible mistake about what it means to acknowledge the law of consequences. We do not properly understand this law if we think it simply means we ought not to trust to luck, the way Godfrey and Arthur do. Instead, the law of consequences is a thing grasped practically, a way of living that minimizes the possibility of self-imposed future dilemmas.

Let me conclude by taking a step back and reflecting on how this account might be developed. Most immediately, it's worth noting that Eliot's objection to consequentialist theories of normative ethics is not a standard one. She is not troubled (or not only troubled) by consequentialism's failure to accord with common moral intuitions or its dismissal of concerns about justice; she instead objects to the basic act of deciding what to do by comparing the contributions to overall welfare made by various alternatives. And this is not just because such calculations are difficult, but because the mere act of considering possible benefits and harms of various alternatives encourages a careful accounting of how precisely various actions might benefit oneself. Attention to one's own benefit in this way cannot help but mislead moral agents, Eliot implies, for two reasons. First, because one will inevitably have more information about one's own circumstances than those of others, it will always seem that benefiting oneself is a more reliable way to increase overall welfare than benefiting others. Second and counterintuitively, careful accounting of one's welfare hinders clear perception of one's reasons, because it emphasizes the narrow benefits of immediate desire-satisfaction over the commitments and aspirations actually fundamental to human lives. This is to say the least a surprising worry – one might think that the simplicity of the utilitarian calculus makes it more resistant to self-deception than other decision procedures – and one would like to know more about how Eliot would defend this objection and how a refusal to consider possible personal benefits interacts with basic norms of prudential rationality.

Then, too, the paradigmatic examples of akrasia in Eliot's mind are interestingly distinct from those common in the scholarship. She is not very interested in standard examples of weakness of will, and while she is more interested in actions that take place against one's intentions – as in the case of Arthur planning to end his relationship with Hetty and embracing her instead – such moments are preliminary stages to the real crises: self-imposed dilemmas where moral agents see how a particular problem could have been avoided if only they had acted in accord with their best judgement all along. What's useful about adding this kind of problem to the literature on akrasia is the way it makes clear how motivational force is within an agent's control even in moments where it appears otherwise. If classic akrasia occurs when an agent's motivational force is not aligned with her all-things-considered judgement, Eliot suggests this state is often a product of an agent's own deliberative history.

Finally and most broadly, there is a great deal more to say about the relationship between sympathy and rationality in light of Eliot's suggestion that the capacity to sympathize is constitutively related to the capacity to overcome akrasia. As I have somewhat briefly suggested here, for Eliot the clearest way to get ahold of oneself is to sympathize selflessly with other people, a capacity that makes it possible for us to look past the distraction of impulse and act on the basis of goals that genuinely matter. That claim introduces a number of questions, perhaps most fundamentally the observation that sympathy often involves an identification with others that does not clarify our goals but rather destabilizes our commitment to them, an aspect of sympathy to which many critics have argued Eliot was quite alive.[11] Moral philosophy has in recent years returned to conceptions of the self similar to Eliot's, and perhaps that renewal will offer resources for puzzling out these and similar tensions in her enormously rich body of thought.

Acknowledgements

I wish to thank Alison Stone for the opportunity to participate here, and the two anonymous reviewers for their penetrating yet generous comments. I am grateful as well to Eileen John for inviting me to a workshop on George Eliot and philosophy at the University of Warwick, where I presented the first version of these ideas; the comments there from the extremely distinguished audience of Eliot scholars were very helpful.

ORCID

Patrick Fessenbecker ● http://orcid.org/0000-0002-4314-2872

Bibliography

Ablow, R. *The Marriage of Mind Reading Sympathy in the Victorian Marriage Plot*. Palo Alto, CA: Stanford University Press, 2007.
Albrecht, T. *The Ethical Vision of George Eliot*. London: Routledge, 2020.
Arpaly, N. *Unprincipled Virtue: An Inquiry into Moral Agency*. New York: Oxford University Press, 2003.
Arnett, J. "Daniel Deronda, Professor of Spinoza". *Victorian Literature and Culture* 44, no. 4 (2016): 833–54.
Atkins, D. *George Eliot and Spinoza*. Salzburg: Institut Für Englische Sprache und Litteratur, 1978.
Beer, G. *Darwin's Plots: Evolutionary Narrative in Darwin, George Eliot, and Nineteenth-Century Fiction*. London: Routledge, 1983.
Bray, C. *The Philosophy of Necessity; or, the Law of Consequences; as Applicable to Mental, Moral, and Social Science*. London: Longman, 1841.
Carlisle, C. "George Eliot's Spinoza: An Introduction". In *Spinoza's Ethics*, edited by Clare Carlisle, 1–60. Princeton, NJ: Princeton University Press, 2020.
Coleman, D. *George Eliot and Money: Ethics, Economics, and Literature*. Cambridge: Cambridge University Press, 2014.
Eliot, G. *Silas Marner: The Weaver of Raveloe*. London: Penguin, 1996.
Eliot, G. *Romola*. London: Penguin, 1996.

---

[11]See especially Ermarth, "George Eliot's Conception of Sympathy", and Ablow, *The Marriage of Minds*.

Eliot, G. *Middlemarch*. London: Penguin UK, 2006.
Eliot, G. *Adam Bede*. London: Penguin, 2008.
Eliot, G. *Essays*. Ed. Thomas Pinney. New York: Routledge, 2015.
Ermarth, E. "Incarnations: George Eliot's Conception of Undeviating Law". *Nineteenth-Century Fiction* 29, no. 3 (1974): 273–86.
Ermarth, E. "George Eliot's Conception of Sympathy". *Nineteenth-Century Fiction* 40, no. 1 (1985): 23–42.
Fessenbecker, P. "Sympathy, Vocation, and Moral Deliberation in George Eliot". *ELH* 85, no. 2 (2018): 501–32.
Fessenbecker, P. *Reading Ideas in Victorian Literature: Literary Content as Artistic Experience*. Edinburgh: Edinburgh University Press, 2020.
Forrester, A. "Aiming to Hit: Archery, Agency, and Doing as One Likes in *Daniel Deronda*". *Victorian Review* 44, no. 2 (2018): 215–31.
Gatens, M. "The Art and Philosophy of George Eliot". *Philosophy and Literature* 33, no. 1 (2009): 73–90.
Gatens, M. "Compelling Fictions: Spinoza and George Eliot on Imagination and Belief". *European Journal of Philosophy* 20, no. 1 (2012): 74–90.
Greiner, R. *Sympathetic Realism in Nineteenth-Century British Fiction*. Baltimore: Johns Hopkins University Press, 2012.
Holton, R. "Intention and Weakness of Will". *The Journal of Philosophy* 96 (1999): 241–62.
Levine, G. "Determinism and Responsibility in the Works of George Eliot". *PMLA* 77, no. 3 (1962): 268–79.
Lin, M. "Spinoza's Account of Akrasia". *Journal of the History of Philosophy* 44, no. 3 (2006): 395–414.
Markovits, S. *The Crisis of Action in Nineteenth-Century English Literature*. Columbus: Ohio State University Press, 2006.
Marshall, E. "Spinoza on the Problem of Akrasia". *European Journal of Philosophy* 18, no. 1 (2008): 41–59.
Mele, A. "Weakness of Will and Akrasia". *Philosophical Studies* 150, no. 3 (2010): 391–404.
Mill, J. S. *Utilitarianism and Other Essys*. Ed. Alan Ryan. New York: Penguin, 1987.
Nemoianu, V. "The Spinozist Freedom of George Eliot's *Daniel Deronda*". *Philosophy and Literature* 34, no. 1 (2010): 65–81.
Newton, K. M. "George Eliot, Kant, and Free Will". *Philosophy and Literature* 36, no. 1 (2013): 441–56.
Rosenthal, J. "The Large Novel and the Law of Large Numbers; or, Why George Eliot Hates Gambling". *ELH* 77, no. 3 (2010): 777–811.
Spinoza, B. *Spinoza's Ethics*. Trans. Marian Evans. Ed. Clare Carlisle. New York: Princeton University Press, 2020.
Stone, W. "The Play of Chance and Ego in *Daniel Deronda*". *Nineteenth-Century Literature* 53, no. 1 (1998): 25–55.
Szirotny, J. *George Eliot's Feminism – the Right to Rebellion*. London: Palgrave Macmillan, 2015.
Stroud, S., and L. Svirsky. "Weakness of Will". In *The Stanford Encyclopedia of Philosophy* (Fall 2019 Edition), edited by Edward N. Zalta. 2008. https://plato.stanford.edu/archives/fall2019/entries/weakness-will/.
Williamson, A. "Against Egology: Ethics and Style in George Eliot and Emmanuel Levinas". *The George Eliot Review* 48 (2017): 33–47.
Zenzinger, T. "Spinoza, *Adam Bede*, Knowledge, and Sympathy: A Reply to Atkins". *Philosophy and Literature* 36, no. 2 (2012): 424–40.

"Count it all joy": black women's interventions in the abolitionist tradition

Lindsey Stewart

ABSTRACT
In her introduction to *Narrative of the Life of Frederick Douglass*, Angela Davis notes that the abolitionist tradition often harboured a "gendered framework" that defined "black freedom" in terms of the "suppression of black womanhood". As such, Davis charges us with the task of "develop[ing] a framework that foregrounds both the complexities of gendered violence under slavery and possible gendered strategies for freedom". In this paper, I engage in this task in two ways. First, I analyse key gendered aspects of the abolitionist tradition that erase black women's agency. One important implication of my argument is that the abolitionist tradition prioritizes physical resistance in how we define 'black freedom' and in narratives of black life. Second, I argue that black women have intervened in this tradition by broadening our sense of agency and extending the landscape of liberation. My primary example will be hoodoo practices that emphasize divine submission rather than resistance in the works of black women abolitionists, such as in *Scenes of the Life of Harriet Tubman* and *The Memoir of Old Elizabeth, a Coloured Woman*.

The difference between us is very marked. Most that I have done and suffered in the service of our cause has been in public, and I have received encouragement at every step of the way. You on the other hand have labored in a private way. I have wrought in the day – you in the night.

(Douglass, *Scenes*, 7)

In the epigraph, Frederick Douglass introduces a stark point of contrast between his abolitionist work and that of Harriet Tubman. Douglass has struggled "in public" in the light of day, while Tubman has "labored in a private way" under the cover of night. Although both were engaged in perilous endeavours, Douglass's work as a writer and lecturer provided a level of publicity that would have thwarted Tubman's journeys to free her fellow enslaved.

In our discipline, Douglass has continued to enjoy his 'public' status through his canonization in the philosophy of race.[1] Indeed, Douglass' recount of his struggle for emancipation has been a rich site for philosophical insights on agency, liberation, and freedom since Angela Davis' "Lectures on Liberation" delivered in 1969. However, there has been considerably less engagement with Tubman's abolitionist work in philosophy. I argue that when we place them in conversation with each other, as Douglass suggests in the epigraph, we gain a crucial insight into agency. Namely, the gendered role of spiritual joy in the struggle for freedom. By spiritual joy, I mean the terms of spiritual ecstasy, divine submission, and spirit possession found in hoodoo practices that inform Tubman's account of her abolitionist work.[2] Most recently, this aspect of Tubman's work has been dramatized in Kasi Lemmon's film, *Harriet*, which portrays Tubman's spiritual experiences as a source of empowerment that fuelled her liberation efforts. "I was most inspired by the fact that she was a mystic", Lemmons reports in an interview, "that was something just really, really interesting that most people didn't know. You really can't do the Harriet Tubman story and ignore the mysticism and the visions" (Hobson and Lemmons, "Black Feminist in Public").[3]

1. "Got a lot to be a man about"

In the philosophy of race, much of the discourse around Douglass' struggle for emancipation, especially his fight with slave-breaker Mr. Covey, considers the existential, ethical, and social political implications of the use of violence in the struggle against oppression.[4] To place Douglass in conversation with Tubman, I want to focus on the gendered aspects of this fight. A pivotal point in the *Narrative*, Douglass writes:

> This battle with Mr. Covey was the turning-point in my career as a slave. It rekindled the few expiring embers of freedom, and revived within me a sense of my own manhood. It recalled the departed self-confidence, and inspired me again with the determination to be free.
>
> (Douglas, *Narrative*, 188)

In this quotation, Douglass draws a relationship between several concepts, freedom and 'manhood', battle and self-confidence. Many philosophers of

---

[1] For an example of such canonization, see Bill E. Lawson and Frank M. Kirkland's incredible anthology of philosophers weighing in on Frederick Douglass' intellectual contributions to the field, *Frederick Douglass: A Critical Reader*.

[2] I borrow Katrina Hazzard-Donald's definition of the term 'hoodoo': "the indigenous, herbal, healing, and supernatural-controlling spiritual folk tradition of the African American in the United States". Hazzard-Donald, *Mojo-Workin'*, 4.

[3] All subsequent section titles from Solange's "Mad" on her album *A Seat at the Table*.

[4] For examples, see Bernard R. Boxill's "The Fight with Mr. Covey", Lewis R. Gordon's "Douglass as an Existentialist", and Frank M. Kirkland's "Is an Existentialist Reading of the Fight with Mr. Covey Sufficient to Explain Douglass' Critique of Slavery?".

race and feminist scholars have noted that Douglass' conception of freedom in this passage is deeply gendered.[5] As Kwame Anthony Appiah writes:

> the driving energy of the book is Douglass's need to live not just as a free person but as a free *man*. And he becomes a man, as we have seen, in part by besting another white man – Covey the slave-breaker – in a fight.
>
>   ("Introduction", xiv)

Deborah McDowell observes that whippings were sexually charged as an attempt to "feminize" the enslaved through submission ("Introduction", xx–xxi). As such, Douglass' refusal to be whipped by Mr. Covey was an assertion of his 'manhood'.

In her introduction to a recent critical edition of the *Narrative*, Davis considers some of the problems posed in the implicit relationship drawn between 'manhood' and freedom for Douglass. Davis admits her earlier reading in "Lectures on Liberation" relied upon "an implicitly masculinist notion of freedom" in her analysis ("Introduction", 28). This is because Douglass' understanding of freedom was defined in terms of "reclaiming his manhood" ("Introduction", 25). Further, Davis argues that "lurking within the definition of black freedom as the reclamation of black manhood is the obligatory suppression of black womanhood" ("Introduction", 24). Put another way, portraying the violence enacted towards enslaved black women was also part of the terms through which black 'manhood' was asserted in abolitionist discourse. Abolitionists "assumed that the violent repression of black women was indirectly an attack on black men", Davis writes, "who were not allowed to protect 'their' women in the way white men might be able to protect 'theirs'" ("Introduction", 26). As such, the violence enacted towards black women in these narratives throws the reclamation of black 'manhood' into relief. For example, within Douglass' *Narrative*, black women are often portrayed as victims of horrific violence rather than as agents capable of independently ensuring their own freedom.[6] As McDowell notes, "Douglass traces his introduction to slavery to the heart-rendering shrieks of his Aunt Hester as she is being beaten" ("Introduction", xxi), and "as the *Narrative* progresses, the beatings proliferate, and the women, no longer identified by name, become

---

[5] For more examples of this type of analysis, see Gooding-Williams, *In the Shadow*, 147–8 and Smith, *Self-Discovery*, 33–4. See also Wallace, "Violence", 76–83, Lawson, "Douglass", 123–7. Joy James's distinction between and discussion of 'feminism' versus 'profeminism' might help us to make sense of the contradiction between Douglass' literary representations of women and his political record of being a strong advocate for women's suffrage. "Here *feminist* refers to women's gender-progressive politics, and *profeminist* denotes male advocates of women's equality", James writes. James, *Transcending*, 37.

[6] Valerie Smith also discusses this dynamic in her comparison of Douglass' *Narrative* with Harriet Jacob's *Incidents in the Life of a Slave Girl*. While Douglass' narrative "extols the hero's stalwart individuality", Jacob's story "is not the classic story of the triumph of the individual will; rather it is more a story of a triumphant self-in-relation". Smith, *Self-Discovery*, 33. Although, as John Stauffer notes, Douglass amends his second autobiography, *My Bondage and My Freedom*, to include a story of slave woman, Nelly, who physically fights her master, she is ultimately unsuccessful in winning that fight. See Stauffer, "Douglass' Self-Making", 34–8, and Douglass, *My Bondage*, 41–2.

absolutized as a bloody mass of naked backs" ("Introduction", xxii). As a result, "Douglass's 'freedom' – narrative and physical alike – depends on narrating black women's bondage" (McDowell, "Introduction", xxii).

For this reason, Davis notes that "literary representations of black women's bodies as targets of slavery's most horrific forms of violence", even while true, "might also tend to objectify slave women and discursively deprive them of the capacity to strike out for their own freedom" (Davis, "Introduction", 26). This type of literary representation is not unique to Douglass, but informs abolitionist writing itself (Davis, "Introduction", 26; McDowell, "Introduction", xxii–xxiii). Consider, for instance, Harriet Tubman's narrative, *Scenes*, which was dictated to and composed by white abolitionist, Sarah L. Bradford. *Scenes* is bookended with scenes of women whipping. Bradford interjects the whip near the opening of the narrative (Bradford and Tubman, *Scenes*, 9–11), and the whip closes the book in an appendixed essay on "woman-whipping" (Hopkins, *Scenes*, 117–29). As such, even a figure whose heroism looms large in our national imagination such as Tubman has a story framed with vignettes of helplessness conveyed through whippings. In both vignettes, the whippings are also used highlight the moral perversion of the Southern white slave mistress who has absolute, arbitrary power over enslaved black women. Unlike Douglass' narrative, the whipping of black women in *Scenes* is not shored up for assertions of black manhood, but as fodder for the development of Southern white women's moral character. However, in both *Narrative* and *Scenes*, the suffering of black women is presented as terms for the development of others (i.e. black men's 'manhood' or white women's moral character) rather than part of a larger story about black women's agency. The point raised here is not about whether black women were actually whipped (we were), but how these stories can be shaped in a way that reinforces the objectification of our bodies and erases our agency. Given these constraints of abolitionist discourse, Davis encourages us to develop frameworks that foreground "both the complexities of gendered violence under slavery and possible gendered strategies for freedom" (Davis, "Introduction", 35).

2. "Count it all joy"

I turn to a discussion of black women abolitionists' religious experiences for such a development of 'gendered strategies for freedom'. In analysing religious experiences of black abolitionists, we also find another way in which approaches to abolitionism were gendered. That is, black women abolitionists often embraced hoodoo practices, or what some called 'roots' at the time.[7] In contrast, many black male abolitionists disavowed such practices in their

---

[7] As Zora Neale Hurston notes: "'roots' is the Southern Negro's term for folk-doctoring by herbs and prescriptions, and by extension, and because all hoodoo doctors cure by roots, it may be used as a synonym of hoodoo". Hurston, "Hoodoo in America", 22.

narratives.[8] For example, in his multiple autobiographies, Douglass is careful to disavow the power of the 'root' that his fellow bondsman, Sandy, had given him for protection from Mr. Covey.[9] Although Douglass indeed carried this 'root' during his fight with Mr. Covey, he goes through great pains to deny any contribution of the 'root' to his success in the fight (Davis, "Introduction", 82). That is, not only does Douglass refer to the "roots" as "absurd and ridiculous, if not positively sinful" (*My Bondage*, 135), but he also distances himself from the 'roots' in developing his resolve to fight. And so, during his famous encounter with Covey, Douglass writes that he "forgot about my *roots*, and remembered my pledge to *stand up in my own defense*" (*My Bondage*, 137).

As several scholars have noted, the conversion of the enslaved to Christianity retained many elements of West African religious expression.[10] Anthropologist Katrina Hazzard-Donald identifies these elements as the 'African Religion Complex', which included 8 central components: "counterclockwise sacred circle dancing, spirit possession, the principal of sacrifice, ritual water immersion, divination, ancestor reverence, belief in spiritual cause of malady, and herbal and naturopathic medicine" (*Mojo-Workin'*, 40). Often blended with Christianity in African American religious expression, these components informed the tradition of hoodoo.[11] I argue that the blending of Christianity and hoodoo for black women abolitionists offered a different form of agency than the resistance modelled by Douglass in his fight with Mr. Covey. As Eddie Glaude notes, the conversion experiences of African Americans presented a form of agency whose terms "was bound up with submission to divine agency" rather than revolt and resistance (*In a Shade*, 109). While Glaude's analysis mainly focuses on Christianity, in what ways did practices of hoodoo also cultivate a relationship of "submission to divine agency"?

I focus on two aspects of black religious experiences during the time to trace the cultivation of divine submission in hoodoo practices: visions and spirit possession via 'shouting'. Zora Neale Hurston observes that visions are "a very definite part of Negro religion" in her essay, "Conversions and Visions" (846). Hurston identifies two contexts for visions in African American religious expression during enslavement and Reconstruction. Namely, the conversion experience and the call to preach. In the conversion experience, Hurston notes that the convert will often go alone to some place that is "most likely to have some emotional affect upon the seeker", such as a cemetery or a swamp ("Conversions and Visions", 846–7). Once there, the convert

---

[8] For an extended discussion of these black male slave narratives and examples of their disavowal of conjure, see Martin, *Conjuring Moments*, 55–60. See also Rucker, *The River Flows On*, 183–6.
[9] See Douglass, *Narrative*, 185–7, Douglass, *My Bondage*, 135–7, and Douglass, *Life and Times*, 77–8.
[10] See Hazzard-Donald, *Mojo Workin'*, 43–4, Martin, *Conjuring Moments*, 89–95, and Chireau, *Black Magic*, 12–13, 25–6.
[11] As Tracey E. Hucks notes, black women's spirituality has a long history of blending Christianity with these West African derived spiritual traditions. Hucks, "Burning with a Flame", 90, 96–96.

will attempt to induce the vision by prayer rites or fasting for three days, "the traditional period for seeking the vision" (Hurston, "Conversions and Visions", 847). While there is immense variation concerning the location and type of vision experienced, a common theme in the experience of conversion is an "unwillingness to believe ... so God is asked for proof" (Hurston, "Conversions and Visions", 847). Hurston concludes that conversion has several stages: (1) conviction of sin, (2) "lyin' under conviction", (3) "Jesus converts the supplicant" (often supplemented with a vision), (4) supplicant's refusal to believe, and (5) "open acknowledgement of God and salvation" (Hurston, "Conversions and Visions", 848). In this way, conversion has a "mixture of external and internal struggles", as stages 1 and 3 are perceived as coming from outside the supplicant, while stages 2, 4, and 5 are seen as coming from within. In contrast, the call to preach is wholly external, as the vision is "involuntary ... the call seeking the man" (Hurston, "Conversions and Visions", 848). Hurston writes:

> Three is the holy number and the call to preach always comes three times. It is never answered until the third time. The man flees from the call, but is finally brought to accept it. God punishes him by every kind of misfortune until he finally acknowledges himself beaten and makes known the call.
> ("Conversions and Visions", 847–8)

Like the experience of conversion, there is a marked reluctance on the part of the person 'called to preach'. This reluctance is ultimately resolved through submission to their vocation.

Another hoodoo practice where submission plays a role is 'shouting'. W. E. B. Du Bois witnessed this practice when he attended a religious revival down south. He defined 'shouting' as the moment "... when the Spirit of the Lord passed by, and, seizing the devotee, made him mad with supernatural joy" (Du Bois, *Souls*, 494). Du Bois notes that "['shouting'] varied in expression from the silent rapt countenance or the low murmur and moan to the mad abandon of physical fervor" (Du Bois, *Souls*, 494). 'Shouting' included physical movements such as "stamping, shrieking, and shouting, the rushing to and fro and wild waiving of arms, the weeping and laughing, the vision and the trance" (Du Bois, *Souls*, 494). As a central practice in African American religious expression during this time, "many generations firmly believed that without this visible manifestation of the God there could be no true communion with the invisible" (Du Bois, *Souls*, 495).[12] As Katrina Hazzard-Donald indicates, 'shouting' is also a central component of the enslaved religious practice of the Ring Shout, sacred dancing performed in a counterclockwise, circular motion, which was often invoked during the conversion experience ("Hoodoo Religion", 147).

---

[12]See also Hazzard-Donald, "Hoodoo Religion", 201.

Although Du Bois ultimately denounces the 'shout' as "vague superstition" (Du Bois, *Souls,* 499), Hurston reminds us that the 'shout' is a retention of African religious expression. For example, Hurston argues that 'shouting' is "a survival of the African 'possession' by the gods" (Hurston, "Shouting", 851). "['Shouting'] is a sign of special favor from the spirit", Hurston continues, "that it chooses to drive out the individual consciousness temporarily and use the body for its expression" (Hurston, "Shouting", 851). This experience of spirit possession is also one of submission, for the body is yielded entirely to the expression of said 'spirit'. In fact, "in every case the person claims ignorance of his actions during the possession" (Hurston, "Shouting", 851). Shouting is also extraordinarily gendered, as Hurston notes that "women shout more frequently than men" (Hurston, "Shouting", 852).

An example of how black women abolitionists embraced these aspects of hoodoo of their religious experience can be found in the *Memoir* of 1863. Like Douglass, Elizabeth was also from Maryland. However, unlike Douglass, Elizabeth's emancipation was not secured by a violent confrontation with her slave master. Rather, she was voluntarily freed by her master when she turned 30 years old (*Memoir*, 34). Perhaps the most striking difference between Elizabeth and Douglass' narrative is that Elizabeth's story focuses upon her struggle for an inward, *spiritual* freedom instead of a struggle for emancipation from enslavement. The terms of that spiritual freedom are bound up with submission as outlined in the practices above. For example, her experience of conversion follows much of the guidelines that Hurston describes. Following her mother's admonition that she had "nobody in the wide world to look to but God" (*Memoir*, 32), Elizabeth reports that at 13 "[she] betook [her]self to prayer, and in every lonely place [she] found an altar. [She] mourned sore like a dove and chattered forth [her] sorrow, moaning in the corners of the field, and under the fences" (*Memoir*, 32). In this period, she experiences "lyin' under conviction" or being made painfully aware of her status as a "sinner" (*Memoir*, 32). She also reports being visited by Jesus after this period by way of a vision, where she "felt that [her] sins were forgiven [her], and the time of [her] deliverance was at hand" (*Memoir*, 33).

During her conversion, Elizabeth also reports the "supernatural joy" that Du Bois ascribes to experiences of 'shouting'. " ... [E]very day I went out amongst the hay-stacks" to pray, Elizabeth informs us, "the presence of the Lord overshadowed me, and I was filled with sweetness and joy, and was as a vessel filled with holy oil" (*Memoir*, 34). There also seems to be a reluctance on her part to believe that she has indeed been "delivered". While going "to [her] old place behind the hay-stacks to pray" (*Memoir*, 34), Elizabeth tells us she was admonished by God for continuing to "weep and pray" for "people whose sins are forgiven ought to be joyful and lively, and not to be struggling and praying" (*Memoir*, 34). This charge to be joyful comes in the midst of her enslavement. For this reason, I argue that Elizabeth's conversion experience shifts the terrain of her struggle for freedom, from a struggle with her master for legal emancipation (she does not report attempting to escape) to an inward struggle for joy (even as she goes about her "work" as a slave (*Memoir*, 34)).

Her lifelong inward, spiritual struggle for joy yielded extraordinary political results. When she began preaching at the age of 42, she often spoke out against various injustices, such as slavery and the sexism and racism she experienced at the hand of several male church leaders. However, her description of such instances of speaking out was often in terms of spirit-possession rather than resistance or revolt. For instance, during one of her spiritual meetings she challenged a white man who took exception to all of their "shouting" and complained that "people round here cannot sleep for the racket" (*Memoir*, 36). As Jon Cruz notes, "Africanist 'shouts'" were often interpreted as noise, "low", "sensual", and "lawless" by even sympathetic whites during this period (Cruz, *Culture*, 105). At first, Elizabeth was disposed to allow this man to break up the meeting for "[a] feeling of weakness came over [her] for a short time" (*Memoir*, 36). But then she "grew warm with *heavenly* zeal", which forced her to push through her intial feelings of "weakness" (*Memoir*, 36). Her experience of this 'heavenly zeal' is akin to spirit possession, for it blurs her sense of boundary between self and God. That is, she describes this experience as "burn[ing] with a zeal not my own" (*Memoir*, 36). Moreover, this 'heavenly zeal' would often make her "so full I hardly knew whether I was in the body, or out of the body" (*Memoir*, 38).

Many in the church found offense in her preaching as a black woman (*Memoir*, 36–40). And she, too, "often felt that [she] was unfit" to take this leadership position (*Memoir*, 37). However, her confidence to do so came from her conviction that she was called by God to preach. As Hurston reports of such callings, Elizabeth also recounts visions where she would travel far and wide to preach to many (*Memoir*, 33, 34). Elizabeth also resists the call to preach for "it was hard for men to travel, and what would women do?" (*Memoir*, 35). "These things greatly discouraged me, and shut up my way", Elizabeth notes, "and caused me to resist the Spirit" (*Memoir*, 35). Although she resisted due to the social limitations of black women, she also found that she "could not quench the Spirit" (*Memoir*, 37). And in submission to God's calling to preach, she found the authority to contest the various systems of oppression she faced. I quote her in full:

> I also held meetings in Virginia. The people there would not believe that a colored woman could preach. And moreover, as I had no learning, they strove to imprison me because I spoke against slavery: and being brought up, they asked by what authority I spake? and if I had been ordained? I answered, not by the commission of men's hands: if the Lord had ordained me, I needed nothing better.
>
> (*Memoir*, 40)

Here, her belief that she had been "ordained" by God grounds her authority to assess and intervene in political issues of her time. Although Elizabeth is a lesser known black woman abolitionist, I provide her story to provide framing to analyse the agency of one of our most famous women in this tradition: Harriet Tubman.[13]

3. "Cause doing it all ain't enough"

As Kate Clifford Larson notes, Tubman participated in this larger network of religious and political agitation on the Eastern Shore, where there was "an emergence of free black women preachers, including Jarena Lee, Maria Stewart, Sojourner Truth, and Zilpha Elaw" (Larson, *Bound*, 48).[14] While we often discuss Tubman's heroism, her valiant rescues of the enslaved and her courageous leadership in the Civil War, we focus less on her internal life, which was ripe with spiritual allusions to practices of divination by way of visions and dreams. In the letters that appendix *Scenes*, many of Tubman's contemporaries attest to the centrality of spirituality in her self-understanding of her work as a "conductor". For instance, abolitionist Thomas Garrett writes of Tubman, "I never met with any person, of any color, who had more confidence in the voice of God, as spoken direct to her soul" (Garrett, *Scenes*, 49). Tubman's first biographer, Franklin Sanborn writes that Tubman "is the most shrewd and practical person in the world, yet she is a firm believer in omens, dreams, and warnings" (Sanborn, *Scenes*, 79). Due to a severe head wound delivered by her slave master in her teens, Tubman often fell into "spells" of "somnolency" or unconsciousness. "When these turns of somnolency come upon Harriet, she imagines that her 'spirit' leaves her body", Sanborn reports, "and visits other scenes and places, not only in this world, but in the world of spirits" (Sanborn, *Scenes*, 56–7). Sanborn considered this aspect of her life so crucial that he claims "her dreams and visions, misgivings and forewarnings, ought not to be omitted in any life of her" (Sanborn, *Scenes*, 54).[15]

Tubman's spiritual life contained several elements of hoodoo as described in the previous section. For instance, Tubman was familiar with 'roots', as can be seen in her work as a nurse (Bradford and Tubman, *Scenes*, 38).[16] And there

---

[13]For other examples of black women abolitionist narratives with similar themes of spiritual submission in a hoodoo-Christian context, see Gilbert and Truth, *Narrative of Sojourner Truth* and Lee, *Religious Experience and Journal*.

[14]As Majorie Pryse notes, "[f]or Jarena Lee and other nineteenth-century black women preachers, religious evangelicalism perhaps provided sufficient sanction of faith to allow them to transcend proscriptions against women's expression". Pryse, "Zora Neale Hurston", 8. For example, we can also see Sojourner Truth appealing to visions and her submission to God's calling as the basis of her spiritual authority. See Gilbert and Truth, *Narrative of Sojourner Truth*, 31–40.

[15]A more recent biographer of Tubman, Kate Clifford Larson, also echoes this sentiment. See Larson, *Bound*, xviii–xix.

[16]Davis notes that Tubman got her rootwork from her father: "[h]e taught her how to walk soundlessly through the woods and how to find food and medicine among the plants, roots and herbs" (Davis, *Women, Race, and Class*, 23). Tubman also attributed her ability to foretell the future to her father

are several reports of her participation in 'shouting'.[17] While she sang, she was even known to shout. Florence Carter reports that "[s]he had a fine voice, that was feminine, and when she sang, as she often did, her lungs opened up widely and she would shout" (Carter qtd. in Humez, *The Life*, 265). She also 'shouted' while she preached. James E. Mason tells us "in a shrill voice, [Tubman] commenced to give testimony to God's goodness and long suffering. Soon she was shouting, and so were others also" (Mason qtd. in Humez, *The Life*, 334). Tubman also encouraged the enslaved to 'shout' when they physically crossed into free territory (Humez, *The Life*, 333). In many instances, Tubman also claimed that God alerted and diverted her from danger with visions and dreams (Garrett, *Scenes*, 50, 52). And she was so confident in God's guidance that she claimed to not fear going down South to rescue the enslaved, even with vigorous efforts of whites to capture her. In *Scenes*, Bradford writes:

> When asked, as she often is, how it was possible that she was not afraid to go back, with that tremendous price upon her head, Harriet always answers, "Why, don't I tell you, Missus, t'wan't *me*, 'twas *de Lord!* I always tole him, 'I trust you. I don't know where to go or what to do, but I expect you to lead me,' an' he always did".
> (Bradford and Tubman, *Scenes*, 35)

As Garret corroborates, Tubman claimed that she "felt no more fear of being arrested by her former master, or any other person, when in his immediate neighborhood" of Maryland than she did in New York or Canada (Garret, *Scenes*, 49). This was because "she never ventured only where God sent her, and her faith in a Supreme Power was truly great" (Garret, *Scenes*, 49). Her confidence, I argue, results from her submission to what she considered was a calling by God.

That is, Tubman described her work as an abolitionist as a life-long vocation delivered by God. Her experience of that calling is similar to what Hurston describes as the call to preach. I quote Tubman in full:

> Long ago when the Lord told me to go free my people, I said 'No, Lord! I can't go – don't ask me.' But he came another time. I saw him just as plain. Then I said again, 'Lord, go away – get some better educated person with more culture than I have; go away Lord.' But he came back the third time, and speaks to me just as he did to Moses, and he says, 'Harriet, I want you.' I knew then I must do what he bid me.
> (Tubman qtd. in Humez, *The Life*, 260)

Like Elizabeth, Tubman claimed to have visions of her future work as an abolitionist, travelling to places she had never been and meeting people

---

(Sanborn, *Scenes*, 80). As Larson observes, these practices of dream and fortune-telling formed part of Asante culture, and it is believed that Tubman was second-generation Asante (Larson, *Bound*, 10–13).
[17] See Bradford and Tubman, *Scenes*, 34–5, 41–2, and 43–4. In particular, the 'spiritual shuffle' described on 43–4 is characteristic of the dance of the Ring Shout. See also Humez, *The Life*, 200, 228–9, 246, and 333.

she had yet to meet. And, like Elizabeth, she also saw herself as unfit for the task at hand and refused the call. And yet, as Hurston describes with the call to preach, Tubman yields to the call the third time, relenting to "do what he bid [her]". In this way, her amazing feats of agency are mediated through a sense of *divine* agency. That is, not only is her work motivated by a sense of divine calling, but her work is *enabled* by what is seen as gifts of divine capabilities (visions, foresight, etc.).

Similar to Elizabeth's inward, spiritual struggle for joy, Tubman's spiritual submission to God had revolutionary impact and tremendous political results. She managed to rescue at least 50 of her fellow enslaved (Larson, *Bound*, xvii). I argue, however, that we are in danger of missing the revolutionary impact of black women abolitionists like her if we privilege Douglass as an exemplar of black agency. As Douglass observes in the epigraph at the opening of my paper, the difference between them is "very marked" (Douglass, *Scenes*,7). I have argued that one way to understand this 'marked difference' is through different approaches to spirituality in slave narratives. While black male abolitionists like Douglass often centred the public, direct, physical resistance to slave masters as an assertion of their 'manhood', black women abolitionists like Elizabeth and Tubman located their sense of agency within spiritual submission to God. The terms of that submission were found in a complex version of Christianity that embraced and incorporated West African forms of religious expression. This was in stark contrasts to some black male abolitionists who tended to disavow hoodoo practices.

But why are these religious engagements seemingly gendered? I argue that the terms of submission within hoodoo practices influenced how they were taken up in abolitionist literature. As Valerie Smith notes, submission is a trait largely ascribed to women during this time period (Smith, *Self-Discovery*, 30–31). However, for black male abolitionists such as Douglass, a wilful assertion of 'manhood' was part of terms by which they established their freedom. Due to the implicit opposition between womanhood and manhood in Douglass' definition of freedom, practices of submission became devalued.

For instance, in "Is It Right" of 1854 we may find clues as to why it was important for Douglass to "forget [his] roots" and "stand up in [his] own defense" (Douglass, *My Bondage,* 137). In this essay, we find Douglass privileging resistance over submission while enslaved. He admits that some might argue that "submission" in this case was "far wiser than resistance" (Douglass, "Is it Right", 279). Nonetheless, Douglass argues that "submission is valuable only so long as it has some chance of being recognized as a virtue" (Douglass, "Is it Right", 279). And on the part of the slave, Douglass insists that, far from a virtue, submission serves as a pro-slavery argument:

> Such submission, instead of being set to the credit of the poor sable ones, only creates contempt for them in the public mind, and becomes an argument in the

mouths of the community, that Negroes are, by nature, only fit for slavery; that slavery is their normal condition. Their patient and unresisting disposition, their unwillingness to peril their own lives, by shooting down their pursuers, is already quoted against them, as marking them an inferior race.

(Douglass, "Is It Right", 279)

In *My Bondage and My Freedom* of 1855, Douglass pits Sandy's rootwork against his act of resistance against Mr. Covey. The roots were offered to provide protection, whereby Douglass relied on divine (or 'magic') power to avoid, rather than challenge, the abuse of Mr. Covey. In this way, for Douglass, the roots did not provoke rebellion of slavery, but encouraged submission in the current system of domination. As such, submission is denied revolutionary impact, even though we have seen it yield emancipatory results in the cases of Elizabeth and Tubman.

We can also see this privileging of resistance over submission in how Du Bois takes up Douglass' gendered framework in his analysis of abolitionism in *Souls*.[18] Many scholars note that Douglass' own views on violence and abolitionism shifted over time, whereby his turn to physical resistance in later years mirrors a religious conversion.[19] Du Bois theorizes about precisely this kind of religious turn. "For fifty years Negro religion thus transformed itself", Du Bois writes, "and identified itself with the dream of Abolitionism" (Du Bois, *Souls*, 501). In this marriage of Christianity and abolitionism, "[f]reedom became to [the enslaved] a real thing and not a dream. His religion became darker and more intense, and into his ethics crept a note of revenge" (Du Bois, *Souls*, 501). As Robert Gooding-Williams observes, Du Bois "approaches the problem of political leadership by way of a discussion of two ethical attitudes that he sees animating Negro religious life in his day" (Gooding-Williams, *In the Shadow*, 147). In opposition to the spirit of revolt and revenge that characterizes this militant, Christian abolitionism is a "hypocritical" compromise that encourages submission to our oppression (Du Bois, *Souls*, 502–4). This opposition between radicalism and compromise is cast within a gendered framework as well as regionalized.[20] As Robert Gooding-Williams notes, this gendered framework is inherited from Douglass. Submission though "hypocritical compromise", for Du Bois, is considered "unmanly", while revolt and rebellion is considered "manly, Douglass-like self-assertion" (Gooding-Williams, *In the Shadow*, 148, 163).

---

[18]For a broader discussion of Du Bois's gender dynamics across his corpus of work, see James, *Transcending*, 35–60, and Carby, *Race Men*, 9–45.
[19]See Wallace, "Violence", 78–9; Martin, *The Mind*, 19–20; and Boxill, "The Fight", 273–6.
[20]William D. Hart writes " ... the [black] church teeters between resistance to white supremacy and submission, between 'manliness' and 'effiminancy.'" Moreover, "[a]s historical sociology, Black Religion is bifurcated geographically between North and South, dispositionally between militant church and submissive church, and ethical-politically between fashionable if trivial pursuits and hard questions". Hart, "Three Rivals", 477–8.
See also Hazel Carby's *Race Men*, 37–40, and West, "W. E. B. Du Bois", 1968.

I point out this gendered aspect of abolitionist discourse not to reify a dichotomy of manly resistance and feminine submission. Rather, my point is two-fold. In abolitionist discourse, there is not only a tendency to reduce black agency to resistance, but also this very resistance is often masculinized.[21] On both accounts, we miss the agential insights that lie within Tubman's abolitionism. Either we render Tubman's abolitionism in masculine terms, where she becomes a militant "female Moses" (Edwards, *Charisma*, 21), or we dismiss the terms by which her abolitionism proceeded – spiritual joy or divine submission. Moreover, there is often further reluctance to appreciate the type of agency that her submission exhibits precisely because there is no guarantee that such submission will be emancipatory. As Douglass worried, submission can indeed lead to quietism, but, as in Tubman's case, it can also lead to revolutions. This is because divine submission had the potential (though not guarantee) to create the mental distance needed to prevent internalization of our oppression (Levine, *Black Culture and Black Consciousness*, 80). Put differently, while hoodoo-Christian divine submission could help produce the "emotional conditions for protest" (Davis, "Introduction", 113), these practices of submission are not protest in and of themselves.

What Douglass and Du Bois miss in their critiques above is that the terms of abolitionist agency exhibited by Tubman and Elizabeth are also bound up with submission, with an important difference. This submission is not to our oppressors, but to the divine through experiences of spiritual joy such as spiritual ecstasy and spirit possession. While Douglass and Du Bois are right to oppose our submission to systems of injustice, their sense of 'manhood' also leaves little room for *other types* of submission. Even though the form of agency that Elizabeth and Tubman exhibit does not fit Douglass' model of resistance, I have argued in this paper that their type of divine submission *also* had revolutionary impact. Although Tubman laboured for the abolitionist cause, this is but one way that she deviated from the abolitionist programme. The gendered differences in Douglass and Tubman's approach to the abolitionist project of slavery provide an occasion to ask larger questions about how abolitionist discourse continues to shape our analyses of black life. In this way, troubling the erasures of black women's agency requires returning to the abolitionist period, taking seriously the 'marked difference' to which Douglass alludes (Douglass, *Scenes*, 7).

Bibliography

Appiah, Kwame Anthony. "Introduction". In *Narrative of the Life of Frederick Douglass, an American Slave and Incidents in the Life of a Slave Girl*, edited by Frederick Douglass and Harriet Jacobs, xi–xvi. New York: Modern Library, 2000.

---

[21] For examples of similar feminist analyses of submission, agency, and resistance in religious contexts, see Mahmood, *The Politics of Piety*, 5–16, and Kelley, *The Hammer and the Flute*, 6–10 and 73–83.

Boxill, Bernard. "The Fight with Covey". In *Existence in Black: An Anthology of Balck Existential Philosophy*, edited by Lewis R. Gordon, 273–91. New York: Routledge Press, 1997.

Bradford, Sarah H., and Harriet Tubman. *Scenes in the Life of Harriet Tubman*. London: Forgotten Books, (1869) 2012.

Carby, Hazel. *Race Men*. Cambridge: Harvard University Press, 1998.

Chireau, Yvonne P. *Black Magic: Religion and the African American Conjuring Tradition*. Berkeley: University of California Press, 2003.

Cruz, Jon. *Cutlure on the Margins: The Black Spiritual and the Rise of American Cultural Interpretation*. Princeton: Princeton University Press, 1999.

Davis, Angela. "Introduction". In *Narrative of the Life of Frederick Douglass An American, Written by Himself*, by Frederick Douglass, edited by Angela Davis, 21–40. San Francisco: Open Media Series, 2010.

Davis, Angela. *Women, Race, and Class*. New York: Vintage Books, 1983.

Davis, Angela. *Blues Legacies and Black Feminism: Gertrude "Ma" Rainey, Bessie Smith, and Billie Holiday*. New York: Vintage Books, 1999.

Douglass, Frederick. *Narrative of the LIfe of Frederick Douglass: An American Slave*. Edited by Angela Y. Davis. San Francisco: Open Media Series, (1845) 2010.

Douglass, Frederick. "Is It Right and Wise to Kill a Kidnapper?". In *Frederick Douglass: Selected Speeches and Writings*, by Frederick Douglass, edited by Philip S. Foner, 277–80. Chicago: Lawrence Hill Books, (1854) 1999.

Douglass, Frederick. *My Bondage and My Freedom*. Edited by John Stauffer. New York: The Modern Library, (1855) 2003.

Douglass, Frederick. "Letter from Frederick Douglass". In *Scenes in the LIfe of Harriet Tubman*, edited by Sarah H. Bradford and Harriet Tubman, 6–8. London: Forgotten Books, (1869) 2012.

Douglass, Frederick. *Life and Times of Frederick Douglass*. Radford: Wilder Publications, (1881) 2008.

Du Bois, W. E. B. "The Souls of Black Folk". In *W. E. B. Du Bois: Writings*, by W. E. B. Du Bois, edited by Nathan Huggins, 357–548. New York: The Library of America, (1903) 1986.

Edwards, Erica R. *Charisma and the Fictions of Black Leadership*. Minneapolis: University of Minnesota Press, 2012.

Garrett, Thomas. "Letter from Thomas Garrett". In *Scenes in the Lfie of Harriet Tubman*, edited by Sarah H. Bradford and Harriet Tubman, 48–53. London: Forgotten Books, (1869) 2012.

Gilbert, Olive, and Sojourner Truth. *The Narrative of Sojourner Truth*. Mineola: Dover Publications, (1863) 1997.

Glaude Jr, Eddie S. *In a Shade of Blue: Pragmatism and the Politics of Black America*. Chicago: University of Chicago Press, 2007.

Gooding-Williams, Robert. *In the Shadow of Du Bois: Afro-Modern Political Thought in America*. Cambridge: Harvard University Press, 2009.

Gordon, Lewis. "Douglass as an Existentialist". In *Frederick Dougalss: A Critical Reader*, edited by Bill E. Lawson and Frank M. Kirkland, 243–310. Malden: Blackwell Publishers, 1999.

Hart, William D. "Three Rival Narratives of Black Religion". In *A Companion to African-American Studies*, edited by Lewis R. Gordon and Jane Anna Gordon, 476–93. Malden: Blackwell Publishing Ltd, 2006.

Hazzard-Donald, Katrina. "Hoodoo Religion and American Dance Traditions: Rethinking the Ring Shout". *The Journal of Pan African Studies* 4, no. 6 (2011): 194–212.

Hazzard-Donald, Katrina. *Mojo Workin': The Old African American Hoodoo System*. Urbana: University of Illinois Press, 2013.

Hobson, Janell, and Kasi Lemmons. "Black Feminist in Public: Kasi Lemmons on Telling Harriet Tubman's Freedom Story." *Ms. Magazine*, March 8. Accessed December 20, 2019. https://msmagazine.com/2019/03/08/black-feminist-public-kasi-lemmons-telling-harriet tubmans-freedom-story/.

Hopkins, S. M. "Woman-Whipping, Ethically and Estehetically Considered". In *Scenes in the Life of Harriet Tubman*, edited by Sarah H. Bradford and Harriet Tubman, 117–29. London: Forgotten Books, (1869) 2012.

Hucks, Tracey E. "'Burning with a Flame in America': African American Women in African-Derived Traditions". *Journal of Feminist Studies in Religion* 17, no. 2 (2001): 89–106.

Humez, Jean M. *Harriet Tubman: The Life and the Life Stories*. Madison: University of Wisconsin Press, 2006.

Hurston, Zora Neale. "Conversions and Visions". In *Zora Neale Hurston: Folklore, Memoirs, and Other Writings, by Zora Neale Hurston*, edited by Cheryl A. Wall, 846–51. New York: The Library of America, (1934) 1995.

Hurston, Zora Neale. "Shouting". In *Zora Neale Hurston: Folklore, Memoirs, and Other Writings, by Zora Neale Hurston*, edited by Cheryl A. Wall, 851–4. New York: The Library of America, (1934) 1995.

Hurston, Zora Neale. "Hoodoo in America". *The Journal of American Folklore* 44, no. 174 (1931): 317–417.

James, Joy. *Transcending the Talented Tenth: Black Leaders and American Intellectuals*. New York: Routledge, (1997) 2013.

Kelley, Mary. *The Hammer and the Flute: Women, Power, and Spirit Possession*. Baltimore: The John Hopkins University Press, 2002.

Kirkland, Frank M. "Enslavement, Moral Suasion, and Struggles for Recognition: Frederick Douglass's Answer to the Question–'What is Enlightment?'". In *Frederick Douglass: A Critical Reader*, edited by Bill E. Lawson and Frank M. Kirkland, 243–310. Malden: Blackwell Publishers, 1999.

Kirkland, Frank M. "Is an Existentialist Reading of the Fight with Covey Sufficient to Explain Frederick Douglass's Critique of Slavery?". *Critical Philosophy of Race* 3, no. 1 (2015): 124–51.

Larson, Kate Clifford. *Bound for the Promised Land: Harriet Tubman, an American Hero*. New York: One World Ballantine Books, 2003.

Lawson, Bill E. "Douglass among the Romantics". In *The Cambridge Companion to Frederick Douglass*, edited by Maurice S. Lee, 118–31. New York: Cambridge University Press, 2009.

Lee, Jarena. *Religious Experience and Journal of Mrs. Jarena Lee, Giving an Account of Her Call to Preach the Gospel*. Philadelphia: Pantianos Classics, (1836) 2017.

Levine, Lawrence. *Black Culture and Black Consciousness: Afro-American Folk Thought from Slavery to Freedom*. New York: Oxford University Press, (1977) 2007.

Mahmood, Saba. *Politics of Piety: The Islamic Revival and the Feminist Subject*. Princeton: Princeton University Press, 2012.

Martin, Kameelah. *Conjuring Moments in African American Literature: Women, Spirit Work, and Other Such Hoodoo*. New York: Palgrave Macmillan, 2012.

Martin Jr, Waldo E. *The Mind of Frederick Douglass*. Chapel Hill: University of North Carolina Press, 1984.

McDowell, Deborah. "Introduction." In *Narrative of the Life of Frederick Douglass*, edited by Frederick Douglass, vii–xxvii. Oxford University Press: Oxford, 1999.

"Memoir of Old Elizabeth, A Coloured Woman." In *Women's Slave Narratives: Annie L. Burton and Others*, 29–42. Mineola: Dover Publications (1863) 2006.

Pryse, Marjorie. "Zora Neale Hurston, Alice Walker, and the 'Ancient Power' of Black Women". In *Conjuring: Black Women, Fiction, and Literary Tradition*, edited by Marjorie Pryse and Hortense J. Spillers, 1–24. Bloomington: Indiana University Press, 1985.

Rucker, Walter. *The River Flows On: Black Resistance, Culture, and Identity Formation in Early America*. Baton Rouge: Louisiana State University Press, 2006.

Sanborn, Franklin. "Excerpt from *Boston Commonwealth*." In *Scenes in the Life of Harriet Tubman*, edited by Sarah H. Bradford and Harriet Tubman, 72–92. London: Forgotten Books, (1863) 2012.

Smith, Valerie. *Self-Discovery and Authority in Afro-American Narrative*. Cambridge: Harvard University Press, 1987.

Stauffer, John. "Douglass's Self-Making and the Culture of Abolitionism". In *The Cambridge Companion to Frederick Douglass*, edited by Maurice S. Lee, 13–30. New York: Cambridge University Press, 2009.

Wallace, Maurice O. "Violence, Manhood, and War in Douglass". In *The Cambridge Companion to Frederick Douglass*, edited by Maurice S. Lee, 73–88. New York: Cambridge University Press, 2009.

West, Cornel. "W. E. B. Du Bois: An Interpretation". In *Africana: The Encyclopedia of the African and African American Experience*, edited by Kwame Anthony Appiah and Henry Louis Gates, 1967–82. New York: Basic Books, 1999.

"Friendly to all beings": Annie Besant as ethicist

Kurt Leland

ABSTRACT
Annie Besant (1847–1933) has rarely been identified as a philosopher. Her work as an ethicist has been obscured by the reaction of critics to her abandonment of Anglican Christianity for serial engagements with theism, atheism, collectivist socialism, and Theosophy – often characterized as fickle and indecisive 'conversions'. However, Besant saw these engagements as stages in a quest for a universally applicable system of morality and conduct founded on empirical principles, and as valid as any scientific law. This article positions Besant as an ethicist working in the virtue ethics tradition, as defined by Rosalind Hursthouse, first by examining Besant's ethical evolution, driven by the philosophical problem of whether ethics can exist without metaphysics (which she sometimes phrased as 'Can morals exist without religion?'), and second, by identifying an anonymously published *Advanced Text Book of Hindu Religion and Ethics* (1903) as the most complete expression of her syncretic ethical system.

Besant as philosopher?

Known during her lifetime as one of the foremost female orators of the English-speaking world, Annie Besant (née Wood) published more than 600 books and pamphlets and countless articles. No stranger to controversy, she defied her physically and emotionally abusive husband, an Anglican clergyman, by refusing the sacrament of communion (1873). After separating from him and becoming an atheist, she joined forces with Charles Bradlaugh, founder and president of the National Secular Society, to advocate free speech by republishing a banned pamphlet on birth-control. During the resulting trial, Besant acted as her own legal defence, thereby losing custody of her daughter over spurious allegations of immorality (1877). Besant also supported working women and trade unionism, engaging in protests against low wages and unhealthy and degrading working conditions during the famous Bryant & May Matchgirls' Strike (1888). In 1889, she joined the Theosophical Society (TS), established in New York in 1875 by Henry Steel Olcott, an American lawyer interested in investigating the psychic phenomena associated with Spiritualism, and a Russian noblewoman, Helena Petrovna Blavatsky, supposedly gifted with psychic powers. Though Blavatsky was accused of fraud by the London-based Society for Psychical Research in 1885, Besant became a devotee and, after her teacher's death in 1891, travelled many tens of thousands of miles to promote the TS, acting as its international president from 1907 until her death.[1] In 1917, she was interned by the British Raj for allegedly seditious activities connected to her advocacy of home rule for India – only to become the first female, non-native president of the Indian National Congress upon her release. Nearly forgotten in Britain, Besant continues to be revered (with controversy) in India as a freedom fighter.[2]

Despite these sensational if incongruous achievements, neither contemporary comment, nor pre- or posthumous biography, nor present-day historiography has seen fit to label Annie Besant as a philosopher. She has primarily been portrayed as a propagandist for various causes, including atheism, women's rights, collectivist socialism, and the Theosophical Society. Writing while Besant was alive, British biographer Geoffrey West (pseudonym of Geoffrey Harry Wells) dismissed her lectures and books so decisively that one wonders why anyone would care to investigate them: "Their matter is everything, their manner nothing, they are contributions to controversy rather than to knowledge" (*Annie Besant*, 168). More recently, Mark Bevir noted that because of Besant's "lack of formal education", she was "effectively excluded [...] from highly intellectual groups". Thus "her niche almost certainly had to be as a populariser and propagandist rather than as a philosopher or scientist" ("Annie Besant's Quest", 74). Carol Hanbery MacKay commented on this tacit denial of Besant as philosopher as follows: "Yet our heroine [...] has never been granted the appellation of sage by previous critics, despite the fact that the body of her lifework and eloquence attest to a spirit and oratorical intelligence that have moved millions" (*Creative Negativity*, 100).

One of the few occasions when Besant was publically acknowledged as a philosopher occurred in 1891, on the eve of her arrival in Boston for her first lecture tour in America. An expectant journalist wrote: "Mrs. Besant differs from the average advanced woman in that she stands out, not as a special pleader for the abolition of special wrongs, but as a philosopher surveying the whole field of growth, domestic, social, industrial, spiritual". The

---

[1] Due to schisms within the TS subsequent to Blavatsky's death, it is necessary to identify the organization with which Besant was associated as the TS (Adyar), meaning that its headquarters is located in Adyar, Tamil Nadu, India. All references in this essay are to the TS (Adyar).

[2] See Pécastaing-Boissière, *Annie Besant*, for a nuanced historiographic treatment of Besant's multifarious achievements.

article listed Besant's topics as education, Malthusianism, marriage, labour, religion, and "the subtle metaphysical principles of Theosophy", identifying Besant as a "sociologist", probably meaning a social philosopher (*Boston Daily Globe*, 14 April 1891). Based on this range of topics, which later expanded to include vivisection, vegetarianism, and women's suffrage, as well as Indian social conditions and politics, a naïve case could be made for viewing Besant as a social philosopher. Though she interrogated social problems in hundreds of lectures, articles, pamphlets, and books, many of these productions might justifiably be called 'contributions to controversy', as West would have it.

Another major focus of Besant's literary output was Blavatsky's Theosophy, an amalgam of Western esotericism, including "ancient religion, magic, Gnosticism, Neo-Platonism, Kabbalah, Freemasonry, and modern spiritualism" with "borrowings from Hinduism and Buddhism" (Goodrick-Clarke, "Western Esoteric Traditions and Theosophy", 288–90). Besant was an early reviewer of Blavatsky's esoteric compendium, *The Secret Doctrine: The Synthesis of Science, Religion and Philosophy* (1888), the reading of which prompted her to meet the author and join the TS in May 1889. Besant's popularizing explications of Theosophy could easily justify her dismissal as a propagandist. If West could conclude that she "leaves no distinct body of writings, no vitally original thought, to carry on her name" (*Annie Besant*, 171), then is there any evidence to warrant calling Besant a philosopher?

The disjunctive conversion narrative

Before we address this question, it is necessary to confront the problem that every study of Besant must contend with – a problem that I call the disjunctive conversion narrative. As early as 1889, Besant's secularist colleague G. W. Foote was writing of Besant's "conversion to Socialism" and "conversion to Theosophy", complaining that "[t]he fact that she has held one thing yesterday, and holds the opposite to-day, does not shake her self-assurance" (Foote, *Mrs. Besant's Theosophy*, 4–5). Foote's characterization of socialism and Theosophy as views directly opposed to those of his own Freethought movement displays the partisan bias behind the notion of sudden conversion to opposite views. Later biographers were to develop a dramatic narrative framework from such apparently disjunctive shuttlings between views. Here is an early prototype, published while Besant was alive:

> Disappointed in her first groping effort to find an emotional haven within the church as a Vicar's wife, she had swung to the opposite extreme of materialism. Thwarted again, she had swung blindly back into an ultimate extreme of mysticism. Her emotions were outwitting her excellent mental equipment and leading her astray.
>
> (Williams, *Passionate Pilgrim*, 346–7)

Though this biographer, journalist Gertrude Marvin Williams, does not use the word 'conversion' here, the lineaments of the disjunctive conversion narrative are present. She portrays Besant's movements from membership in the Church of England to her espousal of atheism and from that to membership in the TS as opposite extremes and sees her as blindly driven from one to another by emotional needs that overpowered her strong intellect and resulted in a plunge into (irrational) mysticism. No allowance is made for logically argued transitions from one phase to another; no attempt is made to perceive continuities between the phases. Unfortunately, the tendency to arrange Besant's biography along such lines has persisted, even among more sophisticated, academic biographers. Muriel Pécastaing-Boissière notes that Arthur H. Nethercot's two-volume biography of Besant, *The First Five Lives of Annie Besant* (1960) and *The Last Four Lives of Annie Besant* (1963), and Anne Taylor's *Annie Besant: A Biography* (1992), characterize Besant's "conversion to Theosophy [...] as yet another fracture in a life thought by these two authors to be fragmented to the point of incoherence" (*Annie Besant*, xi).

Since at least 1988, a body of scholarship has developed with the express purpose of chipping away at the disjunctive conversion narrative. Claiming that Besant's biographers have tended to focus on "her outward activities and affiliations" rather than studying "the records of her thought", Catherine Wessinger was the first to trace the development of Besant's "religious thought" (*Annie Besant and Progressive Messianism*, 1). Wessinger characterizes the trajectory of Besant's political and spiritual career in terms of "progressive messianism", a quasi-Christian messianic drive to change the world that developed in stages from the Victorian social progressivism of Besant's upbringing through various movements and causes to embrace a Theosophically-flavoured millenarianism and the promotion of the young J. Krishnamurti as a new 'World Teacher' or messiah. Yet if we accept Wessinger's view of Besant primarily as a religious figure, there is little incentive to investigate her as a philosopher.

In 1999, Mark Bevir published a seminal essay in which he reinterpreted Besant's life "as a coherent quest for truth in the context of a particular set of problems and commitments" that included Theosophy, not as "an emotional abdication of reason but as a reasonable response to the same crisis of faith that inspired much Victorian secularism" ("Annie Besant's Quest for Truth", 66). Bevir focuses on the evolution of Besant's moral thinking, tracing it through various modes, including a Victorian "humanitarian concern with social duty", altruistic "self-sacrifice", "ethical positivism", "a somewhat mystical concern with truth" that was paired with "an insistence on natural explanations incorporating current scientific knowledge", and a belief in "a just order in which everyone receives what they deserve and from which we can eliminate evil" ("Quest for Truth", 70). Despite Bevir's emphasis on Besant's 'quest for truth' as rational, coherent, and intelligible, his portrayal of her moral development takes place entirely within the domain of belief and again leaves little motivation for investigation of Besant as a philosopher.

In 2001, another stage in deconstructing the disjunctive conversion narrative was undertaken by Carol Hanbery MacKay, who characterizes "Besant's quest" as "a narrative of crisis, deconversion, and conversion" (*Creative Negativity*, 100). The term 'deconversion' was borrowed from John D. Barbour, who uses it to describe a sequence of four stages in the loss of religious faith: "intellectual doubt, moral criticism, emotional suffering, and disaffiliation from community" (*Creative Negativity*, 99). To these, MacKay adds the possibility that conversion and deconversion may alternate cyclically, "leading to increasingly larger and more encompassing belief systems" (*Creative Negativity*, 99). In Besant's case:

> [a]s each belief system she embraces becomes her reality, her passionate drive to pursue truth in turn sows the seeds for seeing through the false guises that that reality assumes, and her honesty compels her to eventually call that reality an illusion.
>
> (*Creative Negativity*, 119)

MacKay's examination of Besant's narrative structures thoroughly supports Bevir's notion of a rational continuity between the phases of Besant's development. However, we are once again operating in the domain of belief rather than philosophy.

Muriel Pécastaing-Boissière's recent biography, *Annie Besant (1847–1933): Struggles and Quest* (2017), not only initiates a discussion of Besant's 'Theosophical ethics' in light of her earlier moral struggles (*Annie Besant*, 238–41) but also demonstrates that the disjunctive conversion narrative has been supplanted by another, characterized as a continuous and progressive 'quest for truth'. This narrative takes its inspiration from the rhetorical flourish with which Besant ended her 1889 lecture, "Why I Became a Theosophist" – and with which Pécastaing-Boissière concludes her book: "I ask no other epitaph on my tomb but SHE TRIED TO FOLLOW TRUTH" (Besant, *Why I Became a Theosophist*, 31; Pécastaing-Boissière, *Annie Besant*, 304; original emphasis in both). Despite the willingness of Bevir, MacKay, and Pécastaing-Boissière to recognize what MacKay calls Besant's "insight into her own evolution" (*Creative Negativity*, 100), none of them have noted the following passage from her 1893 *Autobiography*:

> To a woman of my temperament, filled with passionate desire for the bettering of the world, the elevation of the world, a lofty system of ethics was of even more importance than a logical, intellectual conception of the universe; and the total loss of all faith in a righteous God only made me more strenuously assertive of the binding nature of duty and the overwhelming importance of conduct.
>
> (*Autobiography*, 153)[3]

---

[3] It is interesting to note that the word 'ethic' and its derivatives do not appear in Besant's *Autobiographical Sketches* (1885), whereas 'morality' and its derivatives occur frequently, suggesting that by 1893 Besant had reframed the problem of religion and morality in ethical and metaphysical terms.

This passage occurs in a chapter entitled "Atheism as I Knew and Taught It", dealing with utilitarianism, "the morality and creed that governed my life and thoughts from 1874 to 1886, and with some misgivings to 1889" (*Autobiography*, 169). It suggests that Besant recognized her ethical thought lacked a metaphysical basis – that she had become aware of a need to address the philosophical problem of whether ethics can exist without metaphysics. Furthermore, its focus on duty and conduct suggests that Besant could be investigated as a philosopher working in the field now called value theory. Over the next ten years, Besant would evolve a syncretic philosophical system, mediated by her study of Indian philosophy, which would support her lofty ethical vision with 'a logical, intellectual conception of the universe' and integrate aspects of virtue ethics with deontology and consequentialism in a novel way.

Besant's ethical development

Let us re-examine Besant's ethical development in terms of the problem of whether ethics can exist without metaphysics. Because I will substantially rewrite the disjunctive conversion narrative to foreground its philosophical continuities while challenging the quest for truth narrative as incomplete, I propose to rely entirely on Besant's own words. Here is how she formulated the problem in a 1915 essay entitled *The Basis of Morality*:

> Must religion and morals go together? It is a practical question for educationists […]. But apart from education, the question of the bedrock upon which morals must rest, the foundation upon which a moral edifice can be built that will stand secure against the storms of life – that is a question of perennial interest, and it must be answered by each of us […].
>
> (*Basis of Morality*, 1)

The essay discusses five approaches to the problem: revelation (as in Christian and Indian scriptures), intuition (as an innate moral sense or conscience), utility (as in the 'classical utilitarianism' of John Stuart Mill), evolution (physical, moral, social, and spiritual, as seen through a Theosophical lens), and mysticism (a result of transcending the previous stages through spiritual practice). Presented impersonally as descriptions of historical movements within Western culture and psychological movements within a hypothetical individual, these stages are also (silently) autobiographical. With some overlap, they may be mapped onto the chronology of Besant's life as follows:

(1) **Revelation** – until 1873; self-identifying as Christian; trained and confirmed in the Church of England (Besant, *Autobiography*, 11–140)
(2) **Intuition** – 1872–74; self-identifying as theist; still member of the Church of England (*Autobiography*, 106–40)
(3) **Utility** – 1874–89; disaffiliated with the Church of England; self-identifying as atheist and secularist (*Autobiography*, 141–338), and later as socialist

(*Autobiography*, 299–338); member of National Secular Society (1874–89); Fabian Society (1885–90), and Social Democratic Federation (1888–91)

(4) **Evolution** – after 1889; self-identifying as Theosophist; member of the Theosophical Society (*Autobiography*, 338–64); international president after 1907

(5) **Mysticism** – after a four-month lecture tour of India, 1893–94 (not mentioned in *Autobiography*; to be discussed later)

Besant's crisis of faith developed in 1871, while living with her abusive husband and following the near loss of their daughter to whooping cough (*Autobiography*, 86–9). As she probed such questions as "[t]he endless torture of hell, the vicarious sacrifice of Christ, the trustworthiness of revelation" (*Autobiography*, 94), she experienced "a rebellion of the moral nature rather than of the intellectual, a protest of the conscience rather than of the brain" (*Autobiography*, 100). By 1874, this rebellion had led her to reject the authority of the Church and the revelation of the Bible as a basis of morality. She argued that the ethics of the Bible were inconsistent – those of the Old Testament were inferior to those of the New – and that Christian morality had no basis in reason, since the existence of God could not be proven and the inequalities of nineteenth-century British society clearly demonstrated the failure of this morality (*True Basis of Morality*, 5, 16).[4]

During her brief theistic period (1872–74), Besant read the writings of theistically inclined authors such as British social reformer Frances Power Cobbe, whose *The Intuitive Theory of Morals* (1855) provided Besant with the name of this second stage of moral evolution, 'intuition'. According to Besant, such reading allowed her to perceive that the Church dogmas that revolted her moral conscience "were delusions of the ignorance of man, not the revelations of a God" (*Autobiography*, 107). However, she subsequently realized that because the personal God of Christian revelation was unprovable and thus could not provide "an infallible standard of right and wrong" (*Nature and Existence of God*, 32), there was also no validity in the theistic argument from design (*Nature and Existence of God*, 25–6). All that was left was Victorian convention concerning service and duty and an assumed inborn moral sense or instinct called conscience or intuition, supposed to be "god's voice in the soul of man". But this so-called instinct was "as variable as the various nations of the earth" and thus insufficiently universal to serve as a basis for morality. It was nothing more than "a habit, transmitted from parent to child" (*True Basis of Morality*, 7–8).

During the utility stage (1874–89), Besant made the following claim: "The true basis of morality is utility; that is, the adaptation of our actions to the

---

[4]The authority for the 1874 publication of *The True Basis of Morality* is Besant, *Annie Besant*, 153. I have not seen a copy published before 1882 (http://nzetc.victoria.ac.nz/tm/scholarly/tei-Stout39-t8.html). Elsewhere, Besant states that the lecture took place on 27 September 1874 (*Autobiographical Sketches*, 95).

promotion of the general welfare and happiness; the endeavour so to rule our lives that we may serve and bless mankind". She believed that a "science of morality" could be developed on the basis of "the observation of moral phænomena, facts in sociology, recorded in history" (*True Basis of Morality*, 9). Having studied the writings of John Stuart Mill and August Comte (*Autobiography*, 133), Besant expanded her conception of utility in 1876, calling for a Comte-inspired "religion of Humanity" that would promote loving humanity instead of God and obeying scientifically determined laws of nature instead of God's laws. Science would replace the Bible as a guide to the achievement of general happiness, including physical comfort and the intellectual and moral satisfactions associated with truth, beauty, and justice. Mill-inspired utility would determine whether actions were moral or immoral – useful in promoting human happiness or harmful to self and society. Virtue was the product of devotion and self-sacrifice, which, according to Besant, yielded "the purest forms of happiness to be found on earth". The motto would be "Save others". Moreover, this altruistic/utilitarian morality would evolve, becoming nobler as society climbed "ever higher up the mountain of progress" (*Constructive Rationalism*, 6–12). As Besant noted later, this expectation of progress was based on scientific and sociological views of evolution derived from the likes of Charles Darwin, Herbert Spencer, Thomas Huxley, and William Kingdon Clifford. She now saw "in the evolution of the social instinct the explanation of the growth of conscience and of the strengthening of man's mental and moral nature" (*Autobiography*, 164).

In the mid-1880s, Besant's altruistic urges led her to engage with collectivist socialism, as promulgated by George Bernard Shaw's Fabian Society and the Marxist Social Democratic Federation. Claiming that "the case for Socialism was intellectually complete" in terms of "the economic soundness of its basis" and "ethically beautiful" in terms of its "lofty idea of a social brotherhood" (*Autobiography*, 304), she became an activist in areas such as land ownership and tenant farmer's rights, trade unionism, and rights of female workers, as in the Matchgirls' Strike.[5] Socialistically conceived economics was apparently sufficient as an intellectual foundation for Besant's 'lofty ethics'; the question of a metaphysical basis for morals seems not yet to have occurred to her. Yet, after 1886, her reading about abnormal states of consciousness produced under hypnosis, as well as personal experimentation with hypnosis and Spiritualism, led to "a conviction that my philosophy was not sufficient; that life and mind were other than, more than I had dreamed" (*Autobiography*, 359). In 1889, "Theosophy stepped in finally as a further evolution towards knowledge, rendering rational, and therefore acceptable, the loftiest spirituality that the human mind can as yet conceive" (*Autobiography*, 140).

---

[5] See Terrier, "Annie Besant's Struggles", for a comprehensive discussion of these affiliations and associated outlets for activism.

At this time, Besant was collaborating with William Thomas Stead, editor of the *Review of Reviews*, on developing her cherished notion of a church of humanity, now conceived in terms of socialism (*Autobiography*, 329–34). Stead was responsible for Besant's discovery of Blavatsky's *The Secret Doctrine* (1888), which he asked her to review. After writing the review and joining the TS (*Autobiography*, 340–4), Besant's utilitarian period came to an end with resignations from the National Secular Society, Fabian Society, and Social Democratic Federation. She could now declare, along with Blavatsky, that "Matter is, in its constituent elements, the same as spirit; existence is *one*, however manifold its phenomena; life is one, however multiform its evolution" (*Autobiography*, 141). As we shall see, in this notion of oneness, Besant had at last hit upon a metaphysical basis for the 'intellectual conception of the universe' that would support her 'lofty ethics'.

In 1897, Besant produced a digest of *The Secret Doctrine*, portraying the Theosophical vision of evolution as an æonic, superphysically driven developmental progression of physical, social, and spiritual bodies rising in degree of complexity and perfectibility from the mineral, vegetable, and animal kingdoms to humanity. She defines evolution as the process of "latent potentialities becoming active powers", a gradual "unfolding of the capacities of consciousness" (Besant, *Ancient Wisdom*, 44; 26). Constant reincarnation within each kingdom and graduation from one kingdom to the next is the mechanism of such evolution. A 'law of karma', in which every thought, desire, and action is generated by past causes and generates future ones, is the propulsive force. Evolution occurs as humanity transcends selfish thoughts, desires, and actions and cultivates altruism through a "law of sacrifice" – unselfish service of others without desire for reward.[6]

Besant was now immersed in the period identified as 'evolution' in her five-part schema. In 1899, she replaced utility as the basis for morality with the notion that there is "a divine purpose in the evolution of the universe" as it develops "from the imperfect to the perfect"; what forwards this evolution is right, what delays or frustrates it is wrong (*Dharma*, 53–4). Besant no longer accepts the utilitarian maxim of 'the greatest happiness of the greatest number' because it creates an excluded minority. Moreover, no one's happiness can be fully separated from anyone else's. There will always be individuals whose "happiness fails in perfection so long as one unit is left out" (*Dharma*, 52). In 1903, she raised a further objection: "what constitutes the greatest good of the greatest number is always a debatable point" (*Sanātana Dharma: An Advanced Text Book*, 267[7]).

---

[6]See chapters on reincarnation, karma, and the law of sacrifice in Besant, *Ancient Wisdom*, 234–383.
[7]Henceforth this source will be cited as *Advanced Text Book* to avoid confusion with *Sanātana Dharma: An Elementary Text Book of Hindu Religion and Ethics*.

In 1915, Besant claimed that the Theosophical conception of evolution was "the sure basis of morality", upon which it could be "built as a Science with recognised laws" (*Basis of Morality*, 22). For her, the most basic of these laws was that whatever cooperates with evolution (Theosophically understood) is right, producing happiness; and whatever works against evolution is wrong, producing misery. Furthermore, there are younger, inexperienced persons, souls, and cultures and older, wiser ones. Each developmental level comes with its own set of rights and duties, its own scale of values with respect to right and wrong, its own virtues and vices to strive for or avoid. The goal is universal happiness, achievable only as "the Unity of Life" is recognized by everyone (*Basis of Morality*, 26).

The fifth phase in Besant's schema, 'mysticism', likely corresponds to an alleged conversion to Hindu customs and religion while Besant was touring India in 1893–94. Noted jeeringly in the press, this 'conversion' was subsequently denied (Nethercot, *Last Four Lives*, 21). However, at this time, Besant began learning Sanskrit and exploring the six classical systems of Indian philosophy, especially Yoga and Vedānta. In these philosophies, individuals are said to be *jīvātman* ('separated selves') striving to achieve oneness with *ātman* ('supreme self'), the divine consciousness that pervades the universe. Such oneness is experienced as *ānanda* ('bliss'). The development of *buddhi* ('higher mind') through yogic practices such as meditation is the method by which separated selves cognize that oneness.[8] In her 1895 translation of the *Bhagavad Gītā*, Besant defined *buddhi* as "the faculty above the ratiocinating mind [...] the Pure Reason, exercising the discriminative faculty of Intuition, of spiritual discernment" (*Bhagavad Gītā*, x).[9] Such intuition was not Cobbe's 'voice of God in man' but "the faculty which recognises and realises the Unity of the Self" (*Advanced Text Book*, 327). For Besant, mysticism – and religion itself – meant the development of *buddhi*.

Besant's ethical system

Besant's study of Sanskrit and Indian philosophy was undertaken under the guidance of a younger Indian Theosophical colleague, Bhagavān Dās (1869–1958). Member of an affluent Vaishya-caste family in Benares (now Varanasi), Dās held BA and MA degrees from Queens College, Benares, with focuses on Western philosophy and Sanskrit. He joined the TS in 1885 and met Besant in 1894. In 1898, he joined Besant in founding Central Hindu College, Benares (now Banaras Hindu University), and was active in political causes, including Indian independence. Author of several dozen books in English, three in

---

[8] See *Kaṭhopaniṣad* 1.3 for the role of *buddhi* in cognizing *ātman*.
[9] Besant uses the term *pure reason* in a non-Kantian sense derived from the Platonic notion of *nous* as intuition, possibly received from a popular Victorian-era translation of Plato's *Republic* by John Llewellyn Davies and David James Vaughan.

Hindi, and one in Sanskrit, he was granted Bharat Ratna, India's highest award for civilians, in 1955.[10]

In *The Science of Peace* (1904), Dās pursued a critique of Western philosophy, rejecting the Neo-Hegelianism of his time, with its metaphysical starting point in 'being' versus 'non-being', in favour of developing correspondences between Vedānta and the philosophy of Johann Gottlieb Fichte, with their starting point in 'consciousness of self' ('ego' in Fichte; *ātman* in Vedānta and Dās) versus 'consciousness of not-self' ('non-ego' in Fichte; *anātman* in Vedānta and Dās). From the mutual negation of self and not-self and a further negation of the relation between them, Dās saw the possibility of reconciling an absolute unchanging unity with an ever-changing diversity and thus proposed a novel solution of the problem of the one and the many (*Science of Peace*, 36–95). This book, with its predecessor, *The Science of the Emotions* (1900), became for Besant the 'logical, intellectual conception of the universe' she had been seeking as a basis for her ethical system.

To the extent that Blavatsky's *Secret Doctrine* had drawn from Vedānta, the lineaments of such a conception had been available to Besant since 1889. Indeed, Besant's attention must have been arrested early in the book when Blavatsky declared that "[t]he personal God of orthodox Theism" was clearly neither outside of its creation, nor absolute, infinite and changeless, a situation she deemed as both "unpsychological and, what is worse, unphilosophical" (*Secret Doctrine*, 1:1n). Blavatsky's solution to this problem was to borrow the emanationism of Vedānta metaphysics (with Neo-Platonic highlights) and posit the following: an unchanging 'Absolute Unity' called 'Be-ness'; an impersonal unmanifested deity as 'first cause'; a semi-manifested deity, conceived as a duality of 'spirit and matter' or 'life and form'; and a fully manifested deity, an active force within a realized universe, limited by its laws, author of and subject to evolutionary change, and to some extent conceivable as a personalized god or a host of lesser gods (*Secret Doctrine*, 1:1–17).

Besant adopted this emanationist metaphysics in *The Ancient Wisdom* (1897) but her exposition was apparently not sufficiently developed to act as a basis for her ethical system. In *Dharma* (1899), she made another attempt, more purely aligned with Vedānta metaphysics as expressed in the *Bhagavadgītā* and tackling the problem of the one and the many. As noted, this was her attempt to position the Theosophical notion of evolution as the basis of morality. Having defined the word 'dharma' ('religion', 'truth', 'law', and 'way') "as 'the inner nature of a thing at any given stage of evolution, and the law of the next stage of its unfolding'" (*Dharma*, 16–17), Besant explored it as 'way', in the sense of 'having one's own dharma', seeing in it a basis for a relativistic morality (*Dharma*, 53–5). However, she was not yet

---

[10]See the forthcoming companion to this article, "Annie Besant, Bhagavān Dās, and the *Sanātana Dharma* Project" for further particulars about Dās and the texts discussed in this section.

prepared to take 'dharma' in the sense of 'religion' and declare that religion was the basis of morality. Only after following Dās's reworking of Vedānta metaphysics in draft from 1899 to 1903 (Dās, *Science of Peace*, xix–xxii) was Besant able to assert that "[t]he *first* thing we learn from religion is the Unity of all selves, and this is the foundation of Ethics" (Besant, *Advanced Text Book*, 262; original emphasis). Because Hinduism was based on "the recognition of the Unity of the Self amid the Diversity of the Not-Self" (*Advanced Text Book*, 262), where 'not-self' (*anātman*) is any degree of diversity-creating differentiation from the supreme self (*ātman*) into separate selves (*jīvātman*), this religion, in particular, could provide "the ultimate data upon which Ethical Science may be built" (*Advanced Text Book*, 261). Later, in an unusual admission of limitation, Besant would acknowledge Dās as her philosophical superior – "I am not so good a metaphysician as is the author [...]" (*Introduction to 'The Science of Peace'*, v).

The text embodying Besant's ethical system originated in a plan to produce a series of textbooks on religion and morality for publication by Central Hindu College. The series was to be collectively entitled *Sanātana Dharma* ('eternal religion'), an alternative name for Hinduism that Besant had appropriated, with the approval of a Hindu editorial committee, to connote "the ancient teachings, free from modern [i.e. sectarian] accretions" (*Advanced Text Book*, iii). The series was to include a catechism for elementary school students, an elementary textbook for middle- and upper-school students, and an advanced textbook for college students. The latter was published anonymously in 1903 as *Sanātana Dharma: An Advanced Text Book of Hindu Religion and Ethics*. Working under the supervision of "the Board of Trustees, the Managing Committee and a number of learned Hindus", who supplied quotations from Hindu scripture in Sanskrit with English translation "and other material", Besant "drafted the running text of the book in English [...] in two months, middle of May to middle of June, 1901", at Srinagar, where Dās was working on *The Science of Peace* (Murti, "History of the Sanātana-Dharma Text-Books", ix–x; Dās, *Science of Peace*, xix).

I call Besant's ethical system 'syncretic' because of the difficulties of disentangling the textbook's constituent strands. Part 1, "Basic Hindu Religious Ideas", summarizes aspects of Dās's reworking of Vedānta, especially in the chapters entitled "The One" and "The Many" and recasts in Hindu terms the chapters on reincarnation, karma, and the law of sacrifice from *The Ancient Wisdom*. Part 2, "General Religious Hindu Customs and Rites", is at times mediated by Theosophical teachings on subtle bodies and planes. Part 3, "Ethical Teachings", which introduces Besant's system, overtly cites Dās' *The Science of the Emotions*. Involvement of the editorial committee may be assumed throughout, especially in connection with the copious corroborative citations in Sanskrit and English culled from Hindu scriptures. Yet, when the scriptural citations in part 3 are set aside, Besant's running text evinces ethical preoccupations traceable to her earliest writings. The *Advanced Text Book* may have been published anonymously in deference to these putatively collaborative origins, but more likely to conceal the identity of its controversial author and avoid rejection by traditionalist Hindus unfriendly to Theosophy and the TS.

I can but briefly acknowledge the challenges of contextualizing the existence and collaborative authorship of the *Advanced Text Book* in terms of postcolonial theory. What was Besant doing in attempting to educate young Hindus about their own religion? To what extent was the editorial committee made up of Hindu Theosophists? Was it merely a front for Besant's educational and Theosophical agendas? How do we evaluate Bhagavān Dās's subaltern status as an Indian philosopher and Theosophist critiquing Western philosophy within the context of Besant's agendas? Lacking space to deal adequately with such questions, I propose to summarize the ethical system presented by Besant in part 3 of the *Advanced Text Book* with minimal analysis. To facilitate this summary, I draw upon Rosalind Hursthouse's listing of topics associated with the virtue ethics tradition:

> virtues and vices, motives and moral character, moral education, moral wisdom or discernment, friendship and family relationships, a deep concept of happiness, the role of the emotions in our moral life and the fundamentally important questions of what sorts of persons we should be and how we should live.
> (*On Virtue Ethics*, 3)

Besant never ceased to be a eudaimonist. Considering her emphasis on happiness in earlier texts, it is not surprising that Besant's system is a species of virtue ethics, anchored in and extended by appropriation of Sanskrit terms and confirmed by copious citations from Hindu scriptures. In 1874, at the beginning of her ethical career, she proposed "the production of happiness as the ultimate test of right and wrong", despite criticism that such a theory was "low and despicable" and the "true aim of life" should be virtue. For Besant, this argument was merely "bidding us to resign lower pleasures for higher ones, selfish pleasures for unselfish, physical pleasures for moral" (*True Basis of Morality*, 10–11). Identical views appear in the *Advanced Text Book*, with the refinement of a Sanskrit term for higher pleasures: *ānanda* ('bliss'). According to Besant, "Happiness means the deep, inner, enduring bliss which is satisfaction in the Self" (*Advanced Text Book*, 259). Since individuals are "of the nature of the one Self" though each is "embodied in a separate form", they "seek union with the Self in other forms". Furthermore, "this search for unity, for the bliss of union, is instinctive, and results, when the union is found, in perfect happiness. In this everyone is alike". Even when people choose "wrong things", their motive "is always the same, the desire to be happy" (*Advanced Text Book*, 309). *Ānanda* provides Besant's 'deep concept of happiness'.

According to Bhagavān Dās, emotions develop from the interaction of separated selves (*jīvātman*) in relation to the supreme self (*ātman*) and the not-self (*anātman*). In *The Science of the Emotions* (1900), Dās argues that when separated selves turn towards the diversity of the perceptible universe, they experience attraction (*rāga*) to and repulsion from (*dveṣa*) the things and beings of the not-self. Analogues for *rāga* are desire, pleasure, liking, and wanting to "take in, absorb, embrace" – in other words, love. Analogues for *dveṣa* are repulsion, pain, disliking, and wanting to "throw out, push away, repel" – in other words, hate (*Science of the Emotions*, 19–22). Following Dās, Besant declares that emotions associated with *rāga* tend to become virtues and those associated with *dveṣa* tend to become vices. As manifestations of love, virtues reflect an awareness of "more the unity of the Self than the diversity of the Not-Self". As manifestations of hate, vices reflect an awareness of separateness, selfishness, the diversity of individual selves instead of "the oneness of the Self" (*Advanced Text Book*, 297–8). Thus does Besant's system suggest 'the role the emotions play in our moral life' as the fundaments of 'virtues and vices'.

Hursthouse's topic of 'motive and moral character' is dealt with in terms of *guṇa* ('quality'), an ancient Indian concept positing three qualities or states of matter: *tamas* ('resistance' or 'inertia'), *rajas* ('motion' or 'action'), and *sattva* ('rhythm' or 'harmony'). The moral character dominated by *tamas* is "indolent, dull, inactive and ignorant"; to evolve, it requires curiosity and the motivation of exploring likes and dislikes (*Advanced Text Book*, 285–6). That dominated by *rajas* is driven into "material pursuits" by "cravings", the "motive powers" of likes and dislikes, resulting in "unrest and disquietude"; to evolve, it requires giving up "personal likes and dislikes" through the development of self-control (*Advanced Text Book*, 286, 316). That dominated by *sattva* is able to discriminate "between the real and the unreal, the lasting and the fleeting, the bliss eternal and the pleasures of the moment"; to evolve, it requires the development of *buddhi* so it can move beyond "the barrier of personality", perceived as intrinsically selfish, towards blissful, unselfish oneness with all beings in the supreme self (*Advanced Text Book*, 286, 307, 316).

For Besant, all moral precepts "are founded on this recognition of the unity of the Self". Thus, "if there is only one Self, any act by which I injure my neighbour *must* injure me" (*Advanced Text Book*, 263; original emphasis). Thus the primary other-regarding virtue in Besant's system is *ahiṃsā* ('non-harming'; or as she translates the term, 'harmlessness'). Because the object of ethics is "to establish harmonious relations with others" (*Advanced Text Book*, 311), it is not surprising that the two primary self-regarding virtues in Besant's system, self-control and contentedness, are seen in terms of harmonious other-regarding relations. Hence, one who has mastered self-control and contentedness "will promote harmonious relations with others much more than one who has them not" (*Sanātana Dharma: An Elementary Text Book*, 139).

Under the category of self-control come virtues that uphold Hindu traditions of cleanliness and health of the physical body, especially proper diet; the subdual of "animal appetites" in connection with desire and the senses; and the elimination of "impurities and distraction of the mind" based on likes and dislikes. The goal is to achieve dispassion toward sensual temptations and discernment concerning what is genuinely useful for one's development (*Advanced Text Book*, 316). Such self-control involves thought that "constantly dwell[s] on the Unity of the Self" rather than the pursuit of desires "for personal and selfish ends"; speech that not only is "respectful to superiors, courteous to equals, gentle to inferiors" but also honest and truthful; and actions that do not result in injury to oneself or others or create self-centered social disturbances (*Advanced Text Book*, 326–8). Furthermore, developing ideal self-control allows *rāga* "to expand into universal love" while *dveṣa* is reduced to "an abstract dislike for anything that goes against the law". Thus an individual becomes "strong in his purity, in his rejection of all that is evil" while maintaining "universal love for all beings" (*Advanced Text Book*, 315). Ideal self-control produces a "constant mood of righteousness and performance of duty" (*Advanced Text Book*, 328) – not self-righteousness but "the desire to do what is right", "give every one his due", and "always find out the truth and act according to it" (*Advanced Text Book*, 329).

As indicated, the other important self-regarding virtue is contentedness, which Besant calls "the root of happiness". Contentedness develops from right thought, speech, and action; the recognition and fulfilment of duty (as an expression of the law of sacrifice); and conforming oneself to the "unalterable law" of karma, whose keynote is "justice". Thus one "obtains every thing that he has duly earned, neither more nor less; every debt must be paid; every [moral] cause must be followed by its effect" (*Advanced Text Book*, 331). According to Besant, "To be satisfied with what we have because we have our due is true wisdom, and all dissatisfaction is folly". Equanimity in the face of challenging circumstances is required rather than nerveless acquiescence in some supposedly inalterable fate. For Besant, desires, thoughts, and actions from the past of this lifetime, or a previous incarnation, create one's present situation. Yet desire, as will, may generate "opportunities"; thought, as wisdom, may develop "character – or capacities"; and action, as work within "surrounding circumstances", may allow one to change the situation. Thus "exertion" matters more than "destiny" (*Advanced Text Book*, 115–16). The achievements of ideal self-control and contentedness come under Hursthouse's topic of 'moral education'.

Besant's explanations of conduct, which derive from Dās's *The Science of the Emotions*, deal with Hursthouse's topic of 'friends and family'. Dās's project was to combine *rāga* and *dveṣa* with the family-based relations defined in *Manusmṛti*, (*Laws of Manu*): youngers (inferiors), siblings (equals), and elders (superiors). Such distinctions could be perceived in terms of physical age, psychological maturity, occupational station, social status, and degree of spiritual evolution through multiple lifetimes. Whereas Dās's book was principally concerned with categorization of emotions, Besant devotes several chapters of the *Advanced Text Book* to practical applications of Dās's distinctions. Investigating their effectiveness as guides to conduct, she treats not only family relationships and friendships among equals but also every stage of a (colonial) socio-political and religious scale ranging from family servants to king, country, and God.

Hursthouse's topic of 'moral wisdom or discernment' is dealt with by further distinguishing virtues and vices in a deontological mode and subjugating emotions, vices, virtues, and duty to a consequentialist 'law of karma'. Proper conduct is determined by fulfilment of duty, with duty defined as debts owed to others (including beings inferior or superior to humanity, from animals to gods) "for benefits received" (*Advanced Text Book*, 294–5). Emotions prompting the fulfilment of duties are virtues; those prompting their non-fulfilment are vices. Thus "[h]appiness in any relation depends on the parties to the relation fulfilling their duties to each other; that is, on their practicing the virtues which are the fulfilment of the duties of the relation". Naturally, unhappiness would result from the breakdown of this social contract by practice of vices that violate such duties (*Advanced Text Book*, 297). Meanwhile, the law of karma is always "restoring disturbed equilibrium" in the discharge of duties (*Advanced Text Book*, 295). Hateful actions produce suffering in in this or another lifetime; loving actions produce bliss in this or another lifetime. As the soul evolves through many lifetimes, karma teaches it to eschew hatred and embrace love, to transcend the selfishness of the separated self and achieve union with the supreme self. In all relations between sentient beings, the attitude should be one of "harmlessness" (*ahiṃsā*). Here Besant cites the *Mahābhārata*, in which non-harming is said to be "the highest duty" (*Advanced Text Book*, 333).

The character-building goals of Besant's ethical system are declared in the following baldly Victorian effusion, which further addresses Hursthouse's topics of 'the role of emotions' and 'moral education':

> Emotions, rightly directed by the intelligence, are virtues. In the culture of emotions lies the formation of a man's character, his ethical development. Emotional culture is the highest culture of man, and the training of likes and dislikes is his best evolution. The man of cultured emotions is propelled by them to do what he thinks right; he becomes patriotic, he becomes philanthropic, he becomes compassionate, he becomes friendly to all beings. His emotions become predominantly those of Love, and he takes an ever wider and wider range in the manifestation of that love.
>
> (*Advanced Text Book*, 307)

Yet the key to Besant's ethics lies in the simple phrase 'friendly to all beings'. Such friendliness involves "establishing harmonious relations between all the Jivātmas ['separated selves'] that belong to any special area" (*Advanced Text Book*, 257). By 'special area', Besant means social surroundings. She arranges these surroundings in a continuum of increasing collectivity, listing the degrees as follows, each with its distinctive moral lens (*Advanced Text Book*, 258):

- Family ("family morality")
- Community ("social morality")
- Nation ("national" and "international morality")
- Humanity ("human morality")
- All of earth's inhabitants ("inter-world morality", guiding conduct between all sentient beings, human and nonhuman, including animals)
- Inhabitants of other worlds (also called "inter-world morality", but now guiding conduct between living humans, deceased ancestors, and Hinduism's myriad superhuman gods)

This continuum of increasing collectivity suggests how Besant's ethical system treats what Hursthouse calls 'the fundamentally important questions of what sorts of persons we should be and how we should live'. In Besant's system, spiritual evolution is the sanction of morality; happiness, as bliss (*ananda*), the compelling motive; and the achievement of harmonious relations the altruistic mechanism. In this context, the word 'harmonious' refers to the soul's evolution from inertia (*tamas*) through ceaseless activity (*rajas*) to harmony and inner peace (*sattva*). This evolution occurs by development of *buddhi*, the intuitive faculty that supports an ever-increasing identification of each separated self with the supreme self. *Buddhi* develops through progressive elimination of selfishness. By practicing the law of sacrifice, separated selves rise along Besant's continuum of collectivity. They recognize and act on the duties owed on each of these levels, expanding their moral compass and increasing their level of bliss. They gradually become friendly to all beings, resulting in *mokṣa*, 'liberation' from the limited beingness of a separate self into the unlimited beingness of the supreme self. At every stage of this moral and spiritual journey, non-harming is the key.

Conclusion

Having noted the reluctance of Besant's contemporaries to acknowledge her intellectual contribution, much less her possible status as a philosopher; having demonstrated that her early biographers developed what I call the disjunctive conversion narrative to discount any logical or rational continuity between various phases of Besant's life and organizational affiliations;

having cited more recent scholarship that has attempted to restore continuity to the development of Besant's religious and moral life, I have made a case for acknowledging Besant's "insight into her own evolution" (MacKay, *Creative Negativity*, 100). I have adopted her five-part schema of moral development, mapped details of her biography onto it, and indicated, using her own writings, that each stage could be characterized as a phase in her struggle with the philosophical problem of whether ethics (morals) can exist without metaphysics (religion). I have argued that once Besant had found in Bhagavān Dās a metaphysician who could produce, from correspondences between Vedānta and the philosophy of Fichte, the "logical, intellectual conception of the universe" she sought as a basis for her "lofty system of ethics" (Besant, *Autobiography*, 153), she was emboldened to produce such a system in the anonymously published *Sanātana Dharma: An Advanced Text Book of Hindu Religion and Ethics* (1903). By invoking Rosalind Hursthouse's list of various topics associated with the virtue ethics tradition, I have demonstrated that Besant's syncretic ethical system is a species of virtue ethics and shown not only how it addresses each of Hursthouse's topics but also how it enfolds aspects of deontology and consequentialism. If Besant is to be considered as a philosopher, her field should be identified as that of value theory. Perhaps her project as an ethicist, the education of people to become 'friendly to all beings' along an ever-increasing continuum of collectivity, may yet make a contribution to our politically and environmentally challenged world.

Acknowledgements

I would like to thank Dr Muriel Pécastaing-Boissière and Dr Marie Terrier for encouragement and comment during early stages of this project; and Dr Alison Stone and Dr Charlotte Alderwick for much-needed editorial support in finalizing its form.

References
Primary Sources

Besant, Annie. *On the Nature and Existence of God*. London: Thomas Scott, 1875.
Besant, Annie. *Constructive Rationalism*. London: Freethought Publishing Company, 1876.
Besant, Annie. *The True Basis of Morality* (1874). London: Freethought Publishing Company, 1882.
Besant, Annie. *Autobiographical Sketches*. London: Freethought Publishing Company, 1885.
Besant, Annie. *Why I Became a Theosophist*. London: Freethought Publishing Company, 1889.
Besant, Annie. *Annie Besant: An Autobiography*. London: T. Fisher Unwin, 1893.
Besant, Annie. *The Bhagavad Gītā; or The Lord's Song*. London: Theosophical Publishing Society, 1895.

Besant, Annie. *The Ancient Wisdom: An Outline of Theosophical Teachings*. London: Theosophical Publishing Society, 1897.
Besant, Annie. *Dharma: Three Lectures*. Benares: Theosophical Publishing Society, 1899.
Besant, Annie. *An Introduction to 'The Science of Peace'*. Adyar: Theosophical Publishing House, 1912.
Besant, Annie. *The Basis of Morality*. Adyar: Theosophical Publishing House, 1915.
Dās, Bhagavān. *The Science of the Emotions*. London: Theosophical Publishing Society, 1900.
Dās, Bhagavān. *The Science of Peace: An Attempt at an Exposition of the First Principles of the Science of the Self (Ādhyātma-Vidyā)*. London: Theosophical Publishing Society, 1904.
Sanātana Dharma: An Elementary Text Book of Hindu Religion and Ethics. Benares: Trustees of Central Hindu College, 1902.
Sanātana Dharma: An Advanced Text Book of Hindu Religion and Ethics. Benares: Trustees of Central Hindu College, 1903.

Secondary Sources

Bevir, Mark. "Annie Besant's Quest for Truth: Christianity, Secularism, and New Age Thought". *Journal of Ecclesiastical History* 50, no. 1 (January 1999): 62–93.
Foote, G[eorge]. W[illiam]. *Mrs. Besant's Theosophy*. London: Progressive Publishing Company, 1889.
Goodrick-Clarke, Nicholas. "Western Esoteric Traditions and Theosophy". In *Handbook of the Theosophical Current*, edited by Olav Hammer and Mikael Rothstein. Leiden: Brill, 2014.
Hursthouse, Rosalind. *On Virtue Ethics*. Oxford: Oxford University Press, 1999.
Leland, Kurt. "Annie Besant, Bhagavān Dās, and the *Sanātana Dharma* Project". In *Occult South Asia*, edited by Karl Baier, and Mriganka Mukhopadhyay. Leiden: Brill, forthcoming.
MacKay, Carol Hanbery. *Creative Negativity: Four Victorian Exemplars of the Female Quest*. Stanford: Stanford University Press, 2001.
Murti, G. Srinivasa. "History of the Sanātana-Dharma Text-Books, Compiled from Material Supplied by Dr. Bhagavān Dās". In *Sanātana-Dharma: An Advanced Text-Book of Hindu Religion and Ethics*, 2nd ed., vii–xx. Adyar: Theosophical Publishing House, 1940.
Nethercot, Arthur H. *The First Five Lives of Annie Besant*. Chicago: University of Chicago Press, 1960.
Nethercot, Arthur H. *The Last Four Lives of Annie Besant*. Chicago: University of Chicago Press, 1963.
Pécastaing-Boissière, Muriel. *Annie Besant (1847–1933): Struggles and Quest*. London: Theosophical Publishing House, 2017.
Taylor, Ann. *Annie Besant: A Biography*. Oxford: Oxford University Press, 1992.
Terrier, Marie. "Annie Besant's Struggles Against Political and Social Inequalities: From Radicalism to Socialism (1874–1890)". In *Annie Besant (1847–1933): Struggles and Quest*, edited by Muriel Pécastaing-Boissière, 151–96. London: Theosophical Publishing House, 2017.
Wessinger, Catherine Lowman. *Annie Besant and Progressive Messianism (1847–1933)*. Lewiston, NY: Edwin Mellon Press, 1988.
Williams, Gertrude Marvin. *The Passionate Pilgrim: A Life of Annie Besant*. New York: Howard-McCann, 1931.
West, Geoffrey (Geoffrey Harry Wells). *Annie Besant*. New York: Viking, 1928.

E. E. Constance Jones on the dualism of practical reason

Gary Ostertag and Amanda Favia

ABSTRACT
E. E. Constance Jones (1848–1922), a regular contributor to *Mind* and the *Proceedings of the Aristotelian Society*, and the author of several textbooks and a monograph, worked in both philosophical logic and ethics. The current paper focuses on Jones' central contribution to ethics – her response to Sidgwick's "dualism of practical reason". Sidgwick held that practical reason has an allegiance to two distinct 'methods': self-love and benevolence. Yet, while both methods are independently rational, they may potentially come into conflict. This, for Jones, presented "the most important difficulty of the system of [Sidgwick's] Universalistic Hedonism". Jones returned to this problem a number of times in the course of her career. We discuss the evolution of her thinking on this problem and argue that her work presents an original and promising line of response to the dualism that worried Sidgwick.

1. Introduction

A prominent figure in British philosophy in the late nineteenth and early twentieth centuries, E. E. Constance Jones (1848–1922) is now known, if at all, for her work in philosophical logic. But Jones, who was one of Henry Sidgwick's prize students (Schultz, *Henry Sidgwick*, 745, n. 25), also made important contributions to ethics and moral psychology. These writings, though valuable both for the individual proposals they contain as well as the light they shed on contemporary debates, were largely forgotten in the century following Jones' death. It is our goal in the current paper to redress this neglect.

Jones' writings in ethics are unified by a methodological precept: namely, that the study of normativity should be conducted squarely within the realm of human cognition and experience. She followed Sidgwick (*Methods*, 2–4) in maintaining that the metaphysical basis of ethics is distinct from ethics proper:

> No doubt Ethics, considered as a Science, has what has been called a metaphysical basis, and the determination of this is of the last interest and importance; *but it is not the science itself*, and the great question of scientific Ethics – *what* is it that is Right – has to be discussed separately from the investigation of that basis.
> (Jones, "Rationality of Hedonism", 30; first emphasis added)

For Jones, the study of ethics should be focused on determining the truth of normative claims, not on the metaphysical grounds of such claims. In keeping with this broadly pragmatic, anti-metaphysical orientation, she writes: "the End which we ought to aim at ... must be an End ... which can be attained, or approximated to, by human action, and ... which is desirable to us, being what we are, and limited as we are" ("Rationality", 30). That is, not only should there be a sharp separation of the study of normativity from the study of its metaphysical grounds, the norms themselves should reflect the desires and limitations of human agents.

Our particular focus will be on Jones' response to a problem that Sidgwick never resolved to his satisfaction: the dualism of practical reason. This dualism is between two fundamental 'methods' of practical rationality, self-interest and our duty to others. As Bart Schultz writes, the "attempt to get beyond [the dualism of practical reason] – to effect some form of 'harmonization' – was for Sidgwick [an] element of the deepest problems of human life, one that arose with special urgency with the decline of orthodox religion". Sidgwick, he adds, "could not bear the thought of a universe so fundamentally perverse as to allow that the wages of virtue might 'be dust'" and, indeed, despaired at the idea that the dualism might be irresolvable (Schultz, *Henry Sidgwick*, 15). As we shall see, Jones was more sanguine than her mentor about the possibility of a harmonization.

2. Biographical sketch

Born in Wales to a family of landed gentry, Emily Elizabeth Constance Jones was educated at home until entering Girton College, the then newly-formed women's college at Cambridge University, in 1875. Jones saw her formal education, and the study of 'the moral sciences', as a path to an intellectual life: "I was in a magic world of thought – of great thinkers, of unrivalled teachers – a new heaven and a new earth" (*As I Remember*, 54). Although her undergraduate education at Girton was punctuated with periods of familial duty, Jones succeeded in achieving First Class in the Moral Sciences Tripos in 1880, and, in 1884, was invited back to Girton to become a research student. This led to a life-long career at Girton: first as a Resident Lecturer in the Moral Sciences, then as Librarian. These appointments were followed by her tenure as Vice-Mistress, and finally, as Mistress (1903–16).

While at Cambridge, Jones studied with Henry Sidgwick, James Ward, and John Neville Keynes. Most significant to her work in ethics was her time spent under the supervision of Sidgwick. Initially charged with reviewing Sidgwick's students' papers for Girton and Newnham College and proofreading his writings, Jones became his literary executor, compiling the index for the fourth and subsequent editions of *The Methods of Ethics* and correcting and providing supplementary material for posthumous editions.

Jones was a prominent figure in English philosophy from 1890 until her death in 1922. Not only did she publish several texts, some going into multiple editions, she also published a monograph with Cambridge University Press, *A New Law of Thought and its Logical Bearings* (1911), numerous papers in *Mind* and the *Proceedings of the Aristotelian Society*, and frequently participated in symposia with such distinguished figures as F. H. Bradley, W. E. Johnson, Bernard Bosanquet, and F. C. S. Schiller. While Russell was privately dismissive of Jones, he did think her work sufficiently important to address in a lecture to the Cambridge Moral Sciences Club, subsequently published as "Knowledge by Acquaintance and Knowledge by Description" (this was, in part, in response to a lecture Jones presented to the same group some months earlier).[1] A sense of her importance to the English philosophical community at the time can be gleaned from the obituaries that appeared upon her death in *Mind* (Stout, "The Late"), the *International Journal of Ethics*, now *Ethics* (Mackenzie, "The Late"), and the *Proceedings of the Aristotelian Society* (Anonymous, "In Memoriam"). G. F. Stout, then editor of *Mind*, emphasized both Jones' work in philosophical logic and her contributions to the profession, writing: "No mere reference to her published work will do justice to the service rendered by Miss Jones to philosophy within her own circle of friends and colleagues" (384). While this service interfered with her research, it did benefit Girton. As the Mistress of the college, she helped bring Girton back from a £43,000 debt (equivalent to £5,185,069 in 2020), securing the future financial health of the college and funding several fellowships. Moreover, if her work does not equal that of some of her more celebrated contemporaries, it is also true that none of them faced Jones' particular challenges. Nor can it be said that they rose from such challenges to, among other successes, bring a women's college back from insolvency.

3. The dualism of practical reason

In *The Methods of Ethics*, Sidgwick attempts to provide precisely what its title describes – a "rational procedure by which we determine what individual

---

[1] Ostertag, "Emily Elizabeth Constance Jones", Section 5, provides an account of their exchange.

human beings ought – or what it is right for them – to do" (*Methods*, 1; quoted in Jones, *Primer*, 3). At its conclusion, five hundred or so pages later, he writes:

> I find that I undoubtedly seem to perceive, as clearly and certainly as I see any axiom in Arithmetic or Geometry, that it is 'right' and 'reasonable' for me to treat others as I should think that I myself ought to be treated under similar conditions, and to do what I believe to be ultimately conducive to universal Good or Happiness.
>
> (*Methods*, 507)

While Sidgwick takes himself to have demonstrated with something approaching Cartesian clarity[2] that our actions have as their goal "universal Good or Happiness", he also goes on to acknowledge a gap between what he takes himself to have shown – that rationality dictates that I choose an action that accords with the principle of utility – and something else that a moral theory, ideally, should accomplish – showing that performing such an action is, of necessity, in my interest.

Sidgwick acknowledges, quoting Butler, that "'reasonable self-love and conscience are the two chief or superior principles in the nature of man' each of which we are under a 'manifest obligation' to obey ... " (*Methods*, xiii; Butler, *Works*, 64, 40). Reasonable self-love involves valuing one's own interests somewhat higher than one's neighbour's. (The principle's true content, as will become clear below, is not to be gleaned at face value: it also involves adherence to the "axiom of temporal irrelevance" (Shaver, *Rational Egoism*, 74): genuine 'self-love' mandates "impartial concern for all parts of our conscious life" (*Methods*, 381).) Conscience, on the other hand, dictates that our own interests take a back seat to universal good or happiness.

Both conscience (i.e. universal benevolence) and reasonable self-love are principles – more precisely, methods – of practical rationality.[3] This might not seem obvious in the case of the latter. But Sidgwick argues convincingly of its status as a rational principle:

> We do not all look with simple indifference on a man who declines to take the right means to attain his own happiness, on no other ground than that he does not care about happiness. Most men would regard such a refusal as irrational, with a certain disapprobation; they would thus implicitly assent to Butler's statement that 'interest, one's own happiness, is a manifest obligation'. In other words, they would think that a man *ought* to care for his own happiness. The word 'ought' thus used is no longer relative: happiness now appears as an

---

[2] This is no exaggeration. In order to show that his ethical principles "possess the characteristics by which self-evident truths are distinguished from mere opinions" Sidgwick provides four general conditions (see *Methods*, 338–43) that a proposition must meet in order to possess "the highest degree of certainty attainable" (338).

[3] Sidgwick distinguishes between 'principles' – as in first principles – and 'methods' – "rational procedures for determining right conduct in any particular case" (*Methods*, 78; quoted in Schultz, *Henry Sidgwick*, 150). While we don't strictly follow his usage here, when we speak of self-love and benevolence we take these to be methods in Sidgwick's sense.

ultimate end, the pursuit of which – at least within the limits imposed by other duties – appears to be prescribed by reason 'categorically', as Kant would say, i.e. without any tacit assumption of a still ulterior end.

(*Methods*, 7; note omitted; quoting Butler, *Works*, 40)

But – and here is the problem – the principles do not always point in the same direction. Of course, we can conceive of a universe in which they do. If we believe that there is a god who divvies out rewards and punishments depending on whether or not we have acted in conformity with Sidgwick's utilitarian principles, or, alternatively, that we have evolved in such a way that we innately desire universal good or happiness, then the principles are in harmony. But since we do not know either proposition with the requisite certainty – indeed, we do not 'know' them at all – we don't know if these possibilities are in fact the case.

Again, if we assume (say) that a deity exists then we can suppose that the moral rationalism that Sidgwick defends comes with a benefit: *personal salvation*. In such a case, the principles harmonize. But, as indicated, Sidgwick cannot embrace this idea:

> But I cannot find inseparably connected with this conviction [of the rationality of utilitarianism], and similarly attainable by mere reflective intuition, any cognition that there actually is a Supreme Being who will adequately reward me for obeying these rules of duty, or punish me for violating them. Or, – omitting the strictly theological element of the proposition, – I may say that I do not find in my moral consciousness any intuition, claiming to be clear and certain, that the performance of duty will be adequately rewarded and its violation punished.
>
> (*Methods*, 507; notes omitted)

While the existence of a god would make the convergence not just true but necessary, there is no necessity or *a priori* attaching to the existence of such a being (certainly nothing that meets the self-evidence Sidgwick requires of a premise in an ethical argument). And, considered independently of such a being, there is no necessary connection between behaving in the appropriate manner and receiving a benefit.

We can now sum up the problem posed by the 'dualism of practical reason': Our moral principles must meet a standard of self-evidence. If two or more principles are inconsistent relative to a certain scenario, real or imagined, then the standard is not met: one or another of the principles must be rejected or somehow restricted. In such a situation – "of a recognized conflict between self-interest and duty" – "practical reason, being divided against itself, would cease to be a motive on either side ... " (*Methods*, 507). There would, that is, be no rational method for deciding which principle ought to take priority in an entirely conceivable circumstance. (See further, Crisp, *Cosmos*, 227–34.)

Jones included the following passage, drawn from Sidgwick's lecture notes, in her preface to the (posthumously published) sixth edition of *Methods*:

> [T]he persuasiveness of Mill's exposition veiled for a time the profound discrepancy between the natural end of action – private happiness, and the end of duty – general happiness. Or if a doubt assailed me as to the coincidence of private and general happiness, I was inclined to hold that it ought to be cast to the winds by a generous resolution.
>
> But a sense grew upon me that this method of dealing with the conflict between Interest and Duty, though perhaps proper for practice could not be final for philosophy. *For practical men who do not philosophize, the maxim of subordinating self-interest, as commonly conceived, to 'altruistic' impulses and sentiments which they feel to be higher and nobler is, I doubt not, a commendable maxim; but it is surely the business of Ethical Philosophy to find and make explicit the rational ground of such action.*
>
> (Methods, xvii–vxiii; emphasis added)[4]

Once again, for Sidgwick the inconsistency of self-interest and altruism suggests that the project of the *Methods* cannot be fully realized unless the rational ground of our altruistic impulses is provided along with a rational method for choosing one rational principle – rational self-love or rational benevolence – over the other. For practical purposes, it is fine to opt for the altruistic action. But one who is in the business of providing a "rational procedure" for ethical decision-making must do better than the "practical man" and provide a justification for this choice.[5]

The problem posed by the dualism bears comparison to the well-known problem that practical reason faces irresoluble moral dilemmas. I face a moral dilemma when I cannot choose between competing actions by

---

[4]Note that Sidgwick assumes, with Butler, that the motivation for self-love is rational. The conflict is not between egoism of a purely psychological sort and altruism. It is between two rational principles. Moreover, although in this passage Sidgwick presupposes that altruism, or 'Universal Benevolence', should be subordinated to self-love, our concern in what follows concerns the conflict itself rather than Sidgwick's preferred resolution. As Jones writes, the conflict is "not between Reason and Unreason, but between competing reasonable Ends" ("Rational Hedonism", 36). And Sidgwick is clear that such a conflict cannot be left unresolved: "I ... assume as a fundamental postulate of Ethics, that so far as two methods conflict, one or other of them must be modified or rejected" (*Methods*, 6).

[5]While the dualism of practical reason may provide a basis for skepticism about practical reason, the challenge it presents is not the familiar Humean one. The Humean argument targets *internalism*: the thesis that *if* there exists a normative proposition *p*, then believing *p* entails a desire for *q* to obtain, for some descriptive proposition *q*. If I believe that it's good to keep promises, then, all things being equal, I will desire to keep my promise to pick up my friend at the train station. But, so the Humean (or 'externalist') argues, it is perfectly consistent for me to have the relevant belief and yet lack the corresponding desire, thus throwing into question the idea that there can be contents that are distinctly normative. (This follows Schiffer, *Things*, 240–42; but see also Smith, *The Moral Problem*, Chapter 3.)

While Sidgwick doesn't endorse the extremely strong claim that the normative judgement that *p* implies a particular conative attitude, he does hold that the judgement provides "some degree of motivation to behave accordingly" (Schultz, *Henry Sidgwick*, 154). Thus, although he does acknowledge a potential conflict between benevolence and self-love, this does not, for Sidgwick, call into question the idea that one or the other principles possesses genuine normative force. Indeed, the mere fact that both principles are rational gives them such force.

principled means. In such a circumstance, there will be more than one acceptable course of action. While Sidgwick's worry was indeed that the dualism could, in principle, give rise to irresoluble moral dilemmas, the dualism of practical reason does not – in the first instance – concern a conflict between choices of action relative to a particular method but rather a conflict between *methods*. The worry is not that a single method – e.g. benevolence – is ambiguous, delivering conflicting results in a given context. Rather, it is that – at least potentially – two equally rational methods deliver conflicting results. Moreover, in the case of a moral dilemma, it is at least possible to claim that a resolution exists – although perhaps one the agent facing the dilemma cannot grasp. But if we are faced with a dualism of *methods*, each of which is equally rational, then no such resolution exists. That, at least, was what troubled Sidgwick.

4. Rational hedonism

Sidgwick labelled his form of utilitarianism 'Universalistic Hedonism'. Jones describes her own view as 'Rational Hedonism', but this does not flag a doctrinal shift so much as a shift in emphasis. Her concern is primarily to accentuate the rationalist foundations of utilitarianism. The utilitarian and the Kantian both begin at the same starting point – reason and the good will:

> For the Utilitarian makes a first and paramount appeal to Reason – he goes to Reason with the inquiry: *What* is it that it is right to do? What is the *content* of right action? What is the characteristic by which right action may be recognized? – He acknowledges Reason as sovereign, and it is because, in his view, Reason declares that Happiness is intrinsically worth having, and conduciveness to Happiness, the test of right action – it is *because* of this, that he adopts the so-called 'Hedonistic' End. And if Reason tells us that it is Happiness ... that makes any portion of consciousness intrinsically desirable, then the Volition that promotes Happiness is good; and since we cannot have good conduct without a good will (for conduct involves Volition) it appears that the promotion of the Hedonistic End involves both the supremacy of Reason and the conscious direction of the Will to right.
>
> (Jones, "Rationality", 34–5)

In sum: Hedonism is a rational end and the will is good insofar is it complies with what reason dictates. As we shall argue below, the emphasis on reason informs Jones' resolution of the dualism.

A few pages into the same piece – presented to the Aristotelian Society in 1894–95 – Jones gives succinct expression to the challenge Sidgwick faced:

> In short, it appears that the ever-recurring moral controversy between Pleasure and Virtue, is neither more nor less than a controversy between the *Agent's Happiness and the Happiness of Others* – and is a controversy not between Reason and Unreason, but between competing reasonable Ends; and this inevitable dualism or two-fold aspect of the End commended by Reason, still subsists

> within Utilitarianism ... and in the opinion of its adherents, constitutes the most important difficulty of the system of Universalistic Hedonism.
>
> ("Rationality", 36)

As this makes clear, *the dualism of practical reason* is a conflict between "two competing reasonable Ends" – rational self-love and benevolence. It might be thought that there really are two concerns here: first, that we have distinct principles and, second, that these principles are potentially in conflict. But this misconstrues the situation. The concern is that benevolence should flow from self-love. It is precisely because it does not that that the potential for conflict arises.

Over the course of over twenty years, Jones developed three responses to the dualism.[6] We will describe these in chronological order.

A. The Dualism as Irreducible. Jones' initial response to the charge of dualism is to view it as a problem of "the one in the many and many in one" – "a difficulty in no way peculiar to Universalistic Hedonism" ("Rationality", 36). It is somewhat challenging to assess the response, since the connection to the problem of the one and the many is obscure. Moreover, Jones doesn't elaborate on the analogy. However, a related point is made in her roughly coeval "Rational Hedonism"[7]:

> This dualism is inevitable – as inevitable as the antithesis of subject and object in knowledge, or the unity in difference which characterizes the object of knowledge, or the permanence amid change which is the condition of all growth and development. Hedonism is not responsible for the general difficulty of unity in difference.
>
> (81)

This is a bit more helpful, suggesting that there is an inextricable connection between the two competing principles. To take her final analogy in this passage: to say that an object undergoes change between t and $t´$ presupposes that it is *numerically the same* during that interval. Yet, since it changes during that interval it must also *not* be the same. This duality – of "permanence amid change" – is, presumably, ineradicable and irreducible. And something similar holds for the dualism of practical reason.

The second analogy, concerning *the unity in difference* that characterizes the object of knowledge, draws on her views in philosophical logic. Jones' central contribution to this area is her "law of significant assertion" – the "new law of thought" of her monograph: "Any subject of predication is an identity of denotation in diversity of intension" (Jones, *New Law*, 18). It is easy to read this law as a variation on a Fregean theme – that singular

---

[6] Due to considerations of space we pass over Jones' suggestion that a belief in the "moral government of the world" ("Rationality", 41) provides a resolution.

[7] This point is made parenthetically, in the context of the argument that constitutes Response B, below. Since it is made as an aside, so to speak, we treat it as an independent response.

terms have sense as well as reference and that identity statements are thus informative (when true) because their constituent terms, while co-referential, possess distinct senses. For example, 'Hesperus' and 'Phosphorus', though co-referential, express distinct senses (*star that appears in the evening* and *star that appears in the morning*, respectively). This explains how the identity statement, 'Hesperus is Phosphorus', can be informative in a way that, e.g. 'Hesperus is Hesperus' cannot be.

Despite this important similarity, Jones parts with Frege rather dramatically on a crucial issue: logical form. While grammar suggests that the simple sentence 'Hesperus is a star' predicates a property – being a star – of an individual, the true logical form, for Jones, is in fact that of an identity statement: Hesperus is identical to some star or other.[8] Indeed, Jones maintains, following Hermann Lotze, that the logical form of predicative assertions generally is that of identity (that is, of the form $A = B$) (*Logic*, 62).[9] Apparent predication is therefore really only apparent: what appears to be a context in which *P* plays the role of predicate and *S* that of subject is really one that maintains an identity between certain corresponding extensions.

One unwelcome consequence of Lotze's identity theory of predication is that it threatens to make true predications uniformly trivial. In asserting that Hesperus is a star I do not, appearances to the contrary, predicate being a star of Hesperus. Rather, I assert the identity of Hesperus with itself. Jones objected to this indiscriminate application of the law of identity as "oblivious ... of the needs and actualities of living thought ... " (*New Law*, 8–9). Nonetheless, she showed that Lotze could have it his way, although only if he recognized that identity claims, to be significant, must involve diverse connotations. In assertively uttering 'Hesperus is Phosphorus' one asserts a proposition that is true just in case the sense or connotation of 'Hesperus' and the sense or connotation of 'Phosphorus', while distinct, co-denote – the denotation of one *is identical with* the denotation of the other.

There is thus a dualism at the heart of significant assertion: both identity and diversity play ineliminable but independent roles. We misrepresent the nature of assertion if we elevate one aspect over the other (e.g. identity over diversity). Similarly – returning now to Jones' main point in this passage – we misrepresent the nature of *practical reason* if we elevate one of its guiding methods over the other (e.g. benevolence over self-love). Of course, the fact that there are fundamental dualisms *at all* might be puzzling, but, as Jones points out, the hedonist is not under any special obligation to resolve this puzzle.

---

[8] This is not of course an identity statement in the strict sense, but rather an existential quantification. Since Jones did not see this subtlety, we will ignore it in what follows.
[9] See Beiser, *Late German Idealism*, 185–6, for a useful discussion of Lotze's argument.

For Jones, a theory that reflects the two-fold nature of content gets things just right. Similarly for a theory that reflects the two-fold nature of practical reason. In both cases, the dualism is ineradicable, springing from the nature of things rather than reflecting a failure on our part to grasp the world aright. While there remains a question as to *why* the dualisms of identity and diversity on the one hand and of self-love and benevolence on the other cannot be further resolved, this is a matter for fundamental metaphysics, not for theories of content or of practical rationality.

This is unsatisfying: the problem is clearly deeper than Jones lets on here. Sidgwick's concern, after all, was not simply that there are two methods rather than one, but that the methods potentially come into conflict.[10] What seems to be the case is that Jones was gradually coming to see that an actual response to the problem was needed, as opposed to a dismissal. This is presumably why we have a comparatively superficial response mixed in with a substantive one, to which we now turn.

B. *The Argument from Temporal Irrelevance.* The second line of response concerns the analogy between self-concern – as distinct from mere desire gratification – and concern for others. Jones writes:

> As a conscious individual each is necessarily – not to say rationally – concerned with the quality of his own consciousness throughout; as consciously part of a larger conscious whole, each is rationally and naturally concerned with the quality of consciousness of all the members who compose that whole ... Further, since conscious life as known by us is subject to the condition of time, of realization in successive parts, the goodness of the whole is not independent of the goodness of the parts ... .
>
> ("Rational Hedonism", 81)

The point of the final sentence, following the ellipsis, is straightforward: it simply reaffirms the hedonist's claim that the final criterion of a good life – of the goodness of the whole – is determined by the goodness of the parts, which, for the hedonist, is the balance of pleasure over pain, of the quantity of intrinsically good parts over that of intrinsically bad parts.

The first sentence, however, warrants closer attention. The main point here seems to be that the concern for the quality of my consciousness throughout my life leads inevitably – both "rationally and naturally" – to a concern with "the quality of consciousness" of others. Both self-interest, understood as a concern with the quality of one's own consciousness throughout one's life, and benevolence, understood as the quality of consciousness of others, are presented as equally rational. This is underscored by a parallel drawn between my concern with my own conscious states and my concern with

---

[10] Note that the analogy with dualism in the theory of content doesn't help here, since a parallel conflict does not arise with respect to propositional content.

the conscious states of others: in both cases my states are part of a "larger conscious whole".

This is little more than a restatement of Jones' text. It is our view that Jones' reasoning here implicitly refers to Sidgwick's axioms. In effect, she sees a resolution within Sidgwick's own framework, even if he did not. To make further headway thus requires that we review some of these axioms (here we quote from Shaver, *Rational Egoism*, 62, and adopt their terminology):

> *The axiom of temporal irrelevance*: [T]he mere difference of priority and posteriority in time is not a reasonable ground for having more regard to the consciousness of one moment than to that of another.
> (*Methods*, 381)

> *The axiom of personal irrelevance*: [T]he good of any one individual is of no more importance, from the point of view (if I may say so) of the Universe, than the good of any other ... .
> (*Methods*, 382)

> *The axiom of the whole*: [A]s a rational being I am bound to aim at good generally, – so far as it is attainable by my efforts, – not merely at a particular part of it.
> (*Methods*, 382)

The latter two axioms entail, "as a necessary inference", the following:

> *The principle of rational benevolence*: [E]ach one is morally bound to regard the good of any other individual as much as his own, except in so far as he judges it to be less, when impartially viewed, or less certainly knowable or attainable by him.
> (*Methods*, 382)

The axiom of temporal irrelevance mirrors the axiom of personal irrelevance. Just as no person has priority over another "from the point of view ... of the Universe" so no *moment* in one's life has priority over any that precedes or follows it from the point of view, we might say, of that life taken as a whole. In each case, the axiom of the whole directs us, as rational beings, to be guided by considerations pertaining to the good of the whole – the universe, or one's life considered as a whole, as the case may be – and not to this or that individual or moment.

The point here is that the position of intra-personal temporal neutrality, on which no moment of my life takes precedence over another, leads inevitably to the idea of inter-personal temporal neutrality. If no moment in my life takes precedence over any other moment in my life, no moment in my life takes precedence over any moment in anyone else's life.

We thus have an argument that takes us from rational egoism, properly construed, to benevolence. It might be countered that this merely shows the *rationality* of benevolence and that this was never the issue. The issue, rather, is that there is a competing principle, equally rational. But this misses the point. Jones here argues not that benevolence is rational *simpliciter*, but that it is rational *given* rational self-love.[11] That is, the status of benevolence as a rational principle derives from that of self-love. Establishing that we must adhere to benevolence depends on our first accepting self-love. Again, rational self-love, properly understood, requires an impartiality that is similar to that required by benevolence, only here the impartiality concerns the value placed on moments of a life as opposed to the value placed on the happiness of an individual person.

C. *The Argument from Mutual Dependency*. In her final piece on this topic – indeed, her final published essay – Jones provides a more succinct derivation of benevolence from self-love or egoism:

> I think, however, further, that it is possible to deduce from it [the "Rule of Benevolence"] alone the maxim of Prudence – that the agent's own happiness on the whole is a reasonable end of his action.
> ("Practical Dualism", 323)

Jones reasons as follows:

> Now, a man cannot experience, cannot directly know, any happiness but his own. It must, therefore, be on the ground that *his own* happiness is *to himself* ultimately and intrinsically valuable, valuable in itself, that he can logically regard the happiness of others as ultimately and intrinsically valuable to them. His reasoned belief in the value for others of their own happiness must be based, *it can only be based*, on his recognition of the value for himself of his own happiness.
> ("Practical Dualism", 323; final emphasis added)

Here, we have simply the claim that my grasping of the value of my happiness to me *grounds* my grasping of the value of the happiness of others to themselves. She adds that there is no other possible basis for my coming to value the happiness of others. But she continues:

> All distress at the pain of others, all hatred of cruelty, all indignation at the 'injustice' of undeserved suffering, the irrepressible demand that the 'wages of virtue' should not be 'dust', that there should be a heaven for the good, is based in the last resort on our apprehension of the intrinsic value of Happiness, and this, as we see, *must start from the individual's apprehension of the intrinsic value of his own happiness to him*. But Benevolence, love of others, is as natural as love of self (as Butler has maintained); and, *chronologically*, the impulse of Benevolence is often prior to reasonable Self-Love, and a man's own greatest happiness may often depend on the happiness of others, and his acutest misery be caused by the suffering of others.
> ("Practical Dualism", 323–4; emphases added)

---

[11] Again, Jones is attempting to establish that the dualism is not, or should note be viewed as, a problem for Sidgwick.

Again, Jones first claims that my grasping of the intrinsic value of happiness is grounded in my grasping of the intrinsic value of my happiness to me. This is what explains our distress at the suffering of others. But in the above passage she claims that the selfless concern for others is *as natural* a response as our aversion to our own suffering, adding, somewhat surprisingly, given the context, that *it might even precede it chronologically*.[12]

While these points appear inconsistent, on closer examination they are not necessarily contradictory. Metaphysically speaking, my grasping of my own happiness *grounds* my grasping of others' happiness: there is a metaphysical dependency of my grasping the value of the happiness of others on my grasping the value of my own happiness. But reasonable self-love is not simply the recognition that my happiness has intrinsic value – it involves affirming the proposition that *my overall happiness* should be maximized. One way I might recognize the intrinsic value of happiness and yet deny the principle of reasonable self-love thus understood is if I place greater value on present over future happiness. The fact that happiness has intrinsic value for me does not rule this out. Put another way: my recognition of the intrinsic value of happiness does not entail that, on grounds of logical or conceptual consistency alone, I accept the axiom of temporal irrelevance – which is intrinsic to reasonable self-love.

It is therefore not at all incoherent for Jones to suggest that reasonable self-love originates in our natural response to the suffering or happiness of others. And, indeed, there is some motivation for the point. We are more likely to recognize the truth of the axiom of temporal irrelevance (central, for Sidgwick, to reasonable self-love) when considering others than in our own case. I might convince myself to put off a painful procedure, implicitly judging that, for me, future pain matters less than present pain. But I am far less likely to make this judgement when considering a loved one.

There is a clear sense here that, for Jones, the two principles are not merely consistent but mutually supporting: on the one hand, our attitude towards our own happiness – our grasping its intrinsic value – grounds our attitude towards happiness in others. (This was the thrust of Response B.) But on the other, correctly grasping the *principle* of self-love depends on – is posterior to – the realization of our natural inclination towards benevolence. That is to say, while the intrinsic value of our own happiness is what grounds benevolence, we will not have the proper attitude towards self-love – towards our

---

[12]In suggesting an innate or natural basis for benevolence, Jones echoes Mill:

> If there be anything innate in the matter, I see no reason why the feeling which is innate should not be that of regard to the pleasures and pains of others. If there is any principle of morals which is intuitively obligatory, I should say it must be that. If so, the intuitive ethics would coincide with the utilitarian, and there would be no further quarrel between them.
> (Mill, *Utilitarianism*, Book III; cited in Schultz, *Henry Sidgwick*, 187)

own individual happiness – until we appreciate the value of the happiness of others to themselves.

5. Conclusion: assessing the responses

Jones' initial response (Response A) emphasizes the irreducibility of the dualism. The point is dialectical in nature and is made by appealing to similarly ineliminable dualisms concerning identity over time and the nature of content. While it is effective as a burden-of-proof-shifting manoeuvre, the response does not dig very deeply into the nature of the particular dualism at issue. We thus do not take it to be a response requiring further comment.[13]

More substantive are responses B and C. Response B makes implicit reference to the axiom of temporal irrelevance to establish the connection between self-love and benevolence. This idea recurs in Response C, but it is here part of a more complex picture. Yes, benevolence is grounded in self-love, but our grasping of the value of our own happiness is, at least in many cases, consequent upon our natural grasping of the value of their own happiness to others.

With her responses in place, we can ask whether they succeed in changing the state of play or whether they leave the dualism unresolved. In our view, the former is the case: these responses mark an advance. This can be seen by comparing Jones' response to that of T. H. Green (*Prolegomena*, sects. 226–8). According to Terence Irwin, Green sees "the dualism of practical reason [as] avoidable [once] we set out a true conception of a rational agent's good" ("Eminent Victorians", 281). Irwin reconstructs Green's reasoning as follows:

> (1) A person's good is his self-satisfaction. (2) Self-satisfaction ... consists in the full realization of a rational agent's capacities. (3) The full realization of one person's capacities requires him to will the good of other people for their own sake.
>
> (281–2)

This argument, however, fails to engage Sidgwick, since it is explicitly perfectionist in formulation: on Irwin's reconstruction, Green takes as his starting point the idea that our fundamental obligation is the cultivation of our

---

[13] A referee has suggested to us a more substantive reading of response A, one which places greater emphasis than we have on the mutual dependency of benevolence and self-love. (Jeanne Peijnenburg suggested a similar reading.) On the suggested reading, the resolution of the dualism involves our grasping "the unity of the determinations [i.e. the concepts of self love and benevolence] in their opposition" (Hegel, *Encyclopaedia*, 131). As the referee notes, this has the advantage of unifying the three responses.

Such a reading deserves extended discussion – more than we can provide here. But let us note the following: First, there is no explicit mention of such a dialectical opposition in Jones' writings, including, crucially, her one piece fully dedicated to the dualism (the late-career "Practical Dualism"). In addition, Jones saw herself as a defender and expositor of Sidgwick's views. She would thus have avoided any resolution that would have been unacceptable to Sidgwick – and a dialectical solution surely would have been off the table for him.

virtue. Sidgwick, committed after all to "Universalistic Hedonism", would reject any such approach. What is notable about Jones' response – whether or not it was inspired by Green's – is that it does not share Green's perfectionist assumptions, even if it parallels it in other respects. Jones, in contrast to Green, sees the resolution in explicitly hedonistic terms: "All distress at the pain of others, all hatred of cruelty … is based in the last resort on our apprehension of the intrinsic value of Happiness … " Here, Green's requirement that I "will the good of other people for their own sake" is, in effect, recast as the requirement that *I will the happiness of other people because of the intrinsic value of that happiness to them* ("Practical Dualism", 323). Moreover – and crucially – this requirement does not, *contra* Green, emanate from a prior obligation to develop and cultivate my capacities *qua* rational agent. Rather, it derives from my recognition of the intrinsic value of happiness *per se*. Nothing about my duties to myself need enter into my reasoning.

Jones thus reformulates Green's argument in terms that would have been congenial to Sidgwick – which is not to say that Sidgwick would have accepted her conclusion.[14] Indeed, Jones' response would doubtless not have been the last word on this issue. Still, we think it is equally clear that her contribution to the debate – recasting Green's resolution in a manner consistent with Sidgwick's hedonistic assumptions – presents an original and promising line of response.

Acknowledgements

This paper was delivered at the workshop "Women in the History of Analytic Philosophy", held at Tilburg University on 27 October 2019. Thanks to the participants for their instructive comments and suggestions. Thanks also to Ray Buchanan, Mark Halfon, Jeanne Peijnenburg, Consuelo Preti, Frank Pupa, Katrien Schaubroeck and two anonymous referees for helpful comments on an earlier draft.

Bibliography

Anonymous. "In Memoriam: Miss E. E. Constance Jones". *Proceedings of the Aristotelian Society* 22 (1921–22): 224–5.
Beiser, Frederick C. *Late German Idealism: Trendelenburg and Lotze*. Oxford: Oxford University Press, 2013.
Butler, Joseph. *The Works of Bishop Butler*. Edited by David E. White. Rochester: University of Rochester Press, 2006.
Crisp, Roger. *The Cosmos of Duty: Henry Sidgwick's Methods of Ethics*. Oxford: Clarendon Press, 2015.

---

[14]Sidgwick would presumably have responded that our sympathies are restricted in strength and scope – they generally extend most powerfully only to a limited range of people (see *Methods*, 502). But notice that this concern applies with equal force to rational self-interest: There are very few persons who are as concerned with the quality of moments of their life ten or twenty years hence as they are with the next few days, weeks, or years. But no one would challenge the idea of rational egoism on such a basis. So it is unclear why these same considerations should provide a challenge to benevolence.

Green, T. H. *Prolegomena to Ethics*. Edited by A. C. Bradley. Oxford: Clarendon Press, 1883.
Irwin, Terence. "Eminent Victorians and Greek Ethics: Sidgwick, Green, and Aristotle". In *Essays on Henry Sidgwick*, edited by Bart Schultz, 279–310. Cambridge: Cambridge University Press, 1992.
Hegel, G. W. F. 1991. *The Encyclopaedia Logic*. Translated by T. F. Geraets et al. Indianapolis: Hackett.
Jones, E. E. Constance. *An Introduction to General Logic*. London: Longmans, Green, 1892.
Jones, E. E. Constance. "Rational Hedonism". *International Journal of Ethics* 5, no. 1 (1894): 79–97.
Jones, E. E. Constance. "The Rationality of Hedonism". *Proceedings of the Aristotelian Society* 3, no. 1 (1894–95): 29–45.
Jones, E. E. Constance. *A Primer of Ethics*. London: John Murray, 1909.
Jones, E. E. Constance. *A New Law of Thought and Its Logical Bearings*. Cambridge: Cambridge University Press, 1911.
Jones, E. E. Constance. "Practical Dualism". *Proceedings of the Aristotelian Society* 18 (1917–18): 317–28.
Jones, E. E. Constance. *As I Remember: An Autobiographical Ramble*. London: A. & C. Black, 1922.
Lotze, Hermann. *Logic, in Three Books: Volume One*. Translated by Bernard Bosanquet. Oxford: Clarendon Press, 1888.
Mackenzie, J. S. 1923. "The Late Miss E. E. Constance Jones, Litt. D." *International Journal of Ethics* 33, no. 2 (1923): 228.
Ostertag, Gary. "Emily Elizabeth Constance Jones", *The Stanford Encyclopedia of Philosophy*, Fall 2014 Edition. Edited by Edward N. Zalta. https://plato.stanford.edu/archives/fall2014/entries/emily-elizabeth-constance-jones/.
Schiffer, Stephen. *The Things We Mean*. Oxford: Clarendon Press, 2003.
Schultz, B. *Henry Sidgwick, Eye of the Universe: An Intellectual Biography*. Cambridge: Cambridge University Press, 2004.
Shaver, Robert. *Rational Egoism: A Selective and Critical History*. Cambridge: Cambridge University Press, 1999.
Sidgwick, Henry. *The Methods of Ethics*. 7th ed. Indianapolis: Hackett, 1906/1981, 1902/1988. [abbreviated as *Methods*].
Smith, Michael. *The Moral Problem*. Oxford: Blackwell, 1994.
Stout, G. F. 1922. "The Late Miss E. E. Constance Jones". *Mind* 31, no. 123 (1922): 383–4.

Marietta Kies on idealism and good governance

Dorothy Rogers

ABSTRACT

This paper explores the political philosophy of Marietta Kies (1853–1899), a progressive-era thinker who gained recognition as both a professional academic philosopher and a public intellectual. Kies' philosophy was grounded in neo-Hegelian theory, while also being responsive to the economic and social realities she observed in the world around her. She was one of the first women in the US to formally study philosophy and political theory at an advanced academic level. Yet she also gathered with fellow intellectuals, political activists, and feminists to discuss solutions to contemporary problems at chautauqua-style summer programmes. The paper introduces Kies in her intellectual and political context. It then examines distinctive elements of her thought: specifically her heightened notion of positive rights and her theory of public/political altruism. It also evaluates how effectively Kies intertwined a neo-Hegelian understanding of the state with her commitments to Christian socialism, to progressivism, and to a liberal conception of democracy.

Introduction

In the 1890s, Marietta Kies (1853–99) developed a theory of altruism that anticipated today's ethic of care in that she identified justice as an individualistic and egoistic principle, and objected to its dominance in political discourse. In her view, justice is a principle in political life in which an individual "thinks, feels and acts, and receives the like in kind, nothing better, nothing worse" (Kies, *Ethical Principle*, 1–2). This is not to say her theory was identical to the feminist ethic of care that developed nearly a century later. But like Carol Gilligan and the scores of ethic of care theorists who followed, Kies insisted that we need a more holistic principle in political life than justice alone.[1] She drew not on a concept of care per se, but on the

---

[1] For discussions of the ethic of care as related to social/political theory, see: Gilligan, *Different Voice*, especially 64–105, 128–50; Tronto, *Moral Boundaries* and *Caring Democracy*; Noddings, *Caring*; Held, *Feminist Morality* and *Ethics of Care*. I have previously discussed Kies, along with a contemporary as predecessors of care theorists, in "Before Care".

religious notion of grace, which she considered parallel to altruism. In her system, altruism is not a private individual prerogative, but a public community mandate that will allow all members of society to grow and flourish. Drawing on Hegel's *Philosophy of Right*, Kies asserted that it would be irrational for the state to fail to provide for the good of its members – particularly those who suffer from poverty.[2] In this sense, a degree of empathy is necessary in public life, and a truly rational state will institute policies that encourage and reinforce altruism. I have discussed Kies's theory of altruism as related to state action at some length elsewhere (Rogers, *America's First Women Philosophers*, 138–61). This paper aims to examine her notion of positive rights and human good in the just state.

While some feminist scholars have rightly objected to delving too deeply into the personal biographies of women philosophers (Kendrick and Gordon-Roth, "Recovering Early Modern Women", 2019), it would be naïve to ignore the connection between Kies's social placement as a youth and her work as a political theorist. She was raised in the northeast corner of Connecticut, more than thirty miles from large cities in the region, an area that remained largely a farming community until recent decades. As was fairly common for children in her socio-economic class in the mid-nineteenth century, Kies began working at local textile mills before reaching the age of twelve. Although a memorialist indicated that she came "from a home where she had absolutely no encouragement intellectually",[3] she moved on to teaching in the area's schools when she was fourteen and ultimately became one of the first women to earn a doctorate in philosophy, at the University of Michigan in 1891. Her experiences in this working class/working poor environment no doubt informed the ideas she developed in her work on political altruism, *The Ethical Principle* (1892) and *Institutional Ethics* (1894). In these books, she struggles with the inequalities an increasingly industrialized capital-based economy created in social/political life and attempts to find ways to address those inequalities without introducing unforeseen and damaging consequences into the equation.

Intellectual influences

There were a number of intellectual forces at play in Marietta Kies's life. She became a member of the idealist movement in philosophy through her association with a hometown hero in the region in which she grew up,

---

[2] As noted later in this essay, Kies drew on Hegel's *Philosophy of Right* on this point, especially sections 240–5, until he affirms the practice in Scotland of leaving the poor "to their fate" rather than offering assistance. See Hegel, *Philosophy of Right* (Knox translation), 148–50. Kies fully asserted that it would be unethical for the state to ignore the needs of the poor: *Ethical Principle*, 79.

[3] Rev. S. Sherberne Mathews' Letter to James B. Angell [Nov. 3, 1900], from Marietta Kies's necrology file, Bentley Historical Library, University of Michigan.

William Torrey Harris (1835–1909).[4] A generation older than Kies, Harris was raised in Putnam, Connecticut, and became a prominent educator and public intellectual on the national scene. He first gained recognition as the superintendent of schools in St. Louis, Missouri (1867–80), where he gathered a group of philosophers and educators who discussed pedagogy as well as philosophy proper. The group drew primarily on the ideas of G.W.F. Hegel, but also read and translated the work of other European thinkers: Friedrich Froebel, Karl Rosenkranz, Friedrich Schelling, Johann Gottlieb Fichte, and Hermann Lotze. Harris published *The Journal of Speculative Philosophy*, the first journal in the English language devoted to philosophy (1867–93); established an innovative chatauqua-style summer school in Concord, Massachusetts (1879–87); and was appointed US Commissioner of Education (1890–1906). The idealist movement formed by Harris developed into a loose network of public intellectuals, social/political activists, and academics and had spread to other parts of the country by the 1890s. In United States intellectual history, it served as a bridge, both chronologically and philosophically, between New England transcendentalism and American pragmatism.

Kies was among dozens of women who established successful careers as educators, authors, and activists as a result of their ties to the idealist movement. She studied under Harris at the Concord Summer School of Philosophy and Literature, compiling and giving structure to his scattered lectures, which she published as an introductory philosophy textbook in 1889. During this time, Harris wrote a letter of recommendation for Kies's admission to the University of Michigan,[5] where she studied at the graduate level under faculty who also proved to have influence on her thought: the socialist, Henry Carter Adams, and the not-yet-pragmatist, John Dewey.

This is not to suggest that Kies failed to be an original thinker. In fact, the ideas of each of these men were so divergent that she must have had to deeply examine her own views in order to produce her doctoral dissertation at Michigan and an expansion of that discussion two years later – which she succeeded in doing. Harris was a right-leaning idealist who repeatedly extolled the virtues of Hegel's understanding of society as an organic whole. He also favoured a brand of idealism that saw reality (or rather Reality) as an absolute and monistic unity. Henry Carter Adams was a political economist who appears to have had little use for idealism and its many abstractions from lived experience in the material world. His ideas were fairly well aligned with the economic theories of Henry George, whose

---

[4] I have discussed Harris and his circle of educators, activists, and philosophers in St. Louis elsewhere, and the men in the movement have been well-chronicled. See Goetzmann, *American Hegelians*; Harmon, *St. Louis Hegelians*; Pochman, *German Culture in America*; Snider, *St. Louis Movement*.

[5] Undated letter from William Torrey Harris (from Concord, Massachusetts) to George Sylvester Morris, in papers of James B. Angell, at the time the president of the University of Michigan, in Bentley Library, University of Michigan.

ideas Harris despised.[6] Adams ran a short-lived summer programme, modelled after Harris's Concord School, the Plymouth Summer School of Ethics, which Kies attended along with a mix of academics, activists, and intellectuals, including the pacifist, Lucia Ames Mead (1856–1936). Dewey had not yet distanced himself from neo-Hegelianism, but would do so just a few years after Kies completed her degree. While he does not appear to have been using the language of pragmatism at this early stage in his career, it is evident that Dewey and Kies shared an understanding that it takes a "practical man" to balance competing social, political, or economic interests in society (Kies, *Ethical Principle*, 110–13).

It was in this microcosm of social and intellectual life that Kies developed her ideas, and it is clear that in her discussion of justice and grace, she had a larger project in mind. She sought to address issues and concerns in the everyday world around her. And she aimed to do so by finding a middle ground between a classical liberal political theory of the Lockean and Rousseauean varieties and classical conservative political theory, as embraced by thinkers like G.W.F. Hegel (at least as he was interpreted by Harris and others in the early American idealist movement).

Given what appears to have been Kies's disciple-mentor relationship with William Torrey Harris, establishing herself as an independent intellectual was not necessarily an easy task. By all accounts, Harris was a congenial and gregarious person – particularly in his intellectual life. But he was also a man of his time and assumed a paternalistic tone with younger (female) colleagues, like Kies. Though no correspondence between the two has survived, in letters to Lucia Ames Mead (1856–1936) in the 1870s through 1890s, Harris did his best to coax this increasingly progressive thinker/activist away from the peace advocacy and social justice causes she felt compelled to pursue.[7] He also declined to publish work on Rousseau by the feminist and educator, Grace C. Bibb.[8] Along with another leader of the idealist movement, Susan E. Blow, Harris shared a distaste for Rousseau and other thinkers whose theories they considered too individualistic and/or lacking in a Hegelian organic unity (Blow, *Symbolic Education*, xiv, 20). Even so, Kies developed a political theory that drew on the individualism of John Locke, the social contract theory of Rousseau, and only the elements of Hegel's political theory she

---

[6] Susan Blow was an educator in St. Louis who became prominent as an expert on early childhood education. She invited William Torrey Harris to give a series of lectures and suggested he discuss progressive economist Henry George so as to dismantle George's left-leaning theory: Blow to Harris, 24 December 1886, in William Torrey Harris Papers, St. Louis Historical Society.

[7] Lucia Ames Mead was a public intellectual and peace activist who corresponded with Harris, expressing her liberal/progressive views. Harris tried to convince her that a more conservative approach was preferable. See letters dated 9 June 1894 and 11 November 1894, in William Torrey Harris Papers, Houghton Library, Harvard University.

[8] Grace Bibb was an educator in St. Louis, then the first woman dean at the University of Missouri, Columbia. She discussed doing work on Rousseau in letters to Harris dated 28 January 1884 and 7 February 1884, in William Torrey Harris Papers, St. Louis Historical Society.

agreed with: society as an organic whole and the state as a rational entity. Many of the aspects of Hegel that her mentor enthusiastically embraced, Kies downplayed, transformed, or simply chose to ignore.

Kies and/on socialism

Kies identified with the Christian socialist movement, a network of thinkers and activists at the turn of the twentieth century who believed the duty of the true Christian is to eradicate poverty and injustice, rather than adhere to rigid doctrines or seek eternal salvation. Different iterations of the movement emerged in England, Germany, and the US, and descendants of them remain today. In a sense, elements of the movement continued to be influential in the US throughout the twentieth century – particularly in peace activism and the Civil Rights movement.

Also known as the 'social gospel', generally speaking Christian socialism embraced many progressive causes: economic equality, women's rights, minority and immigrant rights, peace, and social reform. It was a movement that include activists across race and gender: Walter Rauschenbusch, Richard Ely, Charles Sheldon, William D. P. Bliss, George W. Woodbey, George W. Slater, Reverdy Ransom, Mary Church Terrell, Ida B. Wells-Barnett, Jane Addams, and Vida Dutton Scudder.[9] Not surprisingly, Christian socialists de-emphasized piety and abstract beliefs, focusing instead on action. They also often worked alongside atheistic socialists on shared political concerns, and for this reason their allegiance to the Christian faith was questioned by more conservative religionists.

Aware that even in the 1890s, the term 'socialism' was not always well received, Kies was quick to clarify that she embraced 'true socialism' – i.e. not a socialism rooted in authoritarian governance, but in communitarian good (Kies, *Ethical Principle*, 40–2). While she was part of a larger network of thinkers and activists who were exploring similar ideas, it is important to keep in mind how forward-thinking she was as a woman writing in the early 1890s, before the existence of a social safety net in the US. At the time, there were few social welfare provisions, aside from the local poor house in any given community. Labour rights and employee safety protections were minimal, and unemployment compensation was non-existent. Healthcare was available only on an as-needed ad hoc basis, and mortality rates were high for those who became seriously ill. There were no tax-supported retirement savings plans or food programmes for poor families with

---

[9] See Craig, *Religion and Radical Politics*, 116–25, discussing Woodbey, Slater, and Ransom, and their interactions with the like-minded Jane Addams. See Williams, "The Least of These'", regarding Mary Church Terrell and Ida B. Wells-Barnett. See Smith, "Cooperative Commonwealth", regarding Scudder and William D.P. Bliss in the Society of Christian Socialists in Boston.

young children. Child labour and child welfare provisions were barely on the horizon.

Kies saw the wide array of social needs around her and made a compelling case for comprehensive political changes based on philosophical principles. She called for a progressive tax structure that would require the well-to-do to contribute more to public funds than those who are poor and struggling for survival. She also called for anti-trust provisions to limit the social and economic power that large corporations are able to wield, especially over the wage labourers they employ. Her claim was that a society that takes the needs and interests of the poor seriously would enact 'constructive' legislation to secure not only our negative rights but our positive rights as well. 'Protective' legislation safeguards our negative rights – the freedom from interference from others. But Kies's constructive legislation goes a step further, ensuring we have the freedom to pursue our own goals and ideals. Roughly forty years after her premature death from tuberculosis, the majority of the provisions Kies proposed were put into place in the United States, and many more appeared in Canada and across northern Europe.

Kies on rights and just legislation

To fully understand Kies's view of positive rights, we must first understand her view of rights in general. At core, her objection to justice as a stand-alone political principle is based in her understanding of the nature of human life – for both individuals and communities. She articulated the classical liberal view that human individuality and identity entail agency, an ability to recognize and assert moral judgement and act on our own behalf. But human rights are central to Kies's understanding of human identity and human flourishing. As she saw it, "all rights that inhere in the will of [persons] are natural rights" (Kies, *Institutional Ethics*, 108).

A reviewer in *The Dial* lamented that Kies did not further develop the spiritual aspects of this theme, but her goal was not to discuss human will in spiritual or ontological terms (Sharp, "Recent Works", 183–5). Instead, she wanted to explore the nature of will in relation to human agency in social/political life. She wanted to convey the sense that rights are integral to human existence in the deepest sense, because in her view, we truly are political animals. The exercise of human will requires the ability to have full agency in our lives – a wide range of opportunities to form our own life goals and engage in the world (without harming others). This claim is significant coming from a woman in this era – especially a woman in early idealist circles. Hegel famously reinforced Aristotle's archaic notions that women are inherently passive, subjective, and internal. As a result of his ruminations on these ancient ideas, Hegel concluded that women were unsuited for public life, but instead achieved their full realization as persons within the confines of home and family. Women, he added, were incapable of active engagement in the world. If they were to be involved in political life, they would be arbitrary and capricious (Hegel, *Philosophy of Right*, §166). Rather than explicitly reject these notions, Kies simply bypasses them. She was not avidly feminist. In fact, she was lukewarm on the voting rights question, suggesting that perhaps women should vote only on local matters related to family, education, or social welfare (Kies, *Institutional Ethics*, 211). Yet she assumed women could and should be involved in public life. In addition, she spoke as a woman engaging in the very discourse from which Hegel thought women should be excluded.

Kies's understanding of human will is embedded in a classical liberal understanding of property rights. Owning property allows individuals to exercise individual agency. Property rights provide people with territory to inhabit, resources to manage, and materials to produce. As such, property rights allow individuals to participate in social, political, and/or economic exchange, thereby exercising individual agency. In this sense, property is inherent in our ability to exercise human freedom. Kies agrees with this perspective. Yet she gives property ownership a socialist twist, although it takes some understanding of Christian socialist ideals to effectively interpret Kies on this point. The concept of property is nonsensical unless the right to ownership is recognized by the larger society and overseen by an impartial sovereign, i.e. the state. As an element of its oversight of property rights, the state imposes taxes on property owners. In this way, property rights recognize the independence and agency of an individual as well as their social obligations. The state requires property owners to contribute to the overall social good so that it (the state) can protect both negative rights and positive rights. For this reason, Kies favours imposing a greater tax burden on wealthy industrialists or owners of "bonanza farms" (Kies, *Ethical Principle*, 110). Doing so will help prevent them from amassing too much wealth and power as in the days of mediaeval feudalism. Again, in the era in which Kies was writing – the early years of the progressive movement – this is significant. Rather than assume it is appropriate for local empire builders to flex their muscles, so to speak, and become a dominant force, regionally or nationally, Kies suggests here that it is better to hold them accountable to the larger whole by requiring them to pay their fair share of taxes, thereby contributing to the greater social good.

Kies recognizes that property rights have been abused, and offers a word of caution, thus demonstrating that she leaned toward the conservative end of the Christian socialist continuum:

> The excessive greed of a few individuals ... have brought into question the validity of the fundamental right of private ownership. But ... making possible private ownership by a larger number ... [will] furnish opportunities for self-direction and self-development to many [who are] now deprived of them.
> (Kies, *Institutional Ethics*, 129)

In Kies's view, the system of property ownership needs reform, not a full overhaul. More widespread property ownership would provide a greater range of people with a sense of purpose and selfhood. Thus it would ensure their individual fulfilment, contributions to their communities, and societal stability and growth.

Kies does not want to place too much emphasis on property as an expression of individual rights, however. Ultimately, she wants to find a middle ground between classical liberal individualistic ideals and classical conservative communitarian ideals. Note that she does not dismiss the concept of inherent/inalienable rights, but she does want to find ways to discuss them less abstractly and analyse how social/political systems can either inhibit rights on the one hand or facilitate the expression of those rights on the other. And she does so by aligning herself with social contract thinking.

As noted, Kies asserts that we have certain rights "by virtue of [our] existence" (Kies, *Institutional Ethics*, 108). As a sovereign, the government must oversee the expression of rights, but (à la Rousseau) sovereignty emanates from the will of the people. Our participation in society allows us wider expression of selfhood/rights. But we must maintain a balance between "wild freedom" among the populace and a concentration of power in the hands of a few (Kies, *Institutional Ethics*, 110). Overreach by the sovereign yields less freedom for the people. We cannot allow political forces or economic power brokers to alter our public policies or forms of governance in such a way as to curtail the freedom of any class of people. At the same time, a state that is too active in intervening in social/political life can actually weaken a group it intended to help. And on this point, Kies provides several examples of government overreach in the past, most notably, feudal abuses of power in the mediaeval period, poor laws in England, and the establishment of a state church in colonial Massachusetts. Drawing on conservative thinkers like Hegel and perhaps Burke, Kies believes this is the reason why law and culture must evolve slowly. Abrupt or radical changes would disrupt social structures. We need to allow for ever-changing social freedoms and gradually broaden our concepts of justice to develop through the course of time.

On positive rights

Kies's notion of 'constructive' legislation comes into the equation in her discussion of the "so-called field of competitive industrial activity" (*Ethical Principle*, 97), precisely because it is usually considered *the* domain of self-interest. Regarding Kies as a member of the American idealist movement, this is an especially important point. In *The Philosophy of Right*, Hegel asserts that civil society is characterized by individualism and self-interest, recast as a system of wants (Hegel, *Philosophy of Right*, §§184, 187, 188). And in *The Phenomenology of Spirit* he indicates that a formal and abstract notion of "virtue" will contradict itself, because it is in the nature of individuality to assert itself in and through action in the public sphere (Hegel, *Philosophy of Spirit*, §§ 389 and 392). By looking at business/industry as a segment of civil society that must be held in check by the state, Kies is taking seriously Hegel's idea that society is an organic whole. She is further affirming the Hegelian notion that the state unifies all members of society at all levels, reinforcing the 'wholeness' of this organic whole. In her view, the state must intervene to influence the otherwise spontaneous development of civil society in certain cases. Civil society may indeed be the realm of free competition among individuals, but the state is a unity into which all else is subsumed. When competition harms one or more of civil society's members, the state, as the manifestation of reason in the ethical world, must *by its nature* rectify the situation. Allowing competitive forces within civil society to damage and possibly even to destroy the organism as a whole would be irrational. Looked at this way, Kies is simply playing out what it means for the state to be rational in regard to the industrial powers that dominated in her day. In her view, the solution is to implement altruistic public policies:

> The voice of the organic whole, speaking through representatives who see the needs and correct relations of the different individual groups, demands that one class in society who will not voluntarily give up privileges which their position in society enables them to get, must be compelled to act as if they saw the good of others and the true interests of all classes.
>
> (Kies, *Ethical Principle*, 79)

Based on this statement, it is clear that Kies does agree with Hegel's understanding of civil society operating spontaneously as the realm of individualism. But when a corporate entity becomes so powerful that it is able to obliterate the autonomy of those beholden to it – whether for goods, services, or employment – then the state must intervene and provide safeguards against it. Since "the will of man is essentially freedom" (Kies, *Ethical Principle*, 91), neither industrial forces nor state power should infringe upon that freedom.

As noted, Kies accepted many elements of liberal political theory. Yet she was critical of the classical liberal notion of justice that prevailed in political discourse. In part, this is because in her view, at its core justice is an egoistic construct. In a political system focused solely on justice, society is an aggregate of individuals, and social happiness is roughly equal to the sum of the happiness of all individuals within society. This is a mistaken notion in Kies's view, and one that she believes can be repaired by infusing grace into political theory.

On grace or altruism

According to Kies, "grace, is in its very nature the yielding of one's own immediate thoughts for self for those of, and in reference to, another" (Kies, *Ethical Principle*, 2). Yet, she does not endorse self-sacrifice for its own sake. In fact, martyrdom is self-centred in her view, because its primary focus is on the self, rather than on the other. Altruism does not merely seek self-denial as an end in itself. Instead, it focuses on the needs of *others* who need assistance – and in order to ensure their betterment, not simply for self-congratulations or public adulation. Altruistic individuals seek their own good only in the 'reflected good' that arises as a result of their assistance to others. When individuals seek not merely that which will bring them pleasure, but are instead content with seeing the benefits to others that their altruistic behaviour brings, then the good for all of society is possible. It is also worth noting that Kies does not suggest justice and grace correspond to male and female gender stereotypes. In this sense, she stands apart from maternalistic thinkers in her era who made the case for women's involvement in society, based on the claim that their more caring, nurturing tendencies would help ennoble political life.[10] In this regard, her ideas are also distinct from Carol Gilligan and other contemporary care theorists, who have sometimes been charged with gender essentialism. Kies's notion of grace applies to both men and women, and, although it is a concept that has origins in Christian religious thought, it can be used to inform ethics in the public realm.

A central feature of Kies's theory of altruism was a distinction between protective laws and constructive laws, and there are two levels within each type of law in her system. In today's parlance, Kies's protective laws safeguard negative rights as well as a subset of positive rights. The first level of protective laws in Kies's system secures our freedom from interference, by government or by others in society, as we seek our own ideals of the Good. The second level of Kies's protective laws provides a layer of protection and security that human beings need to live in harmony with each other: an environment that allows us the freedom to safely pursue our ideals of the Good. This second level of protective laws in Kies's theory is similar to Hegel's public authority – the provision of public utilities, roadways, a police force, and such.

But as communitarians and virtue theorists have maintained over the centuries, human beings require more than freedom from interference and a reliable infrastructure to fully flourish. With this in mind, Kies developed an understanding of constructive laws that provide us with positive freedoms,

---

[10] Throughout the nineteenth century, a number of women affirmed what I prefer to identify as maternal feminism – the idea that women are innately suited for motherhood and caretaking work, the most vocal proponents of which were Sarah J. Hale and Catharine Beecher, but this strain of thought cut across races and cultures. See Rogers, *Women Philosophers*, 59–61.

but on two different levels. 'Fundamental constructive laws' ensure that social benefits and institutions are accessible to all, thereby providing all members of society the 'freedom to' grow, develop, and achieve. Examples include local and national taxation, public education provisions, and health and safety regulations. 'Special constructive laws' address the needs and interests of a specific class of people who would be disadvantaged, due to temporary circumstances or long-term inequities that are beyond their control. "Such measures compel the class favored by birth or inheritance to restrain the expression of possible rights and power" for the sake of social/political equity (Kies, *Institutional Ethics*, 131). A progressive income tax (versus taxation in general), for example, is a 'special' constructive law, because it recognizes economic inequities in society and places the burden of contributing to the financial well-being of the state on the wealthy – a class of people who are the most able to assist others. All constructive laws presuppose a social contract theory of political and economic life. That is, such laws recognize that we all sacrifice a degree of self-interest for the sake of security, safety, and other benefits when we bind together as a social whole. And in Kies's view, the rational state must require that a certain level of altruism be enforced in order to "provide to a reasonable extent for the needs of its poor and unfortunate classes" (Kies, *Institutional Ethics*, 140–1). Her rationale is prototypically Hegelian: society is an organic unity, and suffering by any of its members harms society as an entity.

It is important to note that Kies is committed to altruistic action by the *state*. She rejects outright the common conservative suggestion that private charitable organizations can adequately address the ills of society. The classical conservative claim is that private localized charitable efforts strengthen community ties by producing relationships of accountability between a benefactor and a recipient. As conservatives see it, a philanthropist cannot help but have compassion for those who are close to them and whose suffering they see in full. A needy person cannot help but express respect and gratitude toward a member of the community who provides assistance when they are under no obligation to do so. In addition, at the local level a needy person is more likely to avoid requesting assistance unless absolutely necessary. But, as Kies observes, "spontaneous private charity", is not "definite and systematized" (Kies, *Institutional Ethics*, 140–1). Private charitable giving is subject to the vicissitudes of emotional commitments to needy others, regardless of how close they are to a would-be benefactor – geographically or relationally. Direct charitable giving also can lead a benefactor to wield their economic and social power over a recipient. By contrast, equitably distributed public funds allow recipients to retain their privacy and thus their dignity in the public square. Kies does not address these issues in detail, but she does assert that altruism can and should be promoted by a rational legal system:

> Since the true aim of a nation is ... to secure a harmonious development of all its members, any legislation which wilfully violates or ignores the rights of any class or group of producers, or forgets to secure the good of an oppressed class, cannot in the long run prove to be correct legislation.
>
> (Kies, *Ethical Principle*, 86)

'Correct legislation' by a rational state requires monitoring in order to reliably facilitate the free development of individuals. In this way the state protects the natural and continuous development of the whole society. As Kies sees it, it is better to err on the side of grace rather than of justice.

Kies recognizes that a robust version of altruism may be an unattainable ideal (Kies, *Ethical Principle*, 15–16). Yet it is still worth pursuing, because although humans are finite creatures, their thoughts and ideals are infinite and therefore aim toward the transcendent, or toward the divine in Kies's parlance. In fact, Kies claimed that altruism is the highest stage in a hierarchy of ethical decision making, because it provides a bridge between human strivings and divine/transcendent ideals. Human understandings of ethics and social good change over time, so we may fall short of our altruistic ideals. But this just means that we will need to re-evaluate our goals from time to time, based on new social conditions (Kies, *Ethical Principle*, 14–16).

Although Kies saw altruism as a public political principle, as a Christian socialist, her idea of 'grace' derived from a religious ethic. Grace, she said, is most fully realized in the church, and has its "strongest historical embodiment" in "the life, teaching, and death of Christ" (Kies, *Institutional Ethics*, 235–6). She also insisted that both grace and justice do and must play a role in the church as well as in the state. "Justice should remain ... in the Church as a background as it were, for the manifestation and revelation of grace" (Kies, *Institutional Ethics*, 248). Meanwhile, the emergence of 'true socialism' in the state demonstrates "that there is opportunity for the exemplification of both justice and grace" in the political world (Kies, *Institutional Ethics*, 269). From a secular perspective in the early twenty-first century, the potential of Kies's theory to blur the boundaries between church and state is problematic. Yet there may be value in borrowing the term grace and the sense of communal accountability to the whole that it conveys. Her plan was that the two – justice and grace – would complement and even inform each other in both Church and State, not that one would usurp the role of the other. And her theory has made space for recognizing the role altruism can play in public life. Long obsessed with 'rationalizing' the state, the most dominant strains of (masculine) western political theory have too readily ignored considerations related to empathy and altruism that could inform and strengthen it. Kies's work calls on us to re-evaluate this tendency and consider what it means for the state to be rational.

Conclusion

Did Kies succeed in the project discussed above? My view is that, as with most theorists, the answer is both yes and no. She succeeded in introducing altruism into political theory as a principle that not only runs parallel to justice, but is able to inform and correct it. Like communitarian and feminist thinkers in recent decades, she rejected the individualism, egoism, and thin conception of justice that was dominant in western liberal political theory for far too long. Justice, she said, failed to fully address economic and political inequality, and she sought to repair this by reaching outside the liberal political tradition. Her development of a system in which there are two levels of positive legal protections – constructive laws, as she called them – took a step in the direction of further making a case for altruism in political life. She deserves credit for these innovations. An additional strength is her ability to remain within political philosophy, despite the fact that she borrowed the term grace from religion. The tendency among Christian socialists and social gospel proponents was to start with theology, of course. They asked what God requires, and imported theological values and ideals into political discourse. By contrast, Kies started with political philosophy and remained there. The concept of grace was simply a tool, not a religious value or theological mandate, in her theory.

We see in Kies some shortcomings, however. She did not engage fully enough with the canonical thinkers who influenced her thought, Locke and Rousseau, in particular. In addition, her attempts to be even-handed led to a lack of clarity at points – a hint of timidity at others. She was well-versed in Hegel, but did she know Marx? If one of her mentors, Henry Carter Adams, was known to embrace socialism and had lectured on Marx, why is it that Kies never mentions this thinker? It seems to me that her avoidance of Marx/marxism is largely due to her interest in remaining within the American idealist fold, which had not embraced left-leaning interpretations of Hegel at the time. Another factor is the limited scope of Kies's work. She was able to write only two monographs before her early death at the age of forty-five. The second work, *Institutional Ethics*, is a more fully developed and robust work than the first, and one can only imagine how her ideas might have developed had she lived into the twentieth century. But while Kies's writing style and forms of argument have a thoroughly nineteenth-century tone about them, she was also ahead of her time in many ways. There certainly were schools of thought in which empathy, sympathy, sentiment, and/or altruism had a place in moral and ethical theory, and, as noted, social gospel thinkers were interweaving theology and politics. Yet, few of Kies's contemporaries were developing a philosophical framework in which altruism was to play a role in public/political life. In this sense, Kies was an anomaly, and her ideas did not have time to germinate and make an impact during her lifetime. Instead, they would lie largely dormant for roughly a century. In the meantime, ethic of care feminists would develop some of the same criticisms of justice as a political construct and put forth theories that, while not identical to Kies's understanding of altruism, certainly resonate with them.

Bibliography

Blow, Susan. *Symbolic Education*. New York: Appleton, 1892.
Craig, Robert H. *Religion and Radical Politics: An Alternative Christian History*. Philadelphia: Temple University Press, 1992.
Gilligan, Carol. *In a Different Voice*. Cambridge, MA: Harvard University Press, 1982.
Goetzmann, William H., ed. *The American Hegelians: An Intellectual Episode in the History of Western America*. New York: Alfred A. Knopf, 1973.
Harmon, Frances A. *The Social Philosophy of the St. Louis Hegelians*. New York: Columbia University Press, 1943.
Hegel, G. W. F. *Philosophy of Right*. Translated by S. W. Dyde. London: George Bell & Son, 1896.
Hegel, G. W. F. *Philosophy of Right*. Translated by T. M. Knox. Oxford: Oxford University Press, 1967.
Held, Virginia. *Feminist Morality: Transforming Culture, Society, and Politics*. Chicago: University of Chicago Press, 1993.
Held, Virginia. *The Ethics of Care: Personal, Political, and Global*. New York: Oxford University Press, 2006.
Kies, Marietta. *The Ethical Principle and Its Application in State Relations*. Inland Press: Ann Arbor, 1892.
Noddings, Nel. *Caring, a Relational Approach to Ethics and Moral Education*. Berkeley: University of California Press, 1984.
Pochman, Henry A. *German Culture in America, Philosophical and Literary Influences, 1600–1900*. Madison: University of Wisconsin Press, 1961.
Rogers, Dorothy. "Before Care: Marietta Kies, Lucia Ames Mead, and Feminist Political Theory". *Hypatia:A Journal of Feminist Thought* 19, no. 2 (Spring 2004): 105–17.
Rogers, Dorothy. *Women Philosophers: Education and Activism in Nineteenth Century America*. London: Bloomsbury, 2020.
Sharp, Frank Chapman. "Recent Works on Ethical Theory and the Moral Life". *The Dial* (October 1, 1895): 183–5.
Smith, Gary Scott. "Creating a Cooperative Commonwealth: Vida Scudder's Quest to Reconcile Christianity and Socialism, 1890–1920". *Anglican and Episcopal History* 62, no. 3 (September 1993): 397–428.
Snider, Denton J. *The St. Louis Movement in Philosophy, Literature, Education, Psychology*. St. Louis: Sigma Publishing, 1920.
Tronto, Joan. *Moral Boundaries: A Political Argument for an Ethic of Care*. New York: Routledge, 1993.
Tronto, Joan. *Caring Democracy: Markets, Equality and Justice*. New York: New York University Press, 2013.
Williams, Joseph Thomas. "'The Least of These': Black Club Women and the Social Gospel". Master's thesis, Depauw University, 2015.

Archival Sources:

James B. Angell Papers, University of Michigan, in Bentley Library, University of Michigan.
Marietta Kies Necrology File, Bentley Historical Library, University of Michigan.
William Torrey Harris Papers, Houghton Library, Harvard University.
William Torrey Harris Papers, St. Louis Historical Society.

Race and the 'right to growth': embodiment and education in the work of Anna Julia Cooper

Kevin Cedeño-Pacheco

ABSTRACT
One of the distinctive features of Anna Julia Cooper's political philosophy and philosophy of education is the frequency with which she uses corporeal and organicist imagery to support her analyses of and arguments against racist and sexist oppression. This paper draws on the work of Black feminist scholars to develop a philosophical analysis of Cooper's use of corporeal and organicist rhetoric across some of her published and unpublished works on politics and education. Part II reviews three exemplary passages from her most known and studied work, *A Voice from the South*, to show the important overlap in the ways Cooper formulates her arguments and insights. Part III provides a similar analysis of several writings preserved in her scrapbook from the 1930s. By closely tracing the themes of vitality and education in Cooper's racial and gender politics, this paper aims to reveal some of the implicit insights and criticisms that might go unseen or under-theorized were it not for sustained analysis.

I. Introduction

Anna Julia Cooper's *A Voice from the South* (hereafter *Voice*) is widely regarded as one of the first book-length analyses of Black women's unique oppression, standpoint, and experience (Gines, "Cooper", 2). In this text, Cooper argues that Black women occupy a unique position in the United States due to the fact that they are subject to racism and sexism, but go frequently unrecognized or unacknowledged in struggles against the two (Cooper, *Voice*, 112; discussed in Gines, "Cooper", 18; and May, *Visionary*, 49, 183). Here she has in mind the Black men and White women who have historically failed to grasp the uniqueness and urgency of the problems faced by Black women and other multiply-burdened subjects. As Karen Baker-Fletcher notes, the book is divided into two distinct parts: part one,

Soprano Obligato, consists of the speeches and writings that specifically pertain to Black women's subjugation and liberation; part two, *Tutti ad Libitum*, are the writings that are more directly addressed to issues concerning the Black race as a whole – especially in relation to the broader, interracial body politic (Baker-Fletcher, *Singing*, 136). Though the split is important for the organization of Cooper's text, it would be a mistake to assume that there is much of a separation between the issues discussed in the two parts, since one of Cooper's recurring arguments concerns the importance that Black women's liberation has for the survival and vitality of the Black race and human society as a whole.

While addressing an all-male Black congregation of the Protestant Episcopal Church in her speech, "Womanhood: A Vital Element in the Regeneration of a Race", Cooper argues that Black women are central to the project of racial uplift, stating that "the fundamental agency under God in the regeneration, the re-training of the race, as well as the ground work and starting point of its progress upward, must be the *black woman*" (Cooper, *Voice*, 62, emphasis in original). Furthermore, she argues that there is "no issue more vital and momentous than this of the womanhood of the race" and that the very *life of the race* depends on its willingness to enact the types of policy changes that would grant Black women greater (or equal) access to church training and the spaces of racial leadership (Cooper, *Voice*, 62, 70). As Kathryn Sophia Belle (formerly Kathryn T. Gines) remarks, one of the central sites for racial uplift and the physical as well as intellectual development of the race is education (Gines, "Cooper", 2). In her theory of education, Cooper concerns herself with the literal education of individual persons and the metaphorical 'education' or development of the race as a whole. Likewise, in her own life's work, Cooper dedicated herself to teaching and educational administration (as principal and college president) at many levels. The frequency with which she returns to the subject of education in her writings also gives us a clear sense of how Cooper's thinking around the subject develops across her career and life experiences. Hence, we find in Cooper's early and late work a progressively expansive sense of education that becomes increasingly identical with the production of human beings by human society in general. As we will see, for Cooper, education names the whole act of producing human beings and communities.

The title of the speech "Womanhood: A Vital Element in the Regeneration of a Race", and the quotations above highlight an important feature of Cooper's work: her frequent use of corporeal and organicist imagery in the justification of her practical political claims. Indeed, in various places throughout her writings, she uses embodied imagery and references to organic growth as metaphors in her social and political observations, views, and principles. One way of interpreting this would be to say that her use of these constructions is primarily for the sake of illustration or rhetorical effect – that is, that they are secondary to the more substantive insights they illustrate. However, Brittney Cooper (hereafter, B. Cooper) identifies Anna Julia Cooper's use of corporeal imagery as a type of 'embodied discourse', wherein Black women use written or spoken invocations of Black bodies to advocate for racial and gender equality. She argues that "though many scholars have examined [*Voice*] as an early black feminist treatise, few have considered Cooper's persistent use of corporeal imagery to press her claims" (Cooper, "A'n't", 40–41; *Beyond*, 3, 9). For B. Cooper, Anna Julia Cooper's embodied discourse functions to signal her long-term normative political commitments to the further inclusion of Black women, the Black race, and neglected people more generally in the spaces where people manifest their growth and self-development.

In *Beyond Respectability* (2017), B. Cooper employs what she calls an "Anna Julia Cooperian approach" to reading the work and lived experiences of Black women intellectuals. This involves two commitments: "(1) a commitment to seeing the Black female body as a form of possibility and not a burden, and (2) a commitment to centering the Black female body as a means to cathect Black social thought" (Cooper, *Beyond*, 3). The first commitment stands in contrast to Anna Julia Cooper's contemporary, Du Bois, "who famously conceptualized the black body as a site of internal striving" (Cooper, *Beyond*, 6). Instead of seeing gendered and racialized embodiment primarily as a burden, Cooper saw it "as a point of possibility" (Cooper, *Beyond*, 6). While the dominant paradigm of racial struggle describes racial embodiment as an "internal battle", Cooper "inverts the logic of black women's racist and sexist social subjugation by arguing that their position makes them spectators who have a powerful and elucidating gaze of their own" (Cooper, "A'n't", 45; *Beyond*, 6).

This paper provides a philosophical examination of central themes and patterns of thought that bind Cooper's earlier work with some of her lesser-known work preserved in her scrapbook from the 1930s. It does this by surveying writings from different periods in Cooper's career and intellectual development. Specifically, it surveys these works with an attentiveness to the points of contact and resonance between them. The points of contact are the common themes like embodiment, education, and the collective life of the Black race. The resonances are the forms of analysis and argumentation that fit the model of embodied discourse identified by B. Cooper. Attention to these allows one to understand how different aspects of Cooper's philosophy work together and to extrapolate certain claims that one might not note or take as significant were it not for focused attention on the theme of embodiment in her work.

Part II examines some of her earlier work included in *Voice* – again, paying attention to embodiment and the development of her notion of education and racial uplift. Part III applies this same method of reading to Cooper's later work. In this context, it is key to note the forms of sexist exclusion Cooper faced and the alternative measures that she took to disseminate and preserve her work. In conclusion, this paper claims that one of the radical criticisms implicit in Cooper's embodied discourse and the various writings examined is that, in addition to all the other wrongs that have been done to African Americans and Black people throughout the African Diaspora more generally, they have also been robbed of their sacred and inviolable right to growth – to free, self-determinative growth. In the same way that Cooper holds that children can be denied this right by adults who try too much to force them into one or another narrow mode of education (be it industrial, classical, or otherwise), she holds that African Americans in the post-Emancipation and post-Reconstruction period were robbed of this very right on a collective scale. For this reason, if Cooper is correct, then it will turn out that any assessment of systemic racism that fails to take into account this historic wrong will be incomplete and ultimately unable to properly articulate the value of what Black people in the US and throughout the African Diaspora have been denied.

II. Education, regeneration, and the life of the Black race

As stated above, this part reviews three examples from *Voice*. One of the things that brings these passages and arguments together in a way that is important for this paper is Cooper's use of vitality as a conceptual basis for judgement and critique – specifically, the way her deployment of vitalistic imagery allows her to form argumentative reversals and critical observations about the objects of her analysis. What differentiates them is the level on which her use of embodied discourse operates and the results of her analyses. In the first case, she addresses the intraracial dynamics between men and women and develops her argument that the vitality of the Black race is contingent on the liberation and empowerment of Black women to participate in the formation of the race – particularly in the context of teaching and education. In the second example, Cooper uses embodiment to reframe the constellation of issues gathered under the notion of 'the race problem'. In this case, she uses embodiment not just as a basis for critique, but also as a goal in political action: for Cooper, true peace is a living and transformative unity that is predicated on the active participation of all parties in a social system or exchange. In her words, it is peace that is "brought about by a proper adjustment of living, acting forces" (Cooper, *Voice*, 121) – meaning that the achievement of peace is, for Cooper, akin to the production of a collective living body. In the final case, Cooper identifies the system of White supremacy as an actor in the violent (mis-)shaping of the Black race. It is also in the work examined here that she develops the deeper systematic sense of education –

as the "working up of raw material" that produces "a value of immeasurable potential" – that occupies her for the remainder of her writings on education (Cooper, *Voice*, 168).

a.

The first example to be considered is an anecdote from "The Higher Education of Women" that regards famed poet and cultural critic, Matthew Arnold. She recounts how, in a lecture at one of the colleges in the United States, Arnold takes the moment to remark in pleasant surprise that the women in the audience seem to have paid attention as well as the men. This remark leads to a back and forth discussion between Arnold and the audience about women in higher education, wherein Arnold clumsily argues that higher education might hurt women's chances at marriage or successful partnering (Cooper, *Voice*, 82). Specifically, he worries that, with higher education, women might adopt higher standards in the partners and company they seek. With higher standards, he maintains, these women will have a harder time being successfully married. This, Cooper states, is the most important argument against women's inclusion in spaces of higher learning (Cooper, *Voice*, 82). It is not that she thinks the argument is cogent or strong. Instead, what she means is that, given the extent to which it functions as a practical justification for discrimination against women – Black women especially – this is effectively the most important argument against women's inclusion in spaces of higher education. It is the most important despite its clear untenability.

Against these sexist attitudes and practices, she argues that "it is the prevalence of the Higher Education among women, the making it a common everyday affair for women to reason and think and express their thought, the training and stimulus which enable and encourage women to administer to the world" and that "righteousness, or *rightness*, man's ideal, – and *peace*, its necessary 'other half' should kiss each other" (Cooper, *Voice*, 76). Given the wrongs done to women by men in patriarchal societies, to some, Cooper's formulation here might seem like a servile or softly critical attitude; however, it is important to note that this notion of 'peace' or a 'kiss' between sexes is not to be confused with the type of nominal 'peace' that might arise from compliance with patriarchal practices of women's suppression and erasure. We should recall that her use of 'peace' is neither trivial nor unmotivated. As stated above, for her, true peace signifies the proper adjustment of living, acting forces. It is a living and dynamic unity between parties. It promotes the ideal of difference without hierarchy – without domination. In line with this, she rejects the types of norms that would relegate women to passive citizenship and the domestic sphere – and she celebrates the influence women have had in various spheres of life and society (Cooper, *Voice*, 116). Likewise, despite her poetic exposition of the point, her demands regarding women's higher education are very concrete: she requests greater financial support for Black women seeking higher education in the form of scholarships and other funding opportunities (Cooper, *Voice*, 87).

One of the things that is important to note for this analysis is that Cooper does not deny that higher education would likely heighten women's standards and expectations of their partners, associates, and colleagues, but argues that men should not view this heightening as a problem and that, in fact, they should regard it as a valuable opportunity for collaborative self-improvement. Indeed, she agrees with Arnold that higher education "renders woman less dependent on the marriage relation for physical support" and likewise broadens her horizons so that "[h]er sympathies are broadened and deepened and multiplied" and she is more capable of independent thought, willing, and feeling (Cooper, *Voice*, 82). What Cooper does deny is that men should view these possibilities for development as a problem. Rather than view women having higher expectations as a problem, Cooper maintains that men should view this as a valuable opportunity for collaborative growth and self-improvement. In this sense, we can see the outline of the methodology B. Cooper identifies and implements in her own work.

Instead of taking a supposed 'problem' for granted, Cooper reinterprets it as a valuable space of possibility, opportunity, or 'privilege'. Rather than being troubled or dismayed at the prospect of women's expectations being raised, Cooper argues men should be eager to help them in reaching that goal. Hence, instead of functioning as a sign of compliance with masculine and hetero-patriarchal norms and expectations, Cooper's figuration of a kiss between genders functions as a basis for forming normative demands regarding gender equity and the possibilities for mutual aid and betterment that would accompany it.

b.

In the first chapter of the second part of *Voice*, "Has America a Race Problem? If So, How can it Best Be Solved?" (Hereafter "Race Problem") Cooper turns to the popular debate regarding the supposed 'race problem' in the United States. Roughly put, the race problem identifies the sum of social-political issues and tensions that arise from the country's legacy of slavery and racialized terror against African Americans and other non-White minorities. In "Race Problem", Cooper applies a structurally similar argument to the one she gives in favour of Black women's higher education. She argues that in countries where there is no race problem, it is due to the fact that their social and political order has given way to despotism and that because in a system of domination, there is no room or need for conflict or tension between races (Cooper, *Voice*, 123). In situations like this, the conflict has been resolved through one group's rule or domination of the other. According to Cooper, then, what is beneficial or generative about having a race problem is that it necessitates and demonstrates the vitality of different races and opens the possibility for collaborative and reciprocal growth between groups that demand more from one another in terms of respect and equal treatment (Cooper, *Voice*, 122).

What she provides here is akin to the gift of the race thesis, that "[e]ach race has its badge, its exponent, its message" (Cooper, *Voice*, 122). Rather than reading this as a gesture of racial essentialism as some might, Belle reads this as a moment where Cooper celebrates difference in a way that is not unlike Audre Lorde's later defense of difference in her spoken and written work (Gines, "Cooper", 20–22). What is principal here is that the notion of difference that Cooper defends here is not a difference with hierarchy. For Cooper, the law of equilibrium holds equally in the world of sociology as it does in the world of matter (Cooper, *Voice*, 126). So, for her, the only way to accomplish the living and transformative unity that is peace in its higher sense is to maintain equilibrium between the different groups present in the national or global political body. It is important to note that the equilibrium Cooper has in mind is not merely material or directly political. It is also social, cultural, and evaluative (that is, it also concerns judgements of worth).

What is key, then, for Cooper's argument is that she again does not deny the central claim being made: that the United States has a set of interracial frictions referred to as 'the race problem'. Instead, she denies that it should be viewed as a genuine problem at all and instead argues the 'race problem' is actually a potential source of collective strength and vitality. In essence, the race problem on the collective scale is, for Cooper, what racialized and gendered embodiment are on the individual scale. Whereas dominant frameworks of oppression tend to view both racialized embodiment and the national race problem as burdens to be overcome, Cooper's approach here is different in that she is more interested in the unique opportunities that are opened up by the specific histories and collective experiences of different peoples within the body politic.

c.

In "What are We Worth?" (hereafter, "Worth") Cooper begins with a racist and damning quotation by Henry Ward Beecher, brother of Harriet Beecher Stowe, in which he asks, "[w]ere Africa and the Africans to sink to-morrow, how much poorer would the world be?" His answer is: "[a] little less gold and ivory, a little less coffee, a considerable ripple, perhaps, where the Atlantic and Indian Oceans would come together – that is all". He concludes that "not a poem, not an invention, not a piece of art would be missed from the world" ("Worth", 161). This is but one of the myriad instances that Cooper witnesses and examines of prominent White intellectuals giving their unsubstantiated fatalist arguments about the character, fate, and future of Black people. What is found here in terms of the political arguments just outlined is a disequilibrium of judgement between one racial party and another. In addition to the material and political inequality between White and Black people in the United States, there is a lack of equality in the amount of attention, thought, and investment given to Black and White representations and evaluations of Black people. These types of imbalances are what need to be remedied in order to ascend to the type of peace or political harmony that Cooper envisions in the writings discussed above – i.e. a type of peace that is not predicated on the erasure and domination of one group by another.

In her response to Stowe, Cooper first points out the extent to which his evaluation fails to take into account the context wherein African people and Black peoples of the African Diaspora have been denied centuries of their own freedom to develop and self-determine (Cooper, *Voice*, 165). She adds that, when one examines the tremendous strides made by Black institutions and organizations since Emancipation (and even before), one finds ample growth to attest to the fact that it is nothing about their race or appearance that has held Black people back from manifesting their capacities, but merely the brutal and subhuman forms of treatment that they were subject to (Cooper, *Voice*, 164). Free from slavery and the terror of absolute despotism, Cooper maintains, Black men and women could have done and accomplished all that other humans were capable of having done and accomplished.

With this clarified, Cooper takes the opportunity to reverse the cold, materialist evaluation Stowe had levelled against African people. If, as she and others have shown, it is true that human beings are equal in their capacities for growth and development, then it follows that what makes up the difference between them are primarily environmental, institutional, and social causes. In this sense, she takes the harsh, calculating logic of Stowe's impatient and uncharitable evaluation of African people and flips it back on the institutions and global economic political systems that have shaped the Black race in her contemporary moment (Cooper, *Voice*, 187). In this sense, Cooper recites the pattern of embodied discourse and critique by inverting the logic of oppression and marginalization to see other aspects of the situation, but she does so in a notably different way. Whereas in the previous writings examined, Cooper uses bodies to signify groups of persons (like Black women or the Black race and other races as wholes), here Cooper projects a sense of embodiment onto an impersonal institution – White supremacist society – and reverses the same type of calculating, productionist logic that had previously been levelled against African people.

One can see from these examples and others then that in Cooper's writings, embodiment does not merely function as a mode of identifying and assessing the life and quality of different groups of people, but also for analysing the patterns and machinations of different social, economic, and political systems. Likewise, one can understand how embodiment provides a guiding thread or basis throughout the various phases of Cooper's social and political philosophy. Specifically, it shows how, for Cooper, education functions as a basis for both individual and collective vitality. The following section continues to examine the themes of education and vitality in Cooper's later works in light of this analysis – specifically, in her scrapbook from the 1930s. In addition to the content of Cooper's writings and analyses, what is key to note here is the way that, given the context of sexist treatment Cooper faced in trying to publish her later work, her alternative means of disseminating and preserving her intellectual work constitutes a form of subversive textual self-preservation.

III. Embodiment, education, and the right to growth of the Black race

In 1958, Anna Julia Cooper deposited a sum of money to the Savings Department of the National Savings & Trust Company to be used in the publication of her work on "The Ethics of the Negro Question" (hereafter "Ethics") and "The Negro's Dialect". The text of "Ethics" was a speech delivered on 5 September 1902 to the Society of Friends in Asbury Park, New Jersey (Lemert and Bhan, *Voice*, 206). In the speech, Cooper continues her critique of generalization and of the tendency among many to try to reduce Black people to an "algebraic formula" (Cooper, *Voice*, 212). In effect, she ends up defending the bottom-up privileging of the individual that she introduces in her early work and sets the groundwork for her later work regarding the fundamental human capacity for growth (May, *Visionary*, 184). Considered in its context and in the broader arc of Cooper's writings then, the work can be seen as developing and furthering her criticisms of White patriarchal society's misrepresentations of Black people and folkways. She pushes against the logic of stereotype, demanding that Black people be treated and respected as individuals who cannot be captured or identified by racist formulas and depictions.

Shirley Moody-Turner calls the 1958 letter regarding the deposit mentioned above an emblem of Cooper's publishing career. In the letter, she says, Cooper "asserts herself once again as the tenaciously active agent advocating for the publication of her own writings and words" (Moody-Turner, "Dear", 47). What Moody-Turner gestures towards here are what she calls the gender politics of Black publishing: the manifold ways in which Black women's presence and ability to participate in Black print culture were artificially limited by outside parties. In her essay, Moody-Turner traces the lettered exchanges between Cooper and Du Bois as the former attempts to secure publication for some of her work in *The Crisis*, the major Black periodical the latter edited. Despite her frequent attempts, Cooper's requests were routinely dismissed or ignored. One of the few times Du Bois chose to include Cooper in *The Crisis* was in printing the photo of her in her regalia after having received her PhD in history from the Sorbonne. In this instance of inclusion without interaction, Moody-Turner claims that Cooper is reduced to a "voiceless voice from the South" (Moody-Turner, "Dear", 51). The sexist gender politics that Moody-Turner outlines then give rise to one of the tragic ironies of Cooper's life: that as she accrued more skills, technical knowledgeability, and experience in various aspects of scholarship, activism, and teaching, it nonetheless became harder for her to secure publication for her written or produced works. Considered with respect to the embodied politics Cooper espouses in her early work, we can see that these types of gendered exclusions are precisely the types of patterns of behaviour that she argues bring death and stagnation to the community. Far from supporting their own livelihood, the men who continuously ignored Cooper and the work of Black women like Cooper partake in the systemic disenfranchisement of their own communities. It is in light of these gender politics that Moody-Turner argues that Cooper's scrapbooking demonstrates a subversive mode of textual politics that circumvents the undue limitations placed on Black women's voices – what is interpreted here as a mode of textual self-preservation (Moody-Turner, "Dear", 48, 57, 59).

In considering Moody-Turner's account of Cooper's scrapbooking as subversive textual political practice alongside comments made by Lemert and Bahn that Cooper's piece "On Education" (dating uncertain; 1930s – hereafter, "Education") is composed as if it were an introduction to a longer, possibly book-length text, the potential for reading Cooper's scrapbooking as a mode of textual self-preservation becomes further expanded (Lemert and Bhan, *Voice*, 248). In the following paragraphs, I examine the ways in which Cooper's earlier theories on education are expounded in the aforementioned piece, and then turn to offer a reading of the lesser-known and under-theorized writings on education gathered in her scrapbooks. This reading thus sees out the implications of textual self-preservation in suggesting the possibility of these writings comprising such a masterwork on education – one which came to fruition 'in print' despite the gendered exclusions of Black publishing.

In "Education", Cooper begins with the expansive definition of education she introduced in "Worth": that it is "the building up of a man, the whole man" (Cooper, *Voice*, 249). Likewise, she immediately draws on and links education to the embodied discourse she had used in her early political philosophy. She compares the citizens of the nation to the state's blood and argues for the necessity of treating each individual as a vital source of potential value (Cooper, *Voice*, 249). The only "sane education" then, is "that which conserves the very lowest stratum" – i.e. those who are of lesser fortunes and lesser means (Cooper, *Voice*, 250). Found here is another instance in which Cooper's concrete material prescriptions are readily entangled with a corporeal logic that prioritizes the bottom up constitution of individuals and communities. This is evident in her ongoing critique of generalization and of "reasoning about people *en masse*" as well as her vocal support for general education and pluralism in early education (Cooper, *Voice*, 250, 256). She calls this placing the 'educative', that which trains the basic faculties of the mind, before the 'occupative', training in preparation for special activities of different occupations or trades (Cooper, *Voice*, 251). Put more strongly, she refers to this as the child's sacred right to growth – to a time period of undetermined, self-reflexive growth. Her plea is for "the sacredness and inviolability of the growing period of the child" and it is here that her introductory comments end.

Though not explicitly linked to "Education", the writings contained in Cooper's scrapbook from 1931 to 1940 pick up on and develop many of the themes, criticisms, and ideas from her earlier writings on education. Many of the writings included in the scrapbook appear to be from an informal column Cooper ran in the *Washington Tribune*, a newspaper for the Black community that was published from 1925 to 1935 (Lemert and Bhan, *Voice*, 308). The significance here is that Cooper would have taken the time to gather writings that, by the nature of the newspaper medium, would have likely been lost in the annals of accumulated print media. Like the pieces gathered in *Voice*, Cooper's assembly and preservation of this ephemeral media requires us to reflect on the important points of contact the pieces have to one another in order to appreciate the broader themes and insights that are threaded through.

For example, in a piece towards the beginning of the Scrapbook titled, "Educational Aims", Cooper broadens the cultural scope of her previous studies on education by consulting an account of African pedagogy given by Julian S. Huxley (Cooper, *Scrapbook*, 5). She lauds African education systems for focusing on 'native development' or general education from an early age and recounts Huxley's claims about the effect such education could have in producing a self-renewing culture of autonomy and self-determination for Africans under colonial rule (Cooper, *Scrapbook*, 5). One of the things that is striking here is the similarity of the language Huxley uses to that used by Cooper in "Worth". Here, Huxley stresses the self-renewing value of education and the surety of the investments that are made to carry it out.

In another op-ed included several pages later, "'Educational Chit-Chat': Speeding", Cooper returns to the question of value and education's link to national production (Cooper, *Scrapbook*, 15). She laments the effect that the 'machine age' has had on education – specifically its tendency to override the individual for the sake of standardization and production volume. She states that "[i]t is most unfortunate that this craze for speeding and top-notching should strike our educational programs. Youth is a time for growth – and growth, to be healthy, should be normal and without artificial forcing" (Cooper, *Scrapbook*, 15). This piece can then be seen as an application and defense of the 'right to growth' Cooper advanced in "Education" and other works. The difference is here that Cooper names the 'craze' for 'speeding' and 'top-notching' as the culprit behind what is interrupting the growing time of Black youths. Significantly, she also adds an explicit concern for the bodily health of students when she states at the end of the op-ed that "we must conserve [children's] health. See that the 'medicine ball' is mixed in with the day's responsibilities. Old and young need it, regularly, systematically, purposefully" (Cooper, *Scrapbook*, 15). In addition to this added concern for the physical health of teachers and students, Cooper also returns to the affective component of teaching and learning when she repeats what she says to her students: "Relax, relax […] Take a deep breath and smile" (Cooper, *Scrapbook*, 15). Though to some this may seem like mundane advice, what needs to be taken into account is the way that it marks a certain extension in Cooper's thought on vitality and education.

The last writing examined is less about education and more about the vital toll it can sometimes take. In an obituary written for her former students Zenola Bundy, Elaine Williams, and Audrey Wright, Cooper laments the "shattered and blasted hope" experienced at the death of exemplary students she had taught (Cooper, *Scrapbook*, 25). Interesting here is the way she regards the loss as "chargeable to overwork and unmitigated application to the pursuit of knowledge" (Cooper, *Scrapbook*, 25). Cooper here brings up the importance of one's bodily and affective constitution in light of some of the dehumanizing tendencies of popular education paradigms. She asks, "[i]s there not a real danger that we take our degrees and our marks too seriously?" She adds:

> [i]t is not the work, but the worry, which eats into the vitality of the student. Deep down beneath all the tasks and achievements, eating its silent way by day and by night, is the terrible strain of lifting a race, and of treading the winepress alone.
>
> (Cooper, *Scrapbook*, 25)

Hence, one sees here the way Cooper retains an unyielding commitment to the lives and bodies of individual teachers and students despite the conceptual growth and development of her theory. In the end, the extent to which racial vitality and education are related analogically always depends for Cooper on the health and well-being of actual Black people.

IV. Conclusion

One of the key lessons from this reading regards the way that Cooper's early ideas around education and racial uplift grow into the principle of the right to growth that she defends in her later op-eds. If it follows that a child can have their right to growth stolen or infringed upon by adults who try too hard to slot them into one narrow programme of study or another, then it also follows that a group of people can be stripped of their right to growth by heteronomy and outside aggression. This is the implicit claim or critique that Cooper is making with respect to African Americans in US society. Since Reconstruction failed and virtually every attempt to substantively better the lives of African Americans has been frustrated and undermined, in addition to all the material rights and goods that they been denied, they have also been denied the sacred right to growth – to free, self-determinative growth. In this respect, one can understand more clearly that, in contrast to representations of Cooper as an intellectual conservative – or as someone who is too uncritical in her uptake of Western European ideals and values – she maintains a strongly critical view of the wrongs to which African Americans and Black people throughout the African diaspora have been subjected. This also provides further insight into the vital stakes with which she approached her own teaching and pedagogy throughout her career as an educator-activist. For Cooper, her teaching did not merely fulfil the direct goal of educating her students, but also contributed to the collective life and vitality of the Black race. Additionally, with these final writings, one can see that for Cooper, education is not an absolute end in itself, but is a good that must be acquired in proper balance with one's bodily health and needs. It is in these respects that one can understand some of the ways in which the body functions dynamically – both as a space of possibility and limitation – in Cooper's work and how images of the body enable some of her insightful, if under-theorized, claims and criticisms.

Acknowledgements

Thank you to Dr. Linda Martín Alcoff, Dr. Kathryn Sophia Belle, Dr. Shirley Moody-Turner, and Dr. AnneMarie Mingo for the various ways in which they contributed to this project.

Bibliography

Alexander, Elizabeth. "'We Must Be About Our Father's Business': Anna Julia Cooper and the In-Corporation of the Nineteenth-Century African-American Woman Intellectual". *Signs* 20, no. 2 (1995): 336–56.

Baker-Fletcher, Karen. *A Singing Something: Womanist Reflections on Anna Julia Cooper*. New York: Crossroad, 1994.

Collins, Patricia Hill. *Black Feminist Thought: Knowledge, Consciousness, and the Politics of Empowerment*. 2nd ed. New York: Routledge, 2000.

Cooper, Anna Julia. *The Voice of Anna Julia Cooper: Including a Voice from the South and Other Important Essays, Papers, and Letters*. Edited by Charles Lemert and Esme Bhan. Lanham: Rowman & Littlefield, 1998.

Cooper, Anna Julia. "Scrapbook No. 2 1931–1940". *Scrapbooks and Albums*. 3 (2017).

Cooper, Brittney. "A'n't I a Woman?: Race Women, Michelle Obama, and the Ever-Expanding Democratic Imagination". *MELUS* 35, no. 4 (2010): 39–40.

Cooper, Brittney. *Beyond Respectability: The Intellectual Thought of Race Women*. Urbana, IL: University of Illinois, 2017.

Gines, Kathryn T. "Anna Julia Cooper". In *The Stanford Encyclopedia of Philosophy*, edited by Edward N. Zalta. 2015. https://plato.stanford.edu/archives/sum2015/entries/anna-julia-cooper/.

May, Vivian. *Anna Julia Cooper, Visionary Black Feminist*. New York: Routledge, 2007.

Moody-Turner, Shirley. "'Dear Doctor Du Bois': Anna Julia Cooper, W. E. B. Du Bois, and the Gender Politics of Black Publishing". *MELUS* 40, no. 3 (2015): 47–68.

Index

Note: Page numbers followed by "n" denote endnotes.

Abernethy, John 18
abolitionist tradition 12, 100–112
African Americans 54, 62, 104, 105, 169, 171, 178
agency 11, 12, 101, 103, 104, 108, 110, 112, 156, 157
akrasia 83–98
altruism 13, 140, 151, 152, 160–164
American Anti-Slavery Society 67
American Slavery 67, 68
American women's rights movement 52–65
animal bodies 19, 29
Anthony, Susan B. 55
Aristotelian Society 137, 141

Barclay, John 17, 18
Beecher, Catharine 3, 160n10
benevolence 43, 78, 141–148
Besant, Annie 5n5, 6, 9, 12, 116–134
best judgements 85, 86, 97
Bichat, Xavier 18
Black male abolitionists 103, 110
Black people 55, 169, 173, 174, 177, 178
Black race 167–169, 173, 174, 178
Black women 12, 13, 102, 103, 166–171, 173–175; abolitionists 103, 104, 106, 110; interventions 100–112
Blavatsky, Helena 5n5
Blow, Susan 5
Blumenbach, Johann Friedrich. 18
bondage 104, 110, 111
Boole, Mary Everest 5
Bosanquet, Bernard 137
Brackett, Anna 5
Bradley, F. H. 137
buddhi 125, 129, 132

causal principle 16, 22, 23
causation 7, 10, 16, 17, 20–25, 32
Child, Lydia Maria 2, 9, 11, 67–80
Christianity 6, 78, 104, 110, 111
Church of England 119, 121
civil society 158, 159
co-adjutors 55, 64
co-authoring 35, 36, 38
Cobbe, Frances Power 6
competition 43, 44, 46–49, 159
conflict 62, 88, 92, 140–142, 144, 171, 172
conscience 68, 75–77, 121–123, 138
conscious modelling 35–39
constant conjunctions 16, 20, 22
constructive laws 160, 161, 163
contentedness 129, 130
Cooper, Anna Julia 2, 9, 13, 166–178
Cooper, Brittney 168
cooperative socialism 35
Cornwallis, Caroline Frances 6
Cruz, Jon 107

Dās, Bhagavān 125, 129
Davies, Emily 4
determinism 11, 83, 90, 91
dharma 124, 126, 127
disjunctive conversion 118–121, 132
diversity 61, 127, 129, 142–144
divine submission 101, 104, 112
domestic slavery 34–49
Donnithorne, Arthur 89, 96
double consciousness 94
Douglass, Frederick 62, 100–104, 106, 110–112
dualism 13, 136, 140–144, 148; of practical reason 135–137, 139, 141, 142, 148
Du Bois, W. E. B. 105

early women's rights movement 52–54, 56, 63
Eddy, Mary Baker 5n5
education 13, 118, 121, 166–170, 174–178
Eliot, George 2, 6, 7, 9–12, 83–98
embodiment 70, 166, 168, 169, 173, 174
emotions 88, 90, 118, 126–131
equality 4, 37, 41–44, 48, 49, 55, 59, 63
ethical development 121, 131
ethical system 125–128, 131–133
ethic of care 151, 164
external objects 25, 26, 30

Feuerbach 6
Foote, G. W. 118
fragility 12, 83–98
free indirect discourse 95
free will 69, 83

German philosophy 67–80
Germans 8, 68–70, 73
good governance 151–164
Grimké, Angelina Emily 3

Hale, Sarah J. 160n10
Harris, William Torrey 153
higher education 3–5, 170, 171
Hurston, Zora Neale 104

idealism 8, 151–164
identity 128, 142–144, 148, 156
intellectual influences 152–155
intellectual life 93, 136, 154
intrinsic value 146, 147, 149
intuition 121, 122, 125, 139
irritability 19, 20, 22, 28, 29

Jacyna, L. S. 27n8
Johnson, W. E. 137
Jones, E. E. C. 2, 5, 9, 10, 13, 135–149

Kantian conscience 75–77
Kies, Marietta 151–164; positive rights 158–159; on rights and just legislation 156–158
knowledge 8, 19, 20, 43, 46, 75, 117, 123, 137, 142, 177

Lawrence, William 10, 17–22, 26, 27, 29
Lee, Vernon 6
lifetime 13, 37, 62, 63, 116, 130, 131, 164

marriage 34–40, 42, 43, 49, 53, 54, 56
Martineau, Harriet 6
McDowell, Deborah 102
Mead, Lucia Ames 154
Mill, Harriet Taylor 2, 9, 10, 34–49
Mill, John Stuart 10, 34, 93, 121, 123
moral feeling 77–80
morality 9, 11, 121–128, 132; true basis of 122, 123, 128
moral life 68, 75, 128, 129, 133
More, Hannah 3n3
Morgan, Thomas Charles 27n8
Mott, Lucretia 9, 11, 52–65
mysticism 69, 101, 118, 119, 121, 122, 125

Naden, Constance 6
National Anti-Slavery Standard 11, 67, 68, 70–72, 76
naturalism 7, 8
Nethercot, Arthur H. 119
Newtonian attraction 26, 27
non-resistance 73, 74, 77

oppression 59, 61, 64, 101, 107, 111, 112, 172, 173

Paul, Jean 69, 70, 72–74, 80
Pécastaing-Boissière, Muriel 120
political life 61, 62, 64, 151, 157, 160, 163
political power 59
positive rights 159
positivism 6, 8, 9
property rights 157
public life 152, 156, 157, 162

race problem 171, 172
radicalism 7, 53, 55, 58, 63, 64, 111
rational egoism 138, 145
rational hedonism 141, 142, 144
rationality 83, 86, 97, 136, 138, 139, 141, 142, 145
reasonable self-love 138, 146, 147
regeneration 167, 169

Schiller, F. C. S. 137
self-control 88, 91, 92, 96, 129, 130
selfishness 93, 95, 96, 129, 131, 132
self-love 138, 142–144, 146–148
servitude 34–49
Shepherd, Lady Mary 9, 10, 16–32
Sidgwick, Henry 135–141, 144, 145, 147–149

INDEX

slavery 3, 4, 39–43, 48, 49, 58, 59, 76, 103, 107, 111
slaves 40–42, 67, 76, 79, 101, 107, 110
socialism 34, 35, 43, 45–47, 49, 117, 118, 123, 124, 155, 162, 163
spirit 41, 47, 70, 77, 79, 105–108, 111, 117, 124, 159
spiritual joy 101, 112
Stanton, Elizabeth Cady 3, 9–11, 52–65
suffrage 42, 53, 57, 59–61
Sunderland, Eliza 5

Taylor, Ann 36, 119
theories of life 17–20
Thompson, William 34–41, 43, 45–49
Tubman, Harriet 9, 10, 12, 100, 101, 103, 108–112

universalistic hedonism 141, 142, 149
utilitarianism 8, 37, 38, 76, 121, 139, 141, 142

vague superstition 106
value 7–9, 146–148, 162, 169, 170, 176, 178
violence 11, 60, 74–76, 101–103, 111
visions 73, 101, 104–106, 108–110
vitality 13, 167, 169, 172, 174, 177, 178
vital principles 18, 26–28

Ward, Mary Augusta 3
Wheeler, Anna Doyle 9, 10, 34–49
whippings 102, 103
women: oppression 39, 43; rights 3, 4, 41, 42, 52–59, 61–63; suffrage 53, 56, 61, 63

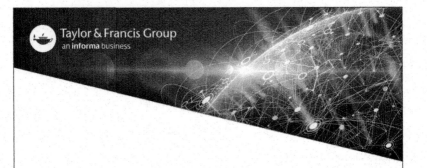